Women Mystics
Confront
the Modern World

Marie-Florine Bruneau

Women Mystics Confront the Modern World

SUNY Series in
Western Esoteric Traditions

David Appelbaum, editor

Marie de l'Incarnation (1599–1672)
and
Madame Guyon (1648–1717)

STATE UNIVERSITY OF NEW YORK PRESS

Production by Ruth Fisher
Marketing by Nancy Farrell

Published by
State University of New York Press, Albany

For information, address the State University of New York Press,
State University Plaza, Albany, NY 12246

Library of Congress Cataloging-in-Publication Data

Bruneau, Marie-Florine.
    Women mystics confront the modern world : Marie de l'Incarnation
(1599–1672) and Madame Guyon (1648–1717) / Marie-Florine Bruneau.
        p.   cm.—(SUNY series in Western esoteric traditions)
    Includes bibliographical references and index.
    ISBN 0-7914-3661-6 (alk. paper). — ISBN 0-7914-3662-4 (pbk.   :
alk. paper)
    1. Marie de l'Incarnation, mère, 1599–1672.   2. Guyon, Jeanne
Marie Bouvier de La Motte, 1648–1717.   3. Mysticism—History—17th
century.   4. Women mystics—Biography.   I. Title.   II. Series.
BV5095.A1B69   1998
248.2′2′0922—dc21   97-19144
                                                                        CIP

10 9 8 7 6 5 4 3 2 1

To M. de C.

Contents

Acknowledgments

My deepest gratitude goes first to my colleague and friend Margaret Rosenthal for her patience and generosity in editing the entire manuscript and for her tireless constructive criticism and judicious advice. I owe a great deal also to the colleagues who have read the manuscript at different stages and offered invaluable suggestions for the fine tuning of the book's argument: Elisabeth Caron, Tom Conley, Martine Debaisieux, Jonathan Dewald, Mitchell Greenberg, Marie-Hélène Huet and Lloyd Moote. I would like to thank the individuals who have read sections of the manuscript and whose ideas, questions, and bibliographical suggestions played a significant role in the development of the work: Sanford Ames, Ann Callaghan, Jean-Jacques Courtine, Maria Letizia Cravetto, Luce Giard, Solange Nobécourt, Mary Beth Rose, Lisa Silverman.

I gratefully acknowledge the unfailing support and encouragement of Albert Sonnenfeld, Chair of the Department of French and Italian, and Marshall Cohen, then Dean of the Humanities at the University of Southern California, as well as my colleagues George Bauer, Ron Gottesman, Marjorie Perloff.

I take this opportunity to honor an old intellectual debt to my sister Michèle Bruneau Fournier who introduced me, when I was a child, to the books that have shaped my mind, my aspirations and my career.

I deeply appreciate the financial support and the research

leave granted by the National Endowment for the Humanities and by the College of Letters, Arts and Sciences at the University of Southern California for the academic year 1989–90, in support of the project. My warmest thanks also go to the Newberry Library and its Renaissance Center, which have provided me at different times between 1987 and 1993 with a carrel, with the title of Associate Fellow, and with a host of opportunities to meet scholars and to participate in events which have been influencial in honing my thinking.

For preparation of the manuscript I especially thank Deanna Curtis, and also Mireille Henneton and Helen Franks, graduate students at USC.

Finally, I want to thank my companion, collaborator and best friend, Charles Krance for his indefatigable editorial work, for his unfailing confidence in me, and for his love, providing me with a continuous source of inspiration and renewal.

Part of Chapter 3 appeared in "L'Amour maternel comme alibi à la production de l'écriture chez Marie de l'Incarnation," in *Etudes Littéraires*, 27:2 (1994):67–76. Portions of Chapter 4 appeared in "A New Perspective on the Historiography of the New World," in *Proceedings of the Western Society for French History*, 18 (1991): 492–97. A brief and early version of Chapter 5 appeared in "Feminité sauvage; feminité civilisée: Marie de l'Incarnation entre la clôture et la forêt," *PFSCL*. 19: 37 (1992): 347–54. Part of Chapter 6 appeared in "Dans les oubliettes de Versailles: Le mysticisme de Madame Guyon," in *Le Labyrinthe de Versailles: Parcours critiques de Molière à Malebranche*, ed. Martine Debaisieux (Amsterdam: Rodopi, 1997). I thank the respective publishers for permission to reprint this material in revised form.

Introduction

The fate of Christian mysticism at the dawn of the modern world has been documented by contemporary historians of religion such as Louis Cognet, Michel de Certeau, Jacques Le Brun, and Georges Gusdorf. Yet many of the dilemmas particular to the decline of a distinctly female mystical tradition at the end of the seventeenth century have not been examined. The challenges Western mysticism encountered at this time produced losses in status and new forms of censorship, but also new opportunities hitherto unavailable to female mystics.

The two mystic writers presented in this study, Marie de l'Incarnation-Guyart (1599–1672) and Madame Guyon (1648–1717), extend, refine, and prolong a literary and spiritual tradition that had begun in the thirteenth century. Yet, because they are situated at a crucial point in the history of Western mysticism, when this movement was at once at its apogee and in the first degrees of its decline, their writings bear the marks of a changing mentality. The subject of this book concerns the transformations their mystical and writing practices underwent during this period, owing to various changes affecting society, knowledge, religious sensibilities,

1

and the perception of the self. I argue, in addition, that these transformations can shed light on the social significance of female mysticism in the Western tradition. Marie de l'Incarnation and Madame Guyon reacted in different ways to the challenges they had to face as they confronted a changing world. The respective stance they took vis-à-vis authority, the opportunities they seized or shunned, and the alliances they formed highlight their maneuvering for power, validation, and autonomy in the midst of the changing perception of mysticism and of the reformulation of gender constraints. But their choices also highlight many contradictions, compromises, and limits imposed upon their self-expression.

My study is inspired by two lines of historical scholarship and theoretical reflection on Western mysticism, which are independent of each other. One is represented by Michel de Certeau, who is well known in France for his vast and complex body of historical and philosophical works and for his articulation of mysticism with psychoanalysis, cultural anthropology, semiotics, linguistics, and contemporary culture. His work is becoming increasingly recognized in the United States through the translation of several of his works.[1] The other line has been initiated by Caroline Walker Bynum, whose historical and feminist scholarship on female mystics in the Middle Ages has come to assume a great importance in the study of female mystics in general.[2] In different ways, and for different periods, both of these scholars have profoundly influenced the study and the interpretation given to mysticism. Although drawing from their works and establishing a three-way debate with them, I also expand on their discussions, vary sometimes from their conclusions, and offer new perspectives.

As a study of two mystics who lived in a period during which Western mysticism was openly challenged, and whose mystical and writing practices were affected by such challenges, my work follows a path opened by that of Michel de Certeau on mysticism in the sixteenth and seventeenth centuries. As such, my analysis is framed by a number of his positions, which it engages. Like most French historians of Western seventeenth-century mysticism, de Certeau asserts the decline of mysticism in this period, emphasizing its loss of prestige and social status. This decline, according to this school of thought, is the consequence of an epistemological shift, which both produced and was produced by the scientific revo-

lution. More importantly, de Certeau situates the mystical movement in the West between two historical ruptures in the organization of knowledge. First, mysticism appeared in Western Europe in
the twelfth and thirteenth centuries as a nostalgic response to the
progressive decline of God as the unique object of inquiry.[3] Indeed,
knowledge, which until the thirteenth century was the domain of
monks and whose unique object was God, became diversified and
professionalized with the creation of the university. It is not by
chance, infers de Certeau, that the love poetry of the troubadours
appeared at the same time as the mystical movement. From this
point forward, God was no longer seen as the unique source of
truth, knowledge, and love. For de Certeau, the loss, which the
mystics characteristically refused to mourn, is of the order of the
cosmological, the epistemological, and the theological.[4]

De Certeau agrees with other historians that the second epistemological rupture that affected the mystical movement and caused
its decline occurred in the sixteenth and seventeenth centuries.
The originality of de Certeau's work on mysticism is that instead of
constructing a chronological account of the Western mystical tradition and then simply accounting for its decline by tying it to the
emergence of modern science, he analyzes the relationship that the
new modes of scientific investigation had with this other mode of
knowing that was mysticism, against which modern science defined itself. He thus establishes how in sixteenth- and seventeenth-
century Europe the emerging modern scientific discourse reified
the mystical as an object of inquiry in accordance with its own categories and methodologies, and that in fact modern scientific discourse defined itself as the *not-that* of mysticism.[5] Whereas before
that period mysticism was regarded as a normal mode of communicating with the divine, in the seventeenth century it increasingly
was regarded first as "extraordinary," then as "abnormal," while
the mystic was seen as a "delusive idealist, a religious fanatic, a
figure of pathology."[6] De Certeau observes that this premodern opposition between the "mystical" and the "scientific" organized not
only scientific discourse on mysticism but also contaminated modern theological, as well as apologetic, conceptualizations of mysticism. While scientific objectification of mysticism pathologized the
visible manifestations of the mystical experience, namely somatizations, theological discourse came to also define itself against mysti-

cal discourse by opposing its ancient tradition to what it perceived was new and heterogenous.[7] Finally, de Certeau claims, modern apologists of mysticism, under the pressure of new modes of scientific and theological investigation, came to discriminate between the somatization of the mystical experience, which they called "sensory mysticism," and the experience of mysticism as it relates to doctrines, which they alternatively called "negative," "apophatic," or again "speculative mysticism."[8] As de Certeau rightly reflects, the believers themselves came to confuse mysticism with the miraculous or extraordinary. In the beginning of the twentieth century, for example, the theologian Father Auguste Poullain, in his *Des grâces d'oraison: Traité de théologie mystique* (1901) indefatigably ennumerated stories of stigmata, levitations, psychological "miracles," and somatic curiosities, as if these manifestations encapsulated the meaning of mysticism.[9]

The extreme position of Father Poullain has been counteracted in the second part of the twentieth century by other apologists and scholars of mysticism, who in turn disregarded somatization and insisted, instead, on the existential experience of mystics. But, as de Certeau states, this "reinvention" of mysticism confined itself too exclusively to the philosophical or theological analysis of textual sources, gladly abandoning the embarrassing symbolic language of the body to psychology or ethnology.[10] In so doing they reiterated the rupture between mystical phenomena and the existential experience itself.

The self-positioning of modern scientific discourse, as the *not-that* of the mystical that echoed in theological discourse, had repercussions, asserts de Certeau, on the discursive pratices of the mystics themselves. First, the mystics arrogated to themselves a tradition.[11] Second, internalizing its reification by the scientific and theological discourses, mystical discourse started to psychologize mystical states. Also, interrogating itself, it consequently migrated toward other genres or created new ones.[12] Third, as a consequence of a renewed and unacceptable loss, the personal practices of the mystics were marked, asserts de Certeau, by a greater importance than ever of somatization.[13]

Keeping in mind de Certeau's historicization of the mystical movement in this period, I locate where a problematic *raison d'être* and a reification of mysticism emerge in Marie de l'Incarnation's and Madame Guyon's writings. I also show how the reception of their writings by theologians of the end of the seventeenth century reveal these same preoccupations. Finally, I demonstrate how their writing practices characteristically not only migrated but also produced other genres, discourses, and perceptions of the self and of the body. Because I take gender as a viable category of historical inquiry, however, and because I consider the whole mystical movement from the perspective of the female mystics, I am able to adumbrate and to extend in different ways some of de Certeau's generalizations.[14]

Using gender as a category of inquiry leads to the realization, for example, that female mysticism has always been characterized by the participation and somatization of the body and that the sixteenth and seventeenth centuries did not innovate on that score, as de Certeau suggests. While it may be true, as he affirms, that starting in the sixteenth century male mystics began to experience more somatization than previously was the case, the same cannot be said for female mystics. In the same vein, de Certeau states that during these two centuries those attracted by mysticism came increasingly from disempowered social and geographical areas.[15] Again, this demographic shift might be applicable to newly disempowered men of this period who were attracted by a movement marked by nostalgia. Recent historical research on female mystics shows that already in the thirteenth century women flocked in great number to the mystical movement and that somatization was particularly (if not exclusively) characteristic of female mystics from the very beginning. Further, as Bynum has shown, women's disempowerment in the thirteenth century was due to specific historical events within the organization of the church. Gender as a category of critical inquiry allows us to see that although disempowerment may be manifested through somatization equally by men and women, they do not necessarily manifest it for the same reasons or at the same time; gender is a social factor that profoundly colors their respective experience of life and events.

My study also refers to some of de Certeau's philosophical reflections on mysticism. De Certeau does not dismiss the mystical experience, as modern science has done. Nor does he follow its modern apologists who, adopting the biases of science, divide mysticism between bodily manifestations (which on the whole they devalue) and disembodied experience and doctrines. De Certeau's confronting modern theological and scientific discourses with mystical discourse allows him to retrieve a space in which the heterogeneity and irreducibility of lived mystical experience can at least partially emerge and which scientific epistemology makes impossible to conceptualize.[16] De Certeau states that we cannot say anymore than the mystics themselves what indeed the mystical experience is. We can only accept that, according to them, it opens up "a space that the mystic can no longer live without," that it is "like throwing open a window into one's dwelling," and allowing "a new sense of ease . . . a breath of fresh air to enter one's life," and that "it seems to rise up from some unfathomable dimension of existence, as from an ocean whose origins precede mankind."[17] Mystical experience seems indeed to bring deep tranformation to existence itself.

What emerges is a radicality that consists in an unrelenting resistance to and an undoing of procedures of reification.[18] This space of the mystical experience which de Certeau retrieves, and which is precisely what scientific discourse excludes in order to found itself in the first place, becomes the repository of "that immense remnant" of everything in human experience that has not been tamed and symbolized by language.[19]

Like Michel Foucault, his contemporary, de Certeau is interested in the workings of the relationships between dominant power structures and oppositional practices of everyday life. But unlike Foucault, he does not believe that dominant power "possesses the capacity of expanding everywhere the policy that it founds."[20] Nor does he believe that the functioning of a whole society can be reduced to a single dominant apparatus. De Certeau articulates this problem in *The Practice of Everyday Life*, in which he distinguishes "strategies of power" from "tactics of opposition." He defines "strategy" as a manipulation on the part of the dominant power to insinuate itself into the social body and even into the smallest recesses of the individual's psyche. A "tactic," however, is the maneuver that the dominated subject deploys to counter the effect of the strategy of dominant power: "A tactic insinuates itself into the other's place [the dominant power], fragmentarily, without taking it over in its entirety, without being able to keep it at a distance."[21] De Certeau shows how those subjected to dominant power poach on it and con-

coct a meaning of their own. In this framework, the mystical experience would be a particularly deep experience of daily practices
that would allow the subject to oppose pernicious and vicious instances of dominant power while transcending, without resolving
them, deep contradictions that would otherwise tear the subject
apart.

My study distinguishes two kinds of "tactics" and their effects
that Marie de l'Incarnation and Madame Guyon use in their resistance to dominant gender power structures: the first one is not different from oppositional tactics women used throughout all of
Western history; the other, nondiscursive, more directly stems from
their practices as mystics.

The chapters that follow also refer to the framework of American historical and theoretical feminist scholarship on female mysticism. Caroline Walker Bynum establishes the existence of a specifically female mystical tradition and motivation within Western
mysticism. She shows how the Gregorian reform in the middle of
the eleventh century placed the church under the control of the
clergy, giving the priests the exclusive privilege of approaching and
touching the Eucharist.[22] In addition, from the eleventh through
the thirteenth century, canons and theologians continually stressed
that women were forbidden to be priests, to preach, to teach, or
even to study at the university. This tendency deprived women of
the quasi-sacerdotal religious functions they had held and of the
independence they had enjoyed before that time. Bynum's studies
give us a more tangible sense of what female mystics had lost and
were refusing to mourn than do those of de Certeau. Given the fact
that women were denied access to education, we may legitimately
ask to what extent they were directly affected by scientific, cosmological, and theological upheavals at the waning of the Middle
Ages. We may thus wonder if the metaphors of loss and refused
mourning that mark the writings and the bodies of female mystics
from the beginning of the movement do not refer to more pressing
realities. We have grounds to believe, indeed, that the melancholy
hidden beneath the metaphors of loss and the refused mourning in
female mystics' texts originated in a situation particular to women.
For women, the losses were indeed specific.[23]

Thus, for Bynum, who directs her attention to the late Middle
Ages, the problem of authority with regard to female mysticism lies

at the heart of the mystical movement. Bynum interprets the predominence of women in the mystical movement and their characteristic bodily manifestations as a creative response to the increased role given to an exclusively male clergy in the church. Thus, for Bynum, mystical union is a substitute or an alternative created by women to counter the newly glorified clerical status denied to them.[24] Mystical union allowed women to experience a direct contact with God that was analogous to or even more privileged than that of the priest who touched the Eucharist. It also permitted the mystic to serve as counselor, mediator, and mystical medium for the sacraments. In other words, it allowed the mystic to serve an apostolic function despite the church's many explicit prohibitions. This movement gave women a charismatic authorization to become agents, despite the fact that dogma and theology denied them any legitimate authorization to do so. In fact, mysticism provided the most intelligent and talented women with opportunities to forge extraordinary careers for themselves and to go far beyond the multiple restrictions that otherwise controlled women's lives.[25] Bynum has indeed forcefully claimed an agency in history for medieval female mystics, attributing to them a central role in shaping the mainstream of late medieval piety, a role that has hitherto not been underscored.

The female mystic's body has become a stake in medieval and feminist scholarship, most recently through the work of Bynum. Bynum has set a new trend by interpreting female mystics' suffering and psychosomatization of piety as a positive and creative manipulation of the body that resulted in self-empowerment, self-affirmation, and religious transcendence. Her positive reevaluation of a mysticism in which the body takes a primordial place and with which women closely identified (and were identified) consequently views the drama of the female mystic's body as an empowering one. By showing how, through the theology of *imitatio Christi*, the body and the flesh took on a positive value as a means of transcendence, Bynum has challenged the traditional assumption held by many medieval scholars, according to whom medieval asceticism is rooted in dualism: that is, the idea that the spirit is opposed, or entrapped by the body.[26] The extravagant penitential practices of the Middle Ages, she affirms, "are not—as historians have often suggested—a world-denying, self-hating, decadent response of a society wracked by plague, famine, heresy, war, and ecclesiastical corruption."[27] For Bynum, these practices represented, on the contrary, the idea that the body and the flesh provided an access to God and to transcendence:

> [These bodily practices were] a profound expression of the doctrine of the Incarnation: the doctrine that Christ, by becoming human, saves *all* that the human being is. It arose in a religious world whose central ritual was the coming of God into food as macerated flesh, and it was compatible with, not contradictory to, new philosophical notions that located the nature of things not in their abstract definitions but in their individuating matter or particularity.[28]

Accordingly, she argues that if we understand what the mystics believe they are experiencing, then, what seem to us, as modern women, to be despicable acts of self-inflicted suffering, become signs of positive empowerment:

> Beatrice of Ornacieux driving nails through her palms, Dorothy of Montau and Lukardis of Oberweimar wrenching their bodies into bizarre pantomimes of the moment of Crucifixion, and Serafina of San Gimignano, revered *because* she was paralyzed, were to their own contemporaries not depressing or horrifying but glorious. They were not rebelling against or torturing their flesh out of guilt over its capacities so much as using the possibilities of its full sensual and affective range to soar ever closer to God.[29]

Where Simone de Beauvoir and her followers could only see victimization,[30] historians such as Bynum can see subversion, strategies, and opportunities, if they focus on the medieval and theological context.

Bynum points out that the favorable light cast upon affectivity, femininity, and flesh by theologians of the twelfth century did not lead, in their minds, to the idea that even though women were flesh they could achieve transcendence; rather, the theologians' attitude was meant to humble men by questioning their own transcendence. She explains, however, that this turn in male religious sensibility opened the possibility of transcendence through the flesh, an idea that gave women an opportunity they seized upon. She shows how medieval women, whom theologians identified with the sins of the flesh, consequently espoused most literally the theology of *imitatio Christi*, pushing identification with the redemptive macerated flesh of Christ to the extreme. She asserts that medieval female mystics' holy inedia, or anorexia, is not an illness but is given its full meaning through the literal understanding of the theology of the Eucharist, which suggests that one is to find true life and redemption by ingesting Christ's body. She adds that, given the increasing interdiction for women to touch the Eucharist, it is not surprising that the host would have assumed a central place in women's religious life. In this perspective, although the outrageous asceticism of female mystics is no less horrible, it takes on another significance; according to Bynum, the mystics are no longer to be viewed as victims, as some feminists scholars would have them,[31] but as agents of their own destiny. Their behavior is thus no longer seen as a symptom of what patriarchy and Christianity needed to repress in order to perpetuate itself but rather as a creative strategy to achieve subjectivity and transcendence. Accordingly, rather than a hapless vehicle for an ideology that oppresses religious women, their writings are a manifestation of their creativity as literary subjects; their spirituality thus reveals a world of positive, regenerative, and fertile symbols.

Bynum's work is a landmark for its strength and originality; her revisions are audacious and at times comforting to the reader of women's history who is weary of dealing with a history of oppression, victimization, and containment. We must also credit Bynum for the impetus she has given to the multidisciplinary study of female mysticism and piety and for her subtle and sophisticated analyses of the mystics' texts. Yet, I feel that her brilliant demonstration that female mystics' desire for hyperbolic suffering is to be viewed as a positive element in the history of women is fundamentally objectionable.

In her preface to *Holy Feast and Holy Fast* Bynum gives us a clue as to what motivates her search for a dignified meaning to medieval female saints' suffering. This motivation seems to originate in her mother's struggle to wrestle dignity and meaning from the sufferings of her own life: "[This book] is also an expression of hope that those future generations of women will not lose the compassion, the altruism, and the moral courage that made Merle Walker's life not a tragedy of self-abnegation but a triumph over meaninglessness and suffering."[32] As Hayden White has observed, history is a set of narratives that create a past of which we would like to be heirs.[33] Indeed, oppressed groups, and among them women, have not failed to write a history from which they would like to be descended. The problem for the oppressed group, however, is that the history they create is ambivalent. It is not always certain that they ought to identify with their past history if they aim to develop their self-esteem. To write a positive and even a triumphant history of the (fore)mother(s) seems, nevertheless, central to Bynum's project, and this leads her to a set of controversial positions regarding what she calls the "received wisdom" of those who do not glorify female mystics' somatization and suffering.

In order to demarginalize women and their suffering bodies by putting them at the center of medieval piety, Bynum must do two things. First, she must counter modern Western scholarship that has denigrated female mystics' bodily drama by reevaluating sensory mysticism in a positive light.[34] Second, she must refute the claims of feminists who affirm that sensory mysticism is self-denying and self-hating and that medieval religious women were victims of misogyny. Bynum's focus on bodily phenomena of the female mystics thus duplicates the logic of modern theological debates on mysticism. According to de Certeau, this modern theological debate, influenced by the scientific reification of mysticism, started either to focus on its bodily phenomena or, on the contrary, dismissing them as unimportant women's problems, focused rather on the existential aspects of the mystical experience.[35] Bynum's response is that these bodily manifestations indeed appear more in women but that they have a positive experiential and theological meaning. She argues that the reason medieval female mystics inflicted suffering upon their bodies was not that the body represented a prison for their soul but that, on the contrary, they used all the affective and sensual possibilities of the flesh in order to attain transcendence: it was thus through the possibility offered *by* the body (and not against it) that they soared ever closer to God. It follows, then, that if the body led them to transcendence, sensory mysticism achieved the same goal as negative mysticism and, along with the female mystics who practiced it, it is thus worthy of scholarly and theological attention. This line of thinking, however, leaves her with the unavoidable task of explaining why a much greater number of women than men took to sensory mysticism, extreme self-inflicted suffering, and parapsychological manifestations. Despite her protestations against possible accusations of essentialism, Bynum nevertheless ends up claiming that women's propensity for somatic piety and suffering is a natural and positive female disposition. I will cite but one example of this constant affirmation and denial that bolster her research:

> First, women's emotionality. This is a matter about which we do well to be careful, for assertions about women's emotionality or sentimentality often simply reflect the sexual stereotypes common in the Western tradition. Nonetheless, it is true that anthropologists have documented the greater prominence of ecstasy and possession in women's religiosity all over the world.[36]

At first, Bynum seems to agree with the need to question stereotypical representations of women as emotional and suffering. But she immediately bypasses her own caution and assumes that if "anthropologists have documented the greater prominence of ecstasy and possession in women's religiosity all over the world," it must be because of women's natural propensity toward such behavior. Her slippages from the cultural to the biological are numerous, affirming, for instance, that if female mystics adopted the same symbols as their male counterparts, they did so, however, in continuity with their "social and biological self."[37]

To be sure, any attempt to understand female mystics' bodily drama and discourse, engaged as they are in issues not only of authority and power but also of resistance in social practices, entails a revision of a conception of female mystics as mere victims of misogyny.[38] But I depart from the conclusions that interpret the contradictory and paradoxical resistance found in female mystics' bodily drama as a subversion of patriarchal order that should thus commend a celebration of female mystics' bodily behavior. For this reason, I challenge the more recent, and it seems prevalent, view that since female mystics manipulated their bodies in response to clerical power—thus creating a version of female piety—they consequently should be seen as absolute agents of their own destinies. This view erases the power inequalities existing between the female mystics and aspects of the church's ideology against which they so vigorously struggled. Bodies are not only strategic sites where gender differences are constructed, but they also serve as signifiers of masculine dominance and feminine subordination. Hence, women's bodies are a locus of contradictory and paradoxical expressions of protest and retreat, of collusion and resistance to their subordinate status, and they reflect both subordination and impulses toward empowerment. Succinctly put, the question I ask concerning the female mystic's body and female mystics' agency is: For the purpose of constructing a history of women, is it possible to rehabilitate the female mystics of the past, together with their ailing bodies, in a positive way as Bynum does, without lapsing into the celebration and the essentialization of women's suffering?

With regard to two mystics who both partook in female mystical practices and reacted to a world that increasingly devalued such practices, the question must be posed as to what is at stake in an examination of female mysticism and its characteristic somatization in the Western tradition: Is female mysticism a possible space for the disruption of the patriarchal order, or, as Sarah Beckwith puts it, does it "exist to act out rigorously . . . [patriarchal order's] most sexist fantasies"?[39] While it is true that female mystics derived a degree of authority from their practices, they also paid dearly for it by revealing self-abnegation and self-hatred. Further, since the forms of resistance deployed by female mystics are often self-destructive or self-denying, it is legitimate to ask whether, in spite of their resistance, they did not ultimately serve to affirm, rather than to challenge, dominant social definitions of women as wicked flesh.

I argue that the ways in which Marie de l'Incarnation and Madame Guyon seized or shunned opportunities and that the ways in which their writings were received by church authorities shed light on the meaning of their mystical practices and allow us a nuanced reading of female agency in Western mysticism. I do not deny an agency to these two women in their struggle to wrestle meaning for themselves out of their oppressors' words. However, the conditions of existence of their dissenting discourse and its limits need to be clarified, especially as these two female mystics were dialogically engaged both with the medieval world that created them and with the modern world that negated them.

But then another question arises: Why be interested at all in women of the past if the lesson we draw is once again that of containment and co-option of female resistance by the gender ideology of any given time? The answer is that individual resistance and attempts to assert subjectivity within the dominant institutional definitions of "femininity" constitute an important object of inquiry in themselves. They can teach us much about the workings of power and survival and about the limits of a resistance, in this case female, which had the capacity neither to deconstruct patriarchy nor to evaluate its effects on women. It is equally interesting to understand how the tensions created by a resistance within established frameworks of femininity most often result in women being at war with their own bodies and minds.

My study blurs the boundaries between literature, religious history, theology, the history of New France, the history of mysticism, and the history of women. Nevertheless, the questions that I address to these texts stem from a literary and theoretical training rather than from the kind of concerns typically found in historical, theological, or philosophical studies of female mysticism.

Chapter One

Female Mysticism

A Historical Perspective

Female Mysticism and the Gregorian Reform

n twelfth- and thirteenth-century Western Europe a charismatic movement known as mysticism[1] emerged within the heart of the Catholic Church. This movement initiated new religious practices as well as new literary and theological traditions. Although historians disagree as to the meaning of mysticism, they do agree that mysticism attracted individuals of both sexes, particularly (if not exclusively) those individuals who had no other source of power.[2] Thus, it is not surprising that women representing all social classes flocked to the mystical movement in great numbers and that they developed a distinctly female mystical tradition. In short, as historians also agree, the movement was both inspired and dominated by women.[3]

Mystics claimed a direct union with God, a union not earthly but reserved for the redeemed after resurrection. Female mysticism was characterized by the importance it gave to the female body in the relationship between the individual and the divine, for it was thought that the female body was a privileged means of ac-

15

cess to God. Historians agree that, when compared to male saints, the body of female saints was more profoundly and more often traversed by psychosomatic and parapsychic manifestations.[4] Women's piety in this movement was most often characterized by corporeal imitation of Christ in his suffering humanity. This could translate into a mixture of self-inflicted suffering, accompanied by a general state of illness interpreted as God's gift. The underlying theological justification for such a practice was that through incarnation, whereby Christ/God descended on earth to save humans, mankind could mystically ascend to God through imitation of his suffering humanity.[5] The mystics' *Imitatio Christi*-piety could also be accompanied by parapsychic phenomena understood as supernatural graces sent by God, such as visions, voices, ecstasies, stigmata, localized bleeding, exudations, levitation, or inedia. The birth of this kind of piety, called affective or sensory mysticism by modern scholars, must be placed within the context of the religious revival experienced by Christianity in the twelfth and thirteenth centuries. A new religious sensibility appeared at that time, which advocated the idea of a more accessible God and thus encouraged a more emotional, more affective, and more internalized form of piety. This new sensibility gave rise to what has been called the feminization of the language of male religious officials of the day; a feminization of religious language which, in all likelihood, had its origin in the masculine desire to view authority no longer simply in terms of discipline but also in terms of love. The feminization of piety was also signaled by an increase in the number of devotions being made to female saints and by an admiration for characteristics that people of the era conceived of as feminine (tears, weakness, compassion, and moral irrationality).

At the same time as sensory mysticism, there flourished what has been called negative or apophatic mysticism. The doctrinal roots of this mysticism go back to early Christianity. It was transmitted throughout the Middle Ages by the translations of the works of Pseudo-Dionysius.[6] These translations from Greek into Latin were done by John Scot Erigenus (852), Jean Sarrazin (c. 1165), and Robert Grossetête (1240–1243).[7] Negative mysticism advocated a mental practice that led to a quieting of the logos and reached beyond memory, language, symbols, images, and representations to permit the meeting with the divine. Modern theologians and scholars who have sought to discern two trends in mysticism have favored negative mysticism as the only true means of access to God, looking with suspicion at sensory mysticism, which they have attributed more to women.[8] Many female mystics, however, seem to have participated in both trends and even to have contributed greatly to the articulation of negative mystical theology, while many men who wrote mystical doctrine also experienced somatization.[9]

There is no question that the male mystic in a Christian, gendered ideology finds himself in a position that might be called "feminine," that is, one of submission vis-à-vis the masculine principle of divinity. The entire symbolism of the soul as God's bride, which we find in the Song of Songs, as well as in the nuptial symbolism developed by the Beguines during the thirteenth century and taken up again by the male mystics during the fourteenth century, bear witness to this assumption. Further, the male mystics—and this is true for Eckhart, Suso, Ruysbroeck, John of the Cross, Bernard of Clairvaux, Surin, Tauler, Rolle, and even Francis of Assisi— adopted a poetical or metaphorical position of loving submission to God the Father, and many of them also demonstrated a spiritual and literary debt to their predecessors, the Beguines. All of this, however, did not prevent them from occupying a position of social and hierarchical power in relation to women, for whom they served as spiritual directors, preachers, or confessors. Female mystics, to the contrary, held a social position of powerlessness, regardless of their social class. Furthermore, male mystics were more often legitimized through canonization even though female mystics were more numerous. Finally, male mystics may have been submissive to God, but they nevertheless wrote for the edification of women from a position of knowledge and authority that was accepted by both the world and the church. Female mystics, instead, wrote for male clerics because the latter were in a position to be guarantors of their legitimacy. God may have confided his most intimate secrets to "simple" women, but it was mostly in educated, religious men, established as their witnesses, that these women confided. Without recognition by at least one member of the clergy, the female mystic could easily find herself rejected as a heretic and a criminal and become a derelict. In addition, although they sometimes counseled their own spiritual directors, female mystics first had to establish credibility by believing, and causing others to believe, that their authority came directly from God.

Caroline Walker Bynum shows that female and male mystics responded to otherworldly demands in a manner underlining their respective social and political powers (or lack thereof). She analyzes specifically male and female mystics' identification with the feminine. She states that for female mystics, who identified with women's poverty, deprivation, and loss, mysticism was a means whereby they could impose their will, deploy their particular genius in the world, exercize influence and power, and manipulate the symbolic to their own advantage. It was a means of recognition and empowerment. To the contrary, for male mystics who identified with women's poverty, mysticism might have been a way to exonerate themselves from the privileges of power and recognition. In a roundabout way this exoneration also allowed them to reaffirm their rights to temporal privileges. Bynum's comparison of female and male mystics precludes their assimilation and therefore precludes the erasure of the sociopolitical specificity of female mysticism.[10] Although I agree with Bynum on this point, I have some reservations concerning what appears to be an assimilation of medieval female piety with female nature.

The church could not accept, without reticence or a sense of paradox, this female-dominated movement in its midst. From the very beginning, the Christian mystics who talked of a union with God that transcended both the intellect and dualism of thought were in conflict with the institution of the church, which feared that their mode of apprehending the divine might bypass the hierarchy, the sacraments, and even the mediation of Christ. By the early fourteenth century, both the themes and forms of female piety were becoming suspect in the eyes of the church. Marguerite Porète, who had been accused of the Heresy of the Free Spirit, was burned in Paris in 1310, and the Beguines were suppressed by the Council of Vienna (1311–12).[11] The watchfulness of the clergy, the tendency to force female mystics to enter convents, and the threat of the Inquisition or of the stake remained constant throughout the history of female mysticism. The suspicion surrounding female prophets reflected that which surrounded all popular or secular religious movements and mysticism in general, whether in the fourteenth or the seventeenth century. This is also the case for Madame Guyon and the new religious consciousness that arose in Europe at the end of the seventeenth century.

Confronted with a growing number of individuals and groups who claimed direct, divine authorization to spread the word of God and reform society, the church kept a close, mistrustful watch on their teaching and behavior; at the same time, it either condemned or encouraged what it saw, according to how useful these individuals or groups could be to the church.[12] Although the church sometimes recognized certain mystics after carefully pruning their teaching of all heterodoxy, it refused to hold them up as examples to the people, preferring to keep them hidden away in cloisters. The most prudent of the female mystics succeeded in gaining acceptance for their exceptional status and, at the same time, in reassuring the church hierarchy of their obedience to the priests and need for the sacraments. This paradoxical situation made the mystics vulnerable to accusations of heterodoxy and anticlericalism, accusations that were all the more easy to hurl at them because women lacked a theological education and therefore could not avoid the pitfall of ratiocination. These fears and the need for caution often resulted in quasi-pathological scrupulousness in the female mystics and in religious women at large. The most vulnerable were those who refused the cloister, thus escaping ecclesiastical supervision, such as the Beguines in the Low Countries, Northern France, and Germany, the Beatas in Spain, and the terciary orders in Italy. Such was also the case of Madame Guyon, who refused any affiliation, whether with religious or lay orders. But cloistered mystics were not safe from the accusation of heresy either, and even Teresa of Avila was harassed by the Inquisition.

Female Mysticism and the Catholic Reformation

In the sixteenth and seventeenth centuries, encouraged by the enthusiasm sparked by the Catholic Reformation, mysticism was revitalized and women were again prominent in the movement. Again, their enthusiasm was closely watched and restricted to convents. Within this confine, religious women, under what Brémond has coined the "mystic invasion," nevertheless made great strides in the early years of the seventeenth century, prying open the Gallican Church and forcing it, by midcentury, to admit a greater number of women into its inner life of prayer. To begin with, a small group of Spanish Carmelite nuns appeared in Paris in 1601, bringing with them the spiritual heritage of Teresa of Avila and John of the Cross. In the next forty years, under the influence and organization of Madame Acarie, fifty-five Carmelite convents were opened in France. These became the center for female spirituality and had much influence on the spiritual life of the upper class.

Other orders were subsequently reformed or founded whose spirituality was influenced by that of the Carmelites and the Oratorians and which also had much influence on contemporary high society. Henri Brémond was right to say that in seventeenth-century France the world and the (female) cloisters intertwined. By midcentury there were more nuns than monks and friars in France; this was an unprecedented occurrence.

The Flemish and German mysticism of the thirteenth and fourteenth centuries, in addition to Spanish mysticism as represented by Teresa of Avila and John of the Cross in the sixteenth century, were claimed as precursors by what has been named the French, or Abstract School, of Mysticism. Marie de l'Incarnation and Madame Guyon's spiritual doctrines are inspired by this school. The two mystics are also heirs of the medieval female mystics' bodily drama, as expressed in their visions, premonitions, ecstasies, prophesies, and illnesses interpreted as God's signs, as well as in their harsh bodily dicipline and self-denial, which they each practiced in a specific period of their respective lives.

Female piety, as identified with both trends of mysticism, enjoyed widespread recognition from the thirteenth to the end of the seventeenth century.[13] For five centuries the church and female mystics had an unwritten contract, agreed to by the rest of society, according to which the church would confirm the mystic's election, would look upon her bodily signs as sent by God, and would accept her charismatic vocation if she, in return, would submit to the church's authority and hierarchy, uphold its dogma, and profess to identify with the church's feminine ideal of humility, passivity, ignorance, silence, and total obedience. This was a powerful double bind. It was a contract productive of paradoxes for which female mystics alone paid a heavy price, notwithstanding the real empowerment they secured for themselves through mysticism. By the

end of the century, that option for charismatic prestige and authority within the church, however problematic, was seriously challenged. Various epistemological and social changes coalesced to
profoundly transform the options available to religious women, the
limits imposed on them by the Tridentine Reformation, as well as
the perception of society regarding mysticism. These changes are
recorded in Marie de l'Incarnation's and Madame Guyon's writings
and were the source of transformations of their mystical discourse.

As Elizabeth Rapley reminds us, it would be a mistake to interpret the wave of women's religious enthusiasm in the sixteenth and
seventeenth centuries as officially part of the Tridentine Reformation.[14] Indeed, when the Council of Trent in the midsixteenth century drew up its plans for reforming the Catholic world, it did not
envisage any role for women. In the sixteenth century, the church
was not better prepared than in the twelfth century to let women
fully participate in religious life, and the Tridentine Reformation
reacted as rigidly to this overflow of female charisma and vocations
as it had to late medieval reforms. The female religious enthusiasm, sparked by the Catholic Reformation, renewed the irksome
problem the church had had to face with the initial female response to mysticism in the Late Middle Ages: what was the church
to do with this enthusiasm and these charismatic inclinations, as
well as with women's desire to have a place in Catholic work outside the convent? Parallels can be drawn between the Catholic re-
formations of the twelfth and sixteenth centuries. Indeed, history
might have repeated itself, for the church tried to respond to this
new wave of female religious invasion with its traditional mar-
ginalization of women. The church maintained that women could
not have any other choice but *Aut maritus, aut murus*, either a
husband or a convent wall.[15] The Council ordered bishops, under
the threat of eternal damnation, to make sure to impose *clausura*
on nuns under their jurisdiction. Nuns were strictly forbidden to
leave their cloister without permission from their bishop.[16] During
the first part of the seventeenth century, the leaders of the Catholic Reformation followed closely the orders of the church, and, despite the resistance to *clausura* on the part of religious women who
desired to participate in the re-Christianization of society, the
church triumphed in cloistering them. The church's prescription for
religious women to return to the strict observance of *clausura*, cou-

pled with the solemn vows of poverty, chastity, and obedience, constituted for them a total separation from the world.

New Options for Religious Women/Repercussions for Female Mystics

The seventeenth century saw the creation of multiple social and charitable institutions that aimed at educating both boys and girls as well as socializing, catechising, and helping the poor. These new social demands would eventually result in the creation of new female religious orders that would include women in the Catholic life of work in the world.

Since not all religious women were satisfied with the prospect of a cloistered and contemplative life but desired, instead, a religious life in a community that would remain open to the world, an organized resistance to *clausura* was felt throughout the seventeenth century. Religious women's desire to ally mystical union with service to others in the world was not new. Prior to this period they had been repeatedly barred from imitating Christ in his apostolic life, leaving them no options other than to imitate his suffering. Their earlier attempts to ally a regulated, religious community life with service to others in the outside world had repeatedly been circumvented by the church, even more so after the Council of Trent with its increased insistence on the total enclosure of women and their isolation from the world. Elizabeth Rapley has authoritatively documented the battle waged in the seventeenth century by several women's congregations to gain the status of religious women within the world. In the early part of the seventeenth century, the *Visitation Filles de Sainte-Marie*, the Ursulines, and both Congregations of the *Filles de Notre-Dame* lost the battle and succumbed to cloistering. Although women in religious orders had not yet won the right to be catechists, they impressed upon the public the need for women teachers for girls. Rapley adds that "the teaching of day pupils, permitted by the Holy See for the first time in 1607, on conditions that preserved *clausura* as much as possible, was a significant advance."[17]

Later in the century, the *Filles Séculières* won a freer life from a begrudging public who needed their services, and the *Filles de*

Montréal were the first congregation to not be confined by *clausura*. While compromising with Pope Urban VIII, local bishops, and elite family clients on several points of organizational and socioeconomic controls, these congregations, together with some of the regular orders of women, created a new tradition of female religious life that lasted well into the nineteenth century. From communal homes or semicloistered convents, these congregations, as well as several regular orders of women, taught poor and well-to-do girls alike catechism classes, set up soup kitchens, took care of the sick in hospitals, and, when not cloistered, assisted their parish priests in several pastoral cares. The impetus for this movement came from middle-class women, and as their work expanded, it began to take on the character of professionalism.[18] Rapley argues that "the complex of social services which developed in the seventeenth century, and especially feminine education, was the creation rather than the creator of feminine religious congregations."[19] The assertion is bold. We need not be as radical as Rapley in crediting women with a great deal of agency in the development of female social services and the opening of the convents. Rather, we can say that religious women took advantage of the era's debate on the education of girls to encourage a need for their education and appointed themselves schoolmistresses. Similarly, we can say that they seized upon the new socializing institutions to render themselves indispensable through their free services, thus creating a need for them outside the cloister. This perspective offers a more nuanced notion of female agency as operative within a society not run by women.

This battle against *clausura* could not have been won without the schism within the church brought about by the Reformation. The Catholic Church was unwittingly forced to respond to the Protestant Church; it could not simply counter it. In the battle to restore Catholicism, it became necessary to use female catechists in order to stem the stream of women into the reformed religion. The schism of the church and the loss of its hegemony thus provided an opportunity for religious women to forge a place for themselves in the Catholic world outside the convents.

Religious women, such as Marie de l'Incarnation, were quick to seize this creation of social institutions as an opportunity to render themselves indispensable and thus to fashion a life for themselves and their orders outside of the cloister. This new avenue for religious women contributed, no doubt, to a displacement or at least to another expression of women's religious experience. The Ursulines and Marie de l'Incarnation were invited to participate in the settling of the French colonies in America *because* they were a teaching order with a mixed *clausura.*

Against various church authorities at different periods of her life, Madame Guyon avoided the convent altogether. Indeed, she conceived of her mission as bringing the spiritual life to people at large despite the clergy who were either ignorant of spiritual life or, if they were not, did not see fit to enlighten people on the subject. Madame Guyon's position illustrates the claims of historians of religion who state that the end of the seventeenth century witnessed the beginning of a divorce between religious sentiments and the church. I contrast Marie de l'Incarnation, who seized opportunities offered her to forge a new self-definition within the church, with Madame Guyon, who forged a self against, and eventually outside the church. In both cases, however, I examine how the self is defined against the demands of motherhood.

A World to Conquer

The enthusiasm of the Catholic Reformation translated into the impulse to conquer or reconquer lost souls for the Kingdom of God. It is in this missionary spirit that the colony of New France was established. However, the New World was to prove a new avenue of expansion for religious women in general and for Marie de l'Incarnation in particular. The settling of the colony of New France in the New World played an important role in demonstrating the incongruency of *clausura* with an expanding world in need of women's work and services. Marie de l'Incarnation's writings reflect the difficulty that *clausura* created for her work as a missionary, even though the *clausura* of the Ursulines, as compared to that of contemplative orders, was somewhat open to the world and in Quebec was even more flexible than in France.

The male missionaries in New France urgently requested the participation of religious women in order to care for the sick and to instruct Indian and French women. This request in itself testified to the fact that women were needed not only to teach catechism but also to render social services for which men felt unfit. This, indeed, was a new perception of women's participation in the social realm. As we have seen, the *Filles de Montréal* were the first French congregation not to be confined by *clausura*.

In the case of Marie de l'Incarnation, I consider how her role as a missionary, dependent on subsidy from France, demanded that she produce discourses other than a mystical one, thus positioning her both as an ethnographer of the New World and as a historiographer of New France. Furthermore, the New World, intrinsically linked to the formation of a new anthropology, was also an element that diversified her mystical discourse. I analyze how at times her representation of Indian women differs sharply from that of male missionaries. In her depiction of Indian women she created a new, positive version of femininity, even if that version conflicted with her offical mission to convert and "civilize" her subjects. Her version of femininity also contradicted the European belief in a universal, essential nature of femininity and the Western ideal of female mysticism as self-sacrificing and hungry for suffering. I speculate on the conditions that made it possible for her to conjure such an image of femininity, and I conclude with the proposition that perhaps what permitted a vision of femininity that escaped all codes known to her was what in mysticism, precisely, escapes language and allows for deep resistance and the emergence of the unknown.

The frontier Madame Guyon set her heart on was Geneva, and her first impulse was the conversion of protestants. Soon, however, she was profoundly disappointed with the whole project of forced conversion, and, eventually, even conversion to a particular confession became irrelevant for her. Geneva was to prove to be a metaphor; Guyon's desire for a fresher spiritual horizon led her to participate in a religious movement that was emerging out of various confessional barriers and was inaugurating a new spiritual and philosophical era.

A Different Epistemology/A Different Body

Parallel to these emerging options for religious women (working orders and missions in the New World), which had an impact on the mystical discourse of Marie de l'Incarnation, an epistemological

shift occurred, as we have seen above, that would profoundly transform not only the way mysticism was perceived but also the way
mystics perceived themselves. The shift of society against mysticism throughout the seventeenth century can be perceived in increasing antimystic feelings, which succeeded in devaluing and
emptying mysticism of the meaning it had held since the thirteenth century. This shift played a major role in Madame Guyon's
tribulations. Even though the outcome of the century-long struggle
between antimystics and proponents of mysticism affected both
male and female mystics, it was all the more devastating for the
latter, since they lost their only means of religious authority within
the church.

Many reasons can be invoked for this turn of events, but beyond matters of dogma and political intrigues, the antimystic cli-
mate and the ensuing decline of mysticism reverberated with a
specifically modern conception and perception of the world. Michel
de Certeau has clearly shown how, in the sixteenth and seventeenth centuries, a revolutionary mode of scientific inquiry emphasizing reason defined itself against mysticism at the same time
that it reified it, reducing it to visible bodily phenomena.[20] It is not
by chance that the new female orders such as the Ursulines (which
emerged in the seventeenth century) were overt in their denigration of the traditional female mystics' bodily practices. Of course,
female working orders needed able-bodied women in their ranks;
but what made it possible for them to openly disdain and oppose
debilitating bodily practices was precisely the emerging perception
of the body issuing from scientific discourse and medical discoveries that were increasingly prevalent in society. Indeed, this epistemological shift moved away from a conception of the body as existing in a premodern analogical relationship with the world (or as a
vessel penetrated with magical, occult, and divine presences) to a
rational, organic, and medicalized perception of the body. I do not
suggest that this new scientific perception of the body has a relation of cause and effect with that of the Ursulines', but rather that
its manifestations in discourses issuing from different disciplines
substantiate the notion of "episteme," or epistemological rupture as
defined by Foucault.

The notion of epistemological discontinuity at work in Foucault
(and also in de Certeau) operates also in the work of those histo-

rians of science who argue that one can witness an epistemological change, a discontinuity, in the way texts produced by different disciplines in the sixteenth, seventeenth, and eighteenth centuries understand the world, the body, or nature.[21] Drawing from the history of science, historians of the body show how a different understanding of the world, coupled with medical discoveries, changed the understanding and the meaning of the body during this period.

Of course, one should not simplistically deduce from the notion of "episteme" or epistemological rupture that an absolute cultural break occurred in the sixteenth, seventeenth, and eighteenth centuries. If we argue that a certain coherence or a different epistemology is present in texts of different disciplines at a given moment of history, this does not mean to suggest that the whole of culture changed overnight. Epistemological shifts penetrate the social fabric slowly and unevenly. This lag of time may account for a mix of premodern and modern elements in seventeenth-century society and in the works of the two mystics I am considering, but the mix does not invalidate the thesis of a rupture. That is why we can witness the survival in scientific texts, and in society at large, of certain practices (stigmata, holy vision, etc.) long after their meaning has changed. Accordingly, although bodily manifestations in female mystics provoked unprecedented repulsion among church authorities at the end of the seventeenth century, this change did not immediately affect cultural practices in general nor did bodily manifestations disappear. On the contrary, these manifestations lasted far into the nineteenth century (and occasionally even occur nowadays); by the end of the seventeenth century, however, they were marginalized by the prevailing culture of modern Western society.

It is within the assumption of an epistemological rupture that is coherently reverberated in different discourses at one given moment that I situate Marie de l'Incarnation's shift in midcourse, from a traditional understanding and practice of bodily phenomena to an explicit condemnation of these practices. It is also within this context that we must view the increasing, prevalent, antimystic feelings of this period, including the Ursulines', Bossuet's, and other theologians' suspicions and aversions for mystics' bodily phenomena or harsh body discipline. This epistemological rupture was dramatically illustrated by Bossuet's acceptance by the public when in his writings he ridiculed Guyon's bodily manifestations.

Finally, it is within this context that I place Guyon's response to the attacks against her.[22] While Marie de l'Incarnation actively sought those situations that resulted in altering her mystical discourse, Guyon reacted to changes that were forced on her. I examine how her mystical writings responded to theologians' attacks upon her during her trial in the Quietist Affair. Forced to interrogate her own practices, she began to relativize and belittle bodily manifestations, without, however, giving them up. These attacks also resulted partly in her elaborating, in collaboration with Fénelon, a tradition for mysticism so as to prove that her doctrine was orthodox.

A New Era

Although a Western European phenomenon, the decline of mysticism occurred in its most spectacular fashion in France as it crystallized into the Quietist Affair at the end of the seventeenth century. Historians of religion agree that France was the center of mysticism throughout this period, as Germany and the Netherlands had been in the thirteenth and fourteenth centuries and as Spain had been in the sixteenth. But France was also the home of Descartes and, by the end of the seventeenth century, was greatly influenced by Cartesian philosophy, a philosophy that was yet another echo of the epistemological rupture and that played a major role in devaluing mystical experience, practices, and doctrine. The epoch was preoccupied with reason and science, and these new conceptual models infiltrated the church itself.

The Quietist Affair, in which Madame Guyon played a major role, marks the decline of Western mysticism and its diffusion into new genres. As a religious quarrel, it placed Bishop Bossuet (who championed the total authority of the church hierarchy in matters of faith) against Archbishop Fénelon and Madame Guyon (who defended mysticism and a more personal faith). Bossuet exemplifies de Certeau's assertions according to which at the end of this period there was an increasing divorce between theology and mystical doctrines, as well as between organized church and those who can be called mystics. Bossuet's triumph in the Affair thus signals a changing epistemology among theologians, and it had a disastrous consequence for the status of mysticism in Western European Christianity.

In opposition to the increasing tyranny of scientific reification of religious life, on the one hand, and the rigidity of established churches, on the other, a religious consciousness emerged, and it grew out of the established religious institutions at the end of the seventeenth century. Tolerance—that is, the respect for individual conscience and lived religious experience allowed to all rather than to just a chosen few—together with a demand for freedom of thought, became the rallying cry of this movement. The new consciousness was shared by individuals whose spiritual hunger could no longer be satisfied by the discourse of knowledge nor by the increasingly rigid orthodoxies of the established churches, whether Catholic, Anglican, Lutheran, or Calvinist. This new religious consciousness profoundly marked European philosophy in the eighteenth and nineteenth centuries.[23]

Opposed to Bossuet's authoritarianism in matters of faith, Madame Guyon was one of the prominent figures of this movement and, through the recognition a younger generation gave her, she exited the history of Western female mysticism and contributed to the philosophical making of a new era.

As for the female mystics, with the dissolution of a philosophical and religious context favorable to them, they were increasingly marginalized, losing their most potent means of making their voices heard and of having their desires taken seriously. It is true that as this option closed down for women, others opened up, such as those we have seen with open congregations (working orders with mixed *clausura* for women of the middle class, such as Marie de l'Incarnation). For upper-class women, new opportunities for education made possible a flourish of activity by female writers, scholars, and literary salons, all of which left their marks on the century. Various cultural historians have brought to light the female sphere of influence in seventeenth-century France.[24]

But the female mystic did not altogether disappear; paradoxically, she resurfaced on the stage of positivism. In its fight for power with the authority of the church, positivistic science amalgamated the medieval female saint with its new creation, the hysteric. In the passage between the medieval and modern eras, the names and the interpretations of female mystics' bodily phenomena became a stake between blocks of power such as the church, the state, and the medical establishment, and women often became caught in a crossfire of interpretations and names. This is already the case with the convulsionary mystics of Saint-Médard (1727–1733), whom the king, upon the advice of medical doctors, decided to prosecute as frauds and sexual perverts, thus eluding altogether the church's dialectic of orthodoxy and heresy.[25] It is even more so the case with one of the last two collective demonic possessions that occurred in the soon-to-be French, backward county of Morzine, in Savoie, between 1873–1875.[26] The collective possession of Morzine resembles others that had convulsed whole populations in the seventeenth century, such as those of Loudun, Louviers, or Auxonne. The difference, however, was that Morzine was a repetition. Occurring in the second part of the nineteenth century, it appeared as if borrowed from another age, the emergence of an anachronism. In Morzine, the old system of belief in possession by the devil was held by the villagers and the possessed women, while the state, its troops, the medical establishment, and the city bishop held out for the new system and treated the possessed women as mad or sick.[27]

The coexistence of competing interpretations of female somatization, along with the lingering occurence of this somatization in marginal sectors of society, explains the peculiar situation of Morzine. It also explains how Catherine Newman, in the second part of the twentieth century, could display inedia and stigmata, characteristics of medieval saints. Whereas medieval people considered the witch to be an ally of the devil and the possessed woman to be unwittingly acted upon by the devil (and in this way akin to the saints who were possessed by God), Charcot and positivistic medical science in general in the nineteenth century thought that the women of the Salpêtrière were sick and/or frauds. Some of the patients about whom Charcot wrote, namely the famous Madeleine de la Salpêtrière, displayed bodily afflictions similar to those manifested by the saints of times past. She, indeed, even attributed meaning to her symptoms according to beliefs expounded by those saints and mystics of former times.[28] What had changed, however, were the values and the beliefs of society at large, and particularly those of the men in authority who controlled these women. Where the psychosomatic manifestations of some of Charcot's patients might have been a proof of God's will for the priest of the late Mid-

dle Ages and the Renaissance, they were, for Charcot and his colleagues, a female pathology having to do with female nature.[29]

Above and beyond the epistemological revolution of the seventeenth century and the different discourses that have been produced about (or have produced) female psychosomatization in
Western civilization, the contract between the suffering woman
and the man having the power to name her is ubiquitous. With the
advent of modern science, women were still expected to suffer and
even had to reproduce suffering when demanded (before by the
priest, now by the psychiatrist), so as to prove that they were worthy of attention and recognition. Charcot learned to reproduce at
will the suffering in his female patients, to the delight of his male
audience. Georges Duby and Philippe Ariès, in their analysis of the
rapport between the female hysterics of the Salpêtrière and their
doctors, state that the therapeutic aim of the doctors (which is not
to be denied) and the necessity to refine clinical observation do not
suffice to explain the complacency of the psychiatrists in soliciting,
stirring up, and even creating in their female hysterical patients
the manifestations of an eroticism suffused with suffering; nor do
these scientific aims alone justify the psychiatrists' reveling in the
hysterics' mimed pleasure.[30] Duby and Ariès further claim that the
theater of hysteria of the nineteenth century might reveal a subtle
economy of masculine desire, and that above all it displays the
symptom of a masculine "dis-ease." What was staged at the Salpêtrière was a complex rapport between exhibitionism and voyeur-
ism, in which both parties were foiled in their attempt to express
their desires.[31] Duby and Ariès's analysis of this drama can also
throw light on the rapport between the female mystic and her ama-
nuensis (almost always a male cleric), who watched, wrote down,
elicited confidences, and expected from the female saint the specta-
cles of her amorous commerce with God. Scientific discourse and
justifications may have replaced the theological explanations of the
premodern period, but male and female desire seems to have been
caught up in the same theatrical arena, by a similar contract: a
demand for love and recognition on the part of the woman; on the
part of man, a quest for a knowledge (God in premodern times,
replaced by the enigma of woman in later times) supposedly channeled, albeit unconsciously, through women. In the medieval as
well as in the modern scenarios, man imposes an orthodoxy, reli-

gious or scientific, on the response he is soliciting from the woman. She mirrors back his desire when she perceives that she is recognized by him. Otherwise, when she perceives she is not recognized, she contradicts his orthodoxy (she most commonly contradicts him because, given the structure of patriarchy, he is always unlikely to recognize her as a subject). It is interesting to note that female psychosomatization adapted to the expectations of dominant conceptions. While the medieval mystic produced stigmata, the nineteenth-century hysteric produced symptoms indicating a repressed sexuality.

The main difference between these competing interpretations of female psychosomatization is, of course, that the late medieval period is the only one that socially and religiously rewarded women for the manifestation of their suffering. We should beware, however, not to fall prey to a nostalgia for an epoch that produced female saints, a nostalgia that reverberates in Bynum's work. Nor should we lament, as she does in *Fragmentation and Redemption*, that when compared to medieval women, who had rich symbols, modern women have lost all of theirs. If, historically, the medieval saints could gain social prestige from such phenomena, even though the hysterics of subsequent centuries could not, let us not forget that they were rewarded for outdoing what was expected of them, that is, suffering. Therefore the symbols they produced justified the system's production of female suffering.

This glimpse at a *longue durée* vision of the history of female psychosomatization allows us to conclude that it was misogyny that gave female medieval saints their agency and a particular shape to their self-empowerment; a vision impossible to have if we restrict the meaning of female mysticism solely to the context of medieval theology, as Bynum suggests we do.[32] We shall see, precisely, how the transformation of the female mystic into the hysteric was already being staged during the Quietist Affair.

Part One

ﬞarie de l'ﬞncarnation
(1599–1672)

arie Guyart was born in 1599 in Tours, a religious me-
tropolis in Western France.[1] She was the fourth of eight
children born to Florent Guyart, a master baker whose
ancestry included a notary. On this side of the family
there was a penchant for sobriety, even a touch of austerity.
Jeanne Michelet, the mother, boasted of a more illustrious connection, that of the higher civil servants of Francis I, the Babous de la
Bourdaisière.

When the time for education came, Marie Guyart went to a
school established by educated but poor women who organized
classes for children of the well-off artisan class. Marie was very
pious, as was the rest of her family, and her only amusements were
church ceremonies. She developed a passion for traveling preachers,
some of whom undoubtedly talked of missions in faraway lands.

Her parents' house was also the site of a commercial establishment. Because women in the artisan class were often in charge of

managing the family business while men did the physical work, Marie early on had the opportunity to deal with business transactions, clients, and tradesmen. She also learned embroidery, a skill at which she later excelled, and by which she earned a living after she was widowed; embroidery, one of the trademarks of the province, was a trade also practiced by men. A woman of many trades, she also learned to wield hammer and saw; later, in Quebec, she carved and painted on wood for the decoration of the convent chapel.

At fourteen, she expressed the desire to enter the Benedictine convent. Her mother refused because she claimed that Marie was too lively and thus would be unhappy cloistered as a nun. At seventeen, her father chose a husband for her, Claude Martin, a man of little character, who did not seek out Marie Guyart himself because he was engaged in a love intrigue with another woman; his mother decided this marriage for him. The abandoned lover eventually took revenge on him by pushing him into bankruptcy. Marie's husband was a *soyeux*, that is a craftsman in silk weaving, and he owned a factory. Only two years after the marriage Claude Martin died, leaving Marie at the young age of nineteen the mother of a boy, penniless and burdened with a bankrupt business. The mastery with which she handled the complicated judicial and financial embroglio of the liquidation of her husband's business made her a highly desirable spouse among the *soyeux*, and indeed many sought to marry her. She refused marriage owing to her allegiance to God, and thus she lived with her father and earned her living by her embroidery.

In 1620 she had her first profound spiritual experience, which decided her future. Through her reading of François de Sales and Teresa of Avila she acceded to the most avant-garde spiritual movement in France. In 1625, her sister requested Marie's assistance in the import-export business she shared with her husband. Marie became the manager of one of the most prosperous establishments of this type in Tours while continuing her spiritual voyage. Her work entailed not only the business management of the enterprise but also dealing with the employees concerning various aspects of the work. She continued this double life until 1631 when she left her son, her family, and the business to enter the Ursulines. During her profession in Tours, she was assistant to the mistress of the novices (*sous-maitresses des novices*) and later mistress of the girls in the boarding school. In 1634, she read the first *Jesuit Relations* dealing with the missions in Huronia in Canada. In 1635, she secretly decided that, if God permitted, she would go to New France. As God always seemed to grant what Marie de l'Incarnation wanted, she arrived with the mission in New France in 1639 with the purpose of founding the first convent of women in French missionary territory, as well as "civilizing" and Christianizing Indian women and educating French girls. She accomplished her goals during the thirty years she lived in Quebec and died there in 1672.

Chapter Two

The Female Mystical Body in Transition

From the Rhetoric of Suffering to the Rhetoric of Health

istorians of the Catholic Reformation typically consider Marie de l'Incarnation as emblematic in her mystical response to the enthusiasm sparked by that movement. In view of her achievements, they also see her as squarely fitting into the aims of the Catholic Reformation. Furthermore, commentators on mystical doctrine consider her parapsychic and psychosomatic manifestations, and her subsequent denigration of them, as characteristic of most female mystics, corresponding to François de Sales's description of the different steps the mystic is supposed to go through. This perceived conformity to what was expected of a saintly woman by church authority has won her the approval of her contemporaries and even of the antimystic theologians of the end of the seventeenth century.

Taking another stance, and agreeing with Donald Weinstein

and Rudolph Bell who claim that the saint is a type that mirrors the changing values of European society from early Christianity to modern times, I aim to show that Marie de l'Incarnation's discourse does not reflect solely the tenets of Catholic Reformation mysticism, but also the concerns of her time that were to change the perception of mysticism.[1]

Historians of the body argue for discontinuity, claiming that there are historical moments when a new understanding of the body was articulated for the first time; the sixteenth and seventeenth centuries constitute such a historical moment in Western history.[2] They further state that one can trace the development of this understanding and witness its effect in social practices, institutions, and texts produced by different disciplines.[3]

In this chapter, I propose to highlight how the new religious perception of the body, infuenced by medical discoveries, is echoed in Marie de l'Incarnation's writing. Mystic, Ursuline, and missionary in the New World, she found herself in the historical conjuncture of the seventeenth century when traditional, medieval, mystical discourse concerning the role of the body in piety encountered new, different religious discourses on the body, challenging the traditional understanding of the body as a vessel channeling God's will.

Weinstein and Bell also posit that although the saints might well serve the church's agenda and although their piety is deeply bound to the requisites of society and culture, they respond primarily to personal, religious impulses, and through their piety they work out conflicts and dilemmas posed to them by their society.[4] Following this line of thought, I further claim that Marie de l'Incarnation not only adopted such a new perception but that she also poached on it in order to concoct a meaning of her own. Indeed, not only did she use the church's ambition and its theological explanations, but she also used new ideas infiltrating theological discourse and women's convents to legitimize her own course of action. I analyze how she deftly adapted her religious impulses to the new religious ideas concerning the role of the body in piety and to various social changes of her time because they conveniently legitimized her choices. My claim is that Marie de l'Incarnation's choice to go along with these new options caused her to claim she stopped experiencing bodily manifestations she had displayed in the first part of her mystic life, manifestations which had been the hallmark of female mysticism since the thirteenth century.

Marie de l'Incarnation and the Female Mystical Body

Dom Guy Oury, whose historical biography of Marie de l'Incarnation was published in 1973, remarks that her spiritual autobiography follows strictly the laws of the genre. Indeed, in it we find the expected ingredients such as austerities, ecstasies, mystical marriage, and the rhetoric of love, pain, and pleasure that one can find in numerous spiritual autobiographies of the female mystical tradition. In the first part of her religious life, before she entered the convent, Marie Guyart behaved and wrote as a typical female mystic:

> God gave her a new spirit of penitence and she treated her body as a slave. She burdened it with hairshirt and chains: she made it sleep on wood with no other blanket but a haircloth. She forced it to spend most of the night in flagellation until much blood flowed. She allowed it just enough sleep so as not to die. Besides all this she made it bear all domestic chores and various other pains attached to her work. She brought it in sight of disgusting decaying carrion so that it might get used to it.[5]

She goes on to explain that this was necessary and demanded by God in order to polish and refine her and to make her worthy for her spiritual marriage to him. She also writes that these austerities brought her pleasure, relief, and an abundance of new, divine favors.[6] There is more, but this will suffice to remind us that we are dealing with the same discourse, the same representation of the body, the same description of piety as that found in female mysticism from the thirteenth century onwards, for which literal *imitatio Christi*, in his suffering, was the paradigm.

This first stage in her piety clearly underscores the link between austerities and control of one's life, as several scholars have recently pointed out.[7] Indeed, through her austerities and consequent mystical experiences, Marie de l'Incarnation succeeded in avoiding remarriage and in obtaining sanctions that allowed her to abandon her son and to enter the convent of her choice as a choir sister, even though she did not have a dowry. This was no small feat, and it represented a gain of personal prestige for her as well as a step up the social ladder. But this first stage also points to the social contract established between the male clerical hierarchy and the female mystic in premodern times. It also points to a link between psychosomatic manifestation of piety and social expectations. Her austerities and ecstasies were not only a creative response, as Bynum claims is the case for female mystics. They were to a certain extent staged by the male clergy and as such were a "proof" of her calling, demanded by the established hierarchy in general, and by her confessor, in particular, who undertook all necessary procedures on her behalf.

The Medieval Female Mystic's Body in Transition

Although she had a propensity for contemplation and austerities and had had mystical experiences for ten years prior to entering the convent, when the time came to choose an order she did not choose to join the Carmelites or the Feuillantines, who invited her and who undoubtedly would have fostered her traditional mystical vocation.[8] Even though the negotiations were quite advanced for her entry into the Feuillantines in Paris, she chose instead the Ursulines. As we have seen, this was both a teaching order emphasizing work and one that was at the forefront of the battle against *clausura*, waged by seventeenth-century religious women who, while they desired to live in a community, also wanted the possibility to work in the world.[9]

In the light of her subsequent choice to go to the New World, one can speculate that the Ursulines satisfied Marie de l'Incarnation on two grounds. However constrained they were, the Ursulines offered her a window to the world, yet retained the class prestige of a cloistered order. Marie de l'Incarnation chose that opening probably for the same reasons that she was a mystic: it offered her an additional way to self-determination and recognition. That small window onto the world, however, was to cause a major shift in her mystical discourse concerning the role of the body in mystical practices.

The Ursulines emphasized work over contemplation, and Marie de l'Incarnation was probably warned that they needed able-bodied women who had no need for disabling austerities.[10] In her autobiography she states that as soon as she was accepted into the Order, she stopped her austerities very easily:

> One of the first things I had to do, in order to follow communal life, was to quit my serge undershirt, my instruments of mortification, my way of sleeping, etc, etc. I was left only with what was accepted in the rule. Although I had loved mortification, and I was attached to all these small exercises of penitence when I was in the world, I nevertheless had no idea or feeling contrary to what was asked. God had given me great love for communal life.[11]

She adds that she abandoned austerities because of her vow of obedience. This argument is repeated by her son in his apology of his mother and by Dom Guy Oury, her twentieth-century biographer and apologist. This is, however, a circular argument, as it was she who chose the Ursulines in the first place over the Feuillantines or Carmelites, with whom she could have maintained her austerities. We can conclude that she easily gave them up when the possibility of rewards was no longer derived from practicing them and when her superiors (whom she had chosen herself) did not expect hyperboles of suffering from her. At this point, however, she still had prophetic dreams and ecstasies even though the Ursulines did not hide their dislike for the usual female mystic's bodily manifestations of piety. Mother de Pommereu, the chronicler of the Ursulines, clearly expressed the distaste in the Ursuline order for what were called "extraordinary graces," and in her *Chronicles* she said bluntly: "As for raptures and ecstasies, Ursulines do not need them."[12] If Marie de l'Incarnation's relinquishment of austerities was just a common response of obedience on the part of any Ursuline of the period (as her apologists contend), we may then ask why she did not at the same time obey the Ursulines' injunction against raptures and ecstasies but instead gave them up only eight years later?

The New World and the Relinquishment of Ecstasy

A second shift occurs in Marie de l'Incarnation's discourse on the body and concerns extraordinary graces on the occasion of her departure for the New World. These changes were recorded not only in her autobiographical accounts, which were written a posteriori and display the expected teleological orientation of the genre, but also in her correspondence written throughout the thirty-two years she lived in Canada.

Desiring a larger horizon more fitted to her apostolic zeal, she conceived the project of becoming a missionary in Canada. The Jesuits had issued an appeal for religious women to establish a house in Quebec and work for the conversion of Indian women and girls. At this point, her ecstasies and her visions, which had survived even after the relinquishment of austerities, proved useful, for she had to convince her spiritual director, her mother superior, and the Jesuits that she had been singled out by God to undertake this unprecedented adventure.[13]

When she was accepted for the mission, however, she abandoned ecstasies, visions, and supernatural graces, and at the end of her life, she indeed clearly expressed a dislike for all such extraordinary experiences. For example, referring to a nun who had just died, she said: "I will speak to you about her virtues, which are for me more important than miracles and feats."[14] Concerning a mystical experience that her son had had, she replied: "It is a greater advantage for you that everything happened in a spirit of faith than if you had had visions or any extraordinary physical experience, which are often an illusion."[15] Then, in 1648 at his request, she sent her son a few maxims that she followed for her daily spiritual guidance. One of these maxims says much about her new attitude vis-à-vis the body: "Mortify certain small appetites, inclinations and natural weaknesses in all manner, without hurting the spiritual or the corporal."[16] This last statement indicates that while she had turned away from a hurtful practice toward the body, she nevertheless did not adopt a Cartesian dualism, which totally separates the mind or soul from the body. Nevertheless, in the latter part of her life, her attitude toward the body constitutes quite a change from the traditional female mystical behavior she displayed during the first eighteen years of her religious vocation.

This shift in her mystical piety is all the more surprising in that New France was established in the wake of mystical and missionary fervor sparked by the Catholic Reformation and that the clergy, the hospital nuns, and the Jesuits themselves partook in all the frenzy of suffering that this fervor inspired. Cornelius Jaenen comments in *Friend and Foe* on the behavior of some members of the religious community in the beginning of New France. He states that the colonial bishop "as an exercise in self-mortification and humiliation sucked in the pus from wounds he dressed" and that a "hospital nun . . . as an exercise in self-denial and complete submission, swallowed caterpillars."[17] As for many of the Jesuits, not only did they glory in martyrdom, but also they acted like the Jesuit Brébeuf, "who added to his arduous labors innumerable sufferings and fatiguing travels many voluntary mortifications: discipline everyday, and often twice each day; very frequent fasts; haircloths, and belts with iron nails; vigil which advanced far into the night."[18] We must add that, imitating their example, some converted Indians had visions, prophetic dreams, and even heard voices.

Given the prestige, the public acceptance and the leverage in negotiating her own life that Marie de l'Incarnation's ecstasies and visions had given her, we must wonder why she abandoned them as soon as she arrived in Canada. Several explanations can be offered.

One could argue that Marie de l'Incarnation's deemphasis of bodily phenomena was common to many mystics as they advanced on the mystical path, and that such was the case with Teresa of Avila and many others.

Or one might be tempted to accept her son's further explanations: "When she went to Canada, God took away from her visions, revelations, and all other communication of this nature and ordered her to lead a common life and be a model for all."[19] God would have taken these gifts from her to show that it is better to be ordinary than to stand out with bodily manifestations. This explanation on the part of the son seems to contradict the claim that her changes merely reflected the steps of a mystic's path, for that progression along the path is supposed to bring the mystic to enjoy in this life the eternal life reserved for the redeemed after their death and resurrection. In other words, the state the mystic is supposed to progressively achieve is anything but ordinary and certainly not a model for all, as the church always had made clear. Her son's argument here seems to break with the understanding of the stages of the mystical path and to be an attempt to ward off criticism by the theologians of his time. The theologians of this period, as we have seen, were suspicious of extraordinary graces and demanded above all obedience and ordinariness from women.

Or, with de Certeau, we could agree that her stance is but one example showing that during the seventeenth century, under the pressure of scientific and theological discourse, mystical discourse relativized bodily phenomena, as was also the case with Teresa of Avila and John of the Cross.

I suggest, however, that none of the above are satisfactory explanations and that Marie de l'Incarnation was pursuing a course of her own while using accepted theological explanations or new conceptions of the body adopted by her order. We could say that faced with the competition of the bishop, the Jesuits, the hospital nuns and the converted Indians, she shifted course. What made her an exception in France was run of the mill in New France. In the circumstances of her life in Canada, opportunities for recognition and power lay elsewhere. It is true that in Quebec she had more power and prestige without austerities, ecstasies, and parapsychological phenomena than she would have had in France with all of the above.[20] I may add that in the seventeenth century martyrdom, rather than bodily manifestations, was considered the most heroic religious act. Marie de l'Incarnation aspired to martyrdom but was prevented from finding it, first because she was cloistered and second because the Jesuits forbade French women (cloistered or not) to go out to the outlying missions where the risk (or promise) of martyrdom lay.

My claims become more convincing when we analyze a last shift in her discourse concerning the body.

From the Rhetoric of Suffering to the Rhetoric of Health

A final important shift from the traditional mystical discourse on the body in Marie de l'Incarnation's texts is the stance she took regarding illness. Usually for mystics, illness had been welcomed and interpreted as a gift from God, as the opportunity to share in Christ's suffering and to glorify the will of God. Although she mentions her physical and mental suffering in her spiritual autobiography, and although these complaints conform to the law of the genre when she says that they were crosses to bear for the greater glory of God, her letters for the most part offer a different dominant rhetoric: that of health. Apart from occasional persistent headaches, she reports being seriously sick for the first time only at the age of fifty. In her letters, she very rarely uses these illnesses within her mystical economy, except to say that she was ready to die or that she would bear them with patience for the love of God. Marie de l'Incarnation is known to have enjoyed unusually sound health, and the mention of it in her letters creates a kind of leitmotif. In a letter to her son in 1644 (she was forty-five years old), she responded to his news of bad health in the following manner: "As for me, God does not inflict me with any corporal infirmity except once in a while a small headache which is a consequence of my past assiduity in embroidery. All my infirmities are spiritual and thus more difficult to cure."[21]

In 1647, she wrote again: "As for my health it is rather good, thanks to God, and I wish you had as strong a voice as mine to express in the world the lights that God gives you."[22]

Then in a letter of 1650, when she was fifty years old and thought her life was close to its end, she wrote: "Even though I have a good constitution and enjoy a good health, at fifty, one should think of life coming to its term."[23] Again in another letter dating from 1654 (she was fifty-five years old), she stated:

As for my health, it is rather good, and I do not yet feel the incommodities of old age, if it were not that my sight is weakening. In order to see better, I use glasses with which I see as well as when I was 25. They also relieve my frequent headaches. I also have become plump: people of my disposition gain weight in this country, where one is more humid than in France, even though the air is more subtle. But let us leave the body for the earth, and let us give our spirit to God.[24]

In 1657 (at fifty-eight), she mentioned a serious illness from which she thought she would die. But she recovered and she closed the chapter, saying: "Finally our sweet Jesus gave me back my health and consequently I am able to fulfill my duties."[25] At sixty-nine, she noted: "My health is better than in the past years."[26] Again the same year she wrote: "I am more or less back to the state of health I held before my long illness, without knowing how long it will last."[27] One year before her death she declared: "I am in rather good health in spite of my age."[28]

The insistant rhetoric of health that we find in her letters might be explained in the following manner. Many people in France looked with a jaundiced eye upon religious women who stepped out of *clausura* and, worse still, left their homes for the colonies. They questioned the propriety and the efficacy of the Ursulines in New France and threatened to force them to return to the motherland. The Ursulines in Paris and in Tours wanted them in New France only if their presence there could bring prestige to the order, and they were sensitive to the slightest criticism. Also, the living conditions of the New World were considered particularly harsh on women, and several nuns had been sent back to France for health reasons. For her part, Marie de l'Incarnation refused to go back to France, even after the destruction of her convent by fire in 1651 and in spite of the threat posed by the Iroquoian attacks. Marie de l'Incarnation valued the New World and the possibilities of development that it offered her, but she was careful above all to legitimize her call to the mission. She had had to convince the world and the church through her dreams, inner visions, and ecstasies that her mission in Canada was part of the divine scheme, and that in the rivalry between convents and nuns to respond to the call of the Jesuits, it was she in particular whom God had designated. To return to France as a result of the failure of her mission would have proved the contrary, putting her in the awkward situation of having to admit that she had made a mistake. She would have been discredited as a mystic; that is, her commerce with God would have been considered illusory. She expressed this clearly to her son, Claude Martin, in 1652:

Last year someone from France, who did not yet know the news of our fire, advised me to negotiate our return to France, telling me that I would be better off if I did so; that I would but suffer some embarrassment, and that for sure, people would laugh a little, but that all would soon be forgotten.[29]

A return to France was exactly what she was trying at all costs to avoid, causing her to reiterate time and time again the divine nature of God's designs for her. After her convent was destroyed by fire and everyone, her son included, called for her return to France, she said: "I am as certain that His divine majesty wanted our recovery, and that the vocation that I had to work here came from Him, as I am assured of dying one day."[30] When the Ursulines were ready to inhabit their new convent after the destruction of the original one, she remarked that the construction of the new building was miraculous, which proved that God wanted the Ursulines in Quebec. When her son insistently asked her how she could be so certain that her presence in Canada and the rebuilding of the convent of the Ursulines were the result of the will of God, she replied:

As for what I told you about my being assured of the will of God in our reestablishment, this results from His powerful touches and His divine movements which possessed me so continually in this affair that I had to obey without question. And I have been even more convinced as a result of what has followed, by His continual assistance which has not been denied me at any moment.[31]

She further insisted that nothing but the will of God alone could make her leave New France: "Until that moment at which it is made known to us that His blessed will is satisfied with our minor services in this country, and that we must go and undertake them for Him elsewhere, we will be constant and unshakable in our resolutions."[32]

Yet in 1650, in view of the serious Iroquoian attacks, she nevertheless devised a way out in case the mission might be forced to leave New France: "the nature of these American savages, even the most holy and spiritual, not being at all suitable for ecclesiastic functions, but only for being instructed and guided in the way of heaven, makes one suspect, in this reversal of affairs, that perhaps God only wanted a temporary church here."[33] In the event that the whole mission to New France had to evacuate, this perspective would leave intact the legitimacy of her mission and, therefore, spare her a shameful return.

So Marie de l'Incarnation had much at stake in Canada and very much wanted to stay; hence her insistence on her good health. Unlike traditional mystics, for whom long illness might be interpreted as a sign of God's predilection, Marie de l'Incarnation found herself in the situation of insisting that she was in good health so as to be allowed to stay in Canada and thus legitimize her claim that God had chosen her in particular for the mission.

There is, however, toward the end of her life for a short time, a dissonant note in her overall rhetoric of health: the reemergence of the rhetoric of illness as a gift of God and of the delight in suffering. In 1667, she wrote: "I am not recovering from my great illness. . . . I am afraid I am attached to the suffering . . . and I am afraid God will take it away from me or make it softer."[34] Again in 1667 she noted: "I would never have believed that there was so much delight in suffering if I had not experienced it for three years."[35] She repeated the same rhetoric in another letter of 1667 in writing: "I say that God in His goodness sent me this illness, and I thank Him for this proof of His love."[36] In 1668, however, she was back to health and talked of her past illness and her present weakness in descriptive tones devoid of religious overtones.

Although the rhetoric of pleasure in suffering is in keeping with female mystical discourse, it diverges from the discourse she developed after her arrival in Quebec. This reemergence at the end of her life of a discourse she had expressly abandoned disproves the claim that Marie de l'Incarnation's relinquishment of bodily manifestations was merely in step with different stages of the mystics' path. Rather it can be read as the return of the repressed. As such, it supports my claim that Marie de l'Incarnation had adopted a rhetoric of health and of disdain of the bodily drama as a strategy better suited for her main purpose, namely, to be allowed to remain in Canada. The return of the rhetoric of illness and of suffering in pleasure testifies that even though there was no place for that rhetoric in her new discourse, suffering was still present in her life; she could, however, only give it meaning through a set of beliefs she was forced (or had chosen) to give up, having been offered no new meaning for it in exchange. In any case, it seems that

Marie de l'Incarnation was at times caught between two attitudes toward female suffering: one being that she ought to embrace this suffering as a gift sent by God to show his election of her, another being that she ought to deny any suffering she experienced so as not to be forced to go back to France and therefore to admit that her mission in Canada was not divinely ordained.

I could conclude this chapter with a representation of Marie de l'Incarnation as a triumphant, self-empowered woman who seized upon the opportunities opened up by a modern discourse on the body. For she did manage to pursue an itinerary of her own while contriving to be acceptable to the authorities, and along the way she did, seemingly, shed the necessity imposed upon women that they suffer in order to be recognized and legitimized, a necessity for female mystics until then. Although that would not be altogether wrong, it would be misleading. For the weakening of a theological justification for women's suffering did not mean that women had no more reason to suffer. In other words, the demand and the reasons that women suffer did not disappear with the theological justification for that suffering, inasmuch as gender ideology persisted while changing its language.

Moreover, Marie de l'Incarnation mentions mental and spiritual suffering when writing of her confrontations with those secular or religious authorities whom she perceived at times as unjust, misdirected, or whimsical. On one such occasion, she confronted the authority of Father Vimont, the Jesuit chief of the Canadian missions. Without consulting her, he had promised the Ursulines (who had arrived from the convent in Paris to join those from Tours) that the rules of Paris would prevail. This put Marie de l'Incarnation at odds with her convent in Tours, which accused her of colluding with Father Vimont in what they considered a betrayal. Losing the support of her home convent would have been disastrous for her, as she depended on it to raise money and to influence officials on behalf of her mission. I also need to stress the importance that seventeenth-century France attached to belonging to a particular order, or even a particular house of an order, so as to appreciate Marie de l'Incarnation's perturbed reaction to Father Vimont's interference in the internal rules of her convent—a reaction all the more perturbed because she had no authority over him, whereas he unquestionably did over her. She won the battle, but not without anguish. She also had to deal with the authority of Bishop Laval, who likewise decided to change the Ursulines' rules without any regard for the inconveniences his changes had on their practical life. After many confrontations in which she had to display outward signs of obedience and humility, she also won that battle. But the Bishop did win on one point: under the pretext that it distracted the priest who officiated, he eliminated singing from the offices of the nuns. This was a great sacrifice for Marie de l'Incarnation, who said that singing the office relieved her of mental and spiritual pains. Father Le Jeune, who was her spiritual director, also treated her roughly. We learn about these circumstances because they involved the rules of the convent, and these are the concerns that she communicated to her convent in Tours. We do not have direct access to the other circumstances in which her will, decisions, and actions were opposed and in which her already difficult work was made more difficult by the whimsical exercise of power on the part of the Jesuits or the Bishop. One can gather, however, from her autobiography that at times the rule of unconditional obedience cost her terrible mental sufferings.[37] But because she had chosen a rhetoric of health and ordinary obedience in order to legitimize her call to the mission, she could no longer negotiate her sufferings against the authority that constrained her will nor assign a theological meaning to them as female mystics of previous centuries had done. Consequently, the suffering she experienced became a hindrance, something to hide and to bear in silence, rather than the occasion to produce bodily phenomena to which she could have given theological meaning and thereby persuade the hierarchy that her will was that of God.

Marie de l'Incarnation's case contradicts de Certeau's generalization that bodily manifestations multiply in the discourse of seventeenth-century mystics as a result of a renewed feeling of loss. We do not sense a feeling of nostalgia in her and her loss was precisely that of bodily manifestations. Her gain was to expand her world, her activities, and her writings. Her case also disproves de Certeau's assertion that mystics of this period relativize bodily manifestations as a defense against scientific and theological discourses' reification of the mystical. She does not simply relativize them, she seems to indict them and to indicate her abandonment of them. Seen this way, Marie de l'Incarnation is anything but a typical Catholic Reformation mystic. My analysis of Marie de l'Incarnation's case also calls into question several of Bynum's assumptions. In her introduction to *Holy Feast and Holy Fast* Bynum states: "My point is to argue that women's behavior and women's writing must be understood in the context of social, economic, and ecclesiastical structures, theological and devotional traditions, very different from our own."[38] Throughout her work her insistence is so strong on this point that it amounts to an injunction and even an interdiction to interpret the mystics' experience outside the medieval and theological economy of the flesh, lest we leave the truth of history and wander off into ideology. Further, Bynum states forcefully and repeatedly that what is important to her is to understand what medieval women thought *they* were doing and the meaning *they* were giving to their behavior:

> My purpose in this book has been to put the behavior, the symbols, and the convictions of women and men in the distant past into their *full* context. Only by considering all the meanings and functions of medieval practice and belief can we explain medieval experiences without removing its creativity and dignity.[39]

Thus, according to Bynum, the meaning female mystics gave to their own behavior necessarily gives it dignity, and this is the only meaning *we* should give to it.

However, Marie de l'Incarnation's maneuvering at the dawn of the modern world between competing medieval and modern theological interpretations of the role of the body in piety allows us a perspective on the female mystical body not available if we restrict our vision solely to the Middle Ages. Further, Bynum's position implies, first, that there is a simple, transparent equation between an individual's behavior and the explanation given by that individual for her/his behavior ("their convictions, their beliefs"). Second, it implies that the socially acceptable discourse in which an individual cloaks her/his behavior (*imitatio Christi*) is, indeed, the only meaning attributable to it—a position Bynum herself contradicts by saying that in reading the medieval texts, "we learn things the past did not understand about itself."[40] What is learned, she says (and in this instance I agree with her), is that the female mystics' behavior signified a desire for empowerment. To my knowledge, however, no female mystic ever declared that her fantastic, unconscious manipulation of the body was aimed specifically at beating the system and empowering herself in spite of the system's interdictions.

As for theological meanings and religious symbols, do they really exhaust the significance of a behavior? One can argue, to the contrary, that theology concealed the oppression that produced such behavior, therefore encouraging female mystics' suffering. Indeed, it was the possibility of theological explanations of female mystics' bodily drama that lured women into creating symbols and meanings for it and, in turn, helped perpetuate the very system that created the injunction that women suffer. Underlying medieval theology was the gender ideology that expected and produced suffering in women. Further, Dom Guy Oury, the biographer and apologist of Marie de l'Incarnation, comments that her choice of a working order over a contemplative one can be attributed to her desire to help souls more directly and to imitate Christ in his apostolic life, thus giving theological meaning to the choice that would lead her to repudiate bodily manifestations.[41] Marie de l'Incarnation herself, along with her son, gave theological meaning to her relinquishing of austerities, ecstasies, visions, and bodily manifestions. However, my analysis suggests that what explains Marie de l'Incarnation's choice is not the theological label "imitation of Christ in his apostolic life" but the fact that the real world offered her, as a religious woman, another avenue besides imitation of Christ in his suffering. The theological explanation appears to be more a socially acceptable justification of her choice than its underlying motive. She justified her choice with a theological argument that emphasized imitation of Christ in his apostolic life rather than in his suffering, until then the sole path that led religious women to recognition.[42] The opportunities offered to her by the modern conception of the body and the New World were predicated on having an able body, and thus made obsolete the theological justifications for female suffering. Marie de l'Incarnation's example makes clear that when female mystics used theological or symbolic meanings, these meanings were most importantly but a rationalization they borrowed from a set of orthodox justifications the church allowed them to use. Just as medieval mystics had given a theological meaning to their suffering bodies, Marie de l'Incarnation gave a theologial meaning to her abandonment of such practices. Analysis of her writings reveals that this move cloaked the more personal reasons she had for such a choice, exposing the theological meaning female mystics gave to their suffering as a subterfuge rather than as the "true," and according to Bynum, exclusive meaning of their choice.

Also, I take issue with Bynum's overemphasis on agency and self-empowerment in female mystics, a bias leading her to a celebratory tone of women's suffering that I find troubling. I thus examine her strong opposition to the idea that female mystics are mere victims of a misogyny that is internalized as self-hatred and masochism.[43] Bynum has rightly shown, against scholarly assumptions of the past, that medieval mystics were not dualists; but an absence of dualism does not necessarily result in an absence of internalization of misogyny as self-hatred. It is true that female mystics did use their bodies as tools to come closer to God and transcendence and in that sense, therefore, were not dualists. But as Beckwith puts it:

> By approximating herself to Christ, misrecognising herself in him, by living a life which is itself a mimesis and remembrance of the Passion, the female mystic may gain access to the Word, or to those more human expedients, words. It is a strategy that never attempts, that is unable to attempt, to break the mould of its subjection. Indeed it cannot, for it is the very equation of victimisation, passivity, subjection with femininity, that allows the Christian inversion its paradoxical triumph.[44]

My aim is not simply to revert to a reductive representation of female mystics as pure victims but to nuance a trend that insists on representing them as pure agents and in viewing their bodily experience as essentially female and necessarily empowering. Bynum's exaltation of female experience makes it possible to retain a simplistic but effective notion of female identity based on the fiction of a coherent, essential female self; this, however, obscures the fact that the body, like experience and gender, is a concept, and that like the self, and even death, it is a culturally determined

conceptual structure. Bynum's exaltation of female experience often works to undermine her own project, which certainly has implications far larger than the simple celebration of female experience
understood as female identity. I propose that what we describe as
"opportunities" or "strategies" on the part of women living in patriarchal societies should not always be considered as triumphant
moves on the part of women, but rather as survival tactics and
adaptive mechanisms. As such, these tactics are compromises
through which women ironically found themselves compromised,
and for which they had to pay a high price even if they did gain
social advantages from them. I understand why historians of
women in the last fifteen years have favored an emphasis on
women's agency. They want not only to modify accepted views of
women as propagated by past historians, but also to valorize those
women's lives by focusing on their production and creativity in
using the options that were available to them. Historians of women
also want to highlight these women's ingenuity in manipulating a
hostile world to their advantage. I think, however, there is a danger in emphasizing women's self-empowerment that was achieved
through extreme suffering and manipulations of the body or through
their utter conformity to negative images that are imposed upon
them. Our desire to create or vindicate a past for women might
lead us to lose sight of the oppressive power that necessitated such
an extreme response on their part and might result only in the
glorification of women's suffering. It might lead us to a miscon-
struction of the negative forms that female self-assertion can take
when constrained and shaped by a patriarchal, sexual ideology. It
is understandable that women were willing to pay a high price for
whatever meaning they could give to their lives. But this very desire to give meaning to their lives with whatever was available to
them also explains their necessary complicity with the very system
that alienated them. The problem of complicity or consent of the
oppressed is not an easy issue and should not imply any moral
blame.[45] We know that women received enormous rewards for supporting the very system that oppressed them and also that many
died when they did not adhere to these strictures. If we eulogize
female mystics' creativity through their capacity to suffer and thus
give meaning to their suffering, we run the risk of extolling an
oppressive order instead of unmasking its workings. In my view,

we must not lure ourselves once more into believing that suffering and madness are indeed women's "natural" ways to self-assertion, self-respect, and wholeness. We must see that that very suffering is a mutilation and an obstacle to any individual's human dignity.

Finally, I critique Bynum's reducing the institutional inequalities between the female mystics and the male mystic or priest to simple "asymmetry" of power.[46] Bynum is right to warn against generalizing about "the status of women" in any period in regard to women's gains and losses. She insists on the need to nuance such a statement with consideration of class, geographical area, and the domain considered.[47] As an illustration of this antiprogressive vision of history, however, she says that, in regard to the religious domain, women, starting with the eleventh century, lose sacerdotal, sacramental, and administrative powers, but that they compensate for these loses by other *kinds* of religious *roles* and *opportunities*:

> Such complex changes in the *kinds* of opportunity and sources of authority available to women, as well as in the kinds of women for whom opportunities were available, make generalizations about "*the* status of women"—statements to which historians have sometimes been tempted—presumptuous and ill-advised.[48]

The problem for me, however, lies precisely in the *kind* of power women gain through charisma. In order to prove that charismatic female piety is not a victim's reaction to oppression but an "opportunity" women seized upon as agents, Bynum finds herself arguing that women lost some and gained some, and that the difference in the *kind* of power lost or gained is of no importance, or, indeed, that the charismatic power they gained was better than the power they lost. Bynum writes:

> Thus, from the thirteenth century on, we find religious women losing roles that paralleled or aped male clerical leadership but gaining both the possibility of shaping their own religious experiences in lay communities and a clear alternative—the prophetic alternative—to the male role based on the power of office.[49]

It seems to me that it is not by chance that women were accorded prophetic power once they had been stripped of all concrete powers, considering that this prophetic power was circumscribed, contained, scrutinized, or channeled by the clergy and that it was paid for with due suffering.

Bynum reproaches critics who have insisted on the negative stereotypes of female sexuality and on the lack of sacerdotal power of women and who, thus, have not accounted for the positive aspect that sensory mysticism offered to women. She could, in turn, be reproached for insisting on the positive aspects of female mysticism to such a degree that her representation sometimes borders on the grotesque, as if the strength, endurance, and desire for recognition on the part of some individuals or groups could be glorified to the point of glossing over or even rejoicing at the circumstances that gave them the "opportunity" to deploy their "strategies" for survival.

Marie de l'Incarnation's choice as a mystic disproves, on the one hand, Bynum's claim that somatic piety and suffering are a natural and positive female disposition. On the other hand, it also proves that the hyperbolic suffering of medieval mystics has to do with total constraint and social expectations and, therefore, gender oppression, for suffering was the only means available to make oneself noticed and thereby obtain a modicum of self-determination. In this light, the medieval female mystic's hunger for pain and suffering, which Marie de l'Incarnation had adopted in the first part of her religious life when she was given no other opportunity for claiming charismatic prestige, appears not, primarily, as a sign of empowerment, as Bynum would have it, but largely as one of alienation.

Chapter Three

From France to Canada/ From Motherhood to Subjecthood
Mystical Writing as Distancing

The geographical distance Marie de l'Incarnation was able to put between her motherland and her land of choice resulted in the distance she took from the typical medieval or Catholic Reformation female mystic regarding the role of the body in mysticism. This geographical distance also allowed her to distance herself from her son and the social expectations of motherhood. This chapter concerns itself with the ways Marie de l'Incarnation's mystical writing maintained the distance between son and mother, transforming her reluctant and skeptical son into her public relations man, editor, and apologist. We must recall that most of her autographs were destroyed, probably during the French Revolution and that without her son's diligence, she may have disappeared from history altogether.

Indeed, the boldest, the most interesting, and the bulk of Marie de l'Incarnation's writings were composed in New France and addressed to her son back in France. These included not only numerous letters concerning the New World, the colony, and the Indians, but also her spiritual writings, which form the subject of an autobiographical account she wrote in 1654 at his request. Elements of her spiritual writings are also to be found here and there, imbedded in her letters to him.

According to her biographer, this outpouring of writing to her son originated in her love for him and from her suffering because she abandoned him as a child, even though (as her biographer claims) she was the most tender of mothers.[1] It would appear, then, that her authorial creation is indeed the fruit of her son's insistent request that she reveal to him her private relationship to God so as to instruct him—a request with which she supposedly complied out of a mother's tenderness and guilt for having abandoned him when he was twelve, when she entered the Ursulines' convent, and again when he was twenty, when she left France to satisfy her missionary hunger for the New World. This is certainly how her son interpreted her motives for writing him, and it was also his intention that her readers follow suit.[2] Had his interpretation been correct, Freud's would-be-universal pronouncement according to which "a mother is only brought unlimited satisfaction by her relation to a son; [and that] this is altogether the most perfect, the most free from ambivalence of all human relationships," would indeed here be vindicated.[3]

But, if we look closer at the dialectic underpinning of this mother-son epistolary relationship of more than thirty years, a somewhat different pattern emerges. Notwithstanding the undoubtedly sincere pain she claimed to have experienced on abandoning her son, Marie de l'Incarnation is definitely not a *mater dolorosa*. It appears instead that his curiosity and avidity to know everything that concerned his mother was pricked by his need to justify, in his eyes, her double abandonment. For the mother, however, it appears that their separation gave her an unexpected excuse to communicate to an official member of the church (in the person of her own son) everything that was of importance to her, and to make it known publicly. This situation enabled her, precisely, to circumvent the official channels of publication, which were inaccessible to her. Her writings to him, then, whether on the topic of the colony, or more largely on spirituality, although seemingly aimed at justifying her abandon, in fact, accomplished a threefold purpose. Given his priesthood (in accordance with her will), he was in a position, first, to bestow upon her an official recognition of her work in New France and, second, to provide her with a clerical legitimization of her mystical calling to the mission in the New World. Third, clerical legitimacy thus served to deflect the reproaches of her abandoned son.

Marie de l'Incarnation accomplished this reversal by playing on, and twisting, two topoi that are characteristic of the female mystic autobiographical tradition: the abandonment of children for the love of God and the authorization to write based on a clerical injunction.

Abandonment of Children for the Love of God

Scholars agree that mysticism was often used by women who entered its avenues as a way to negotiate a measure of freedom from their family's demands, from forced marriage and even from their children's needs. Portrayals of children thought to be a barrier between the female mystic and God, together with claims of great suffering on the part of a mother who feels compelled to obey God's calling, are often present in female mystical writings. Jeanne de Chantal's farewell gesture in 1620, as she stepped over the prostrate body of her son to enter the convent, is legendary. Madame Guyon also thought that she was beyond reproach when she used God's will to justify her rejection of all her familial and maternal responsibilities in order to pursue her religious desire. That this act is not without precedents is made clear by Angela of Foligno's admission (1249–1309) on the occasion of the death of her whole family: "It was God's wish to remove my mother who was an obstacle to my progress towards Him. My husband and children also died within a short space of time. Their deaths were a great consolation to me for when I had entered the mystic way, I had prayed to God to rid me of them all."[4] Marie Guyart herself caused a public scandal by abandoning her son in order to enter the convent, even though several church figures endorsed her decision, based on the observation that her vocation was overwhelming.[5] The theme of the abandonment of children for the purpose of pursuing a religious vocation is not to be confused with the educational ideology of the aristocracy in the seventeenth century, which endorsed raising children away from home, under the belief that it would better prepare them for the social role they were called to perform. The fact that the theme of the abandonment of her son and of the suffering she endured on this occasion recurs as a leitmotif throughout Marie de l'Incarnation's writings, shows that it was not just a custom taken for granted by her or by society at large.[6] Notwithstanding, the fact that she often repeated the theme does not, for all that, constitute a *mea maxima culpa* on her part.

From the outset, Marie de l'Incarnation counteracted her son's reproaches with her own desire. The first letter she sent him from Quebec in 1640 is a rather curt letter of reprimand, in which she instructed him to be less pusillanimous about his calling and not to abandon his vocation to the priesthood.[7] At the same time she asked him to pray to God, to thank him for calling her to such a lofty vocation, and to ask him to grant her the strength to persevere in her mission in Canada until her death. She not only curtailed her son's reproaches and his attempts to excuse his weakness by attributing it to her abandonment, but she also immediately pursued the argument that the difficulties he was experiencing in no way cast any doubt on the legitimacy of her vocation and personal religious mission. To this she added that, since she intended to stay in Canada until her death, he would not see her again. After her son complied with her wishes concerning his vocation to the priesthood, her tone softened; her line of self-justification, however, never swayed.

She mentioned her abandonment of her son for the first time in the second letter, which she wrote to him in September 1641, when he was twenty-two years old and had just been accepted into the religious community of Saint-Maur:

> You were abandoned by your mother and your family. Did this abandonment not stand you in good stead? On leaving you when you were not yet twelve years old I experienced strange convulsions which God alone witnessed. I had to obey His divine will that things should take place in this way, in the hope that He would look after you. I hardened my heart in order to overcome that which had been an obstacle to my entry into the religious life for ten whole years. Nevertheless it

required Reverend Father Dom Raymon and my voices, which I cannot disclose in writing but which I will tell you about in private, to persuade me of the necessity of this action.[8]

She initiated here an argument she used each time he reported to her an honor he received on the temporal level or an advance he made on the spiritual one. She reminded him that she had been right to forsake him, for without her abandonment he would not be what he now was, a man of God, honored by his order, which in her mind was the most precious thing in the world for him to be. In this letter she also told him that when the time came for her to carry out her intention and to abandon him, she had to surmount the obstacle he represented: "I hardened my heart in order to overcome that which had been an obstacle to my entry into the religious life for ten whole years."[9] She overturned the argument put forward by her son, who reproached her for having abandoned him at such a tender age, by stating that she loved him so dearly that she waited ten years to carry out her wishes instead of acting when he was but two years old.

Responding to what obviously constituted a long-lasting and persistent reproach on his part, she tells him in 1647:

I cannot endure you reproaching me with want of affection without retorting accordingly: for it is God's will that I am still alive. You are in a sense entitled to complain, that I left you. I too would willingly complain if it were allowed, about Him who divided the earth so strangely with His sword. It is true that even though you were the only thing left on this earth to which my heart felt bound, He nevertheless wanted to separate us while you were still at the breast, and I had to fight to keep you for twelve years, and even then I had to share half of that time with Him. At last I had to give way to the power of divine will; this did not stop me from feeling on countless occasions like the cruellest of mothers. I ask your forgiveness, my dearest son, for I have brought you great suffering. Let us draw consolation from the thought that this life is short and that, through the mercy of Him who separated us in this life, we shall have the whole of eternity in which to see each other and to rejoice in Him.[10]

She presents the abandonment as the result of a struggle between motherly love and the love of God, and she seems to be asking for forgiveness, while leaving no doubt as to the legitimacy of her choice.

In 1669 she repeated the first separation scene: "You came with me [to the convent], and when I left you it seemed as if my heart and soul were being so painfully rent asunder."[11] However, as she goes on to explain, while with him, she was already elsewhere:

> Note that even from the age of fourteen I had a very powerful religious vocation which was not pursued because my parents did not act in accordance with my wishes. However, since the age of nineteen or twenty, I have been spiritually committed, and my body alone has remained in the world in order to raise you until the time came to carry out God's will for us both.[12]

Further on, as she described the heart-rending scenes when her son would come in tears to the convent begging for her return, she fully admitted not only that she was heartbroken, but also that she was afraid lest her son's tears might move the Mother Superiors to the point of sending her back into the world to look after him.[13]

In the spiritual account she wrote for him in 1654, she even admitted that she had premeditated this abandonment, and for that reason, after he was two, she no longer caressed him to lessen the pains of the coming separation.[14] In another letter she somewhat cruelly quoted to him the example of a young Indian, whom she called her son and who was martyred by the Iroquois, thus intimating to Claude that if he wished to be loved by his mother, he must conform to this model:

> One of those for the love of whom I am writing you this article has singled himself out by his zeal and fervor. (He was about twenty-two years old and was my spiritual son who loved me as much, if not more, than his own mother) . . . . He was called Joseph and had been brought up in the faith almost since childhood by Father Le Jeune. Do you not think that he is a good son to me? More, he is my Father and Advocate before God.[15]

The letter of August 9, 1654, deserves particular attention for it summarizes the mother-son struggle and marks a dialectical shift in her favor. It is the letter in which she informed him that she was at last sending him the great account of her mystical states he had been requesting for over ten years and which she had been avoiding sending him all this time. In this letter she enumerated the arguments which, since the beginning of their correspondence, her son had employed in his persuasive claims to his mother's writing:

> This delay which you interpreted as an outright refusal did not deter you. You have implored me again using the most pressing motives and touching reasons which your spirit could devise, gently reproaching me with lack of affection and suggesting: that I abandoned you when you were so young that you hardly knew your mother and that, not satisfied with this initial abandonment, I left France and forsook you forever; that when you were a child, you were not sensitive to the instruction which I gave you, and now that you have reached the age of understanding, I could not deny you the insights granted to me by God; that having embraced a similar state to mine, we both belonged to God and that our spiritual goods should be held in common; that in the state in which you found yourself, I could not refuse you, without being unjust or hard, that which might console you or be of use to you in the way of perfection which you have professed; and that finally, if I granted you this consolation, you would help me to bless Him who has given me such a large share of His graces and heavenly favors.[16]

All of the son's requests appear to be of an emotional nature. He demanded reparation for the abandonment he had suffered. He demanded an explanation and a proof of the legitimacy of the powerful desire that had pushed her toward something other than him. Since he had become a priest in accordance with her wishes, she owed it to him to give back the gifts God has given her. As a priest, he was experiencing great crises and she was therefore exhibiting cruelty by depriving him of that which could console him: her words, her letters, and her secrets.

Marie de l'Incarnation did not yield to her son's emotional blackmail, to the guilt he tried to provoke, or to the right he invoked. She skillfully undermined the validity of his accusations and rejected the grounds for guilt on which they were founded. She extricated herself, as usual, by hiding her own will behind that of God. By a rhetorical twist common to all mystics, she refuted the logic of her son's claims and denied the need to seek forgiveness for abandoning him. She went on:

> If on reading the writings which I am sending, you should think to question what it is which could have moved God in His goodness to show me such great mercy and to apprize me of the blessings of His gentleness in this way: Let me tell you that I have often reflected on this too, and after much thought, I could find nothing in me but misery and unworthiness; and if there could be a more human reason, I can think only that it is because of you whom I abandoned for the love of Him, at a time when, by human reckoning, you needed me the most, and more especially because I had decided to do so before you were even born.[17]

The abandonment of her son thus became the source of her personal glory and a sign that she had been chosen by God to receive his special favor. She even was so bold as to tell him that he ought to rejoice in the fact that he had been abandoned by his mother:

> For if, divinely inspired, I abandoned you while you were still a child, leaving you no other recourse but His providence, He placed you under His paternal protection and provided richly for you, granting you the distinction of calling you to His service at the moment preordained by His eternal wisdom, exactly as He had promised me with honor and grace. You have gained much by losing me, and my abandonment has been of benefit to you.[18]

In order to free herself still further from any possible blame, she admitted that before abandoning him she had made a pact with God, promising that if her son were ever to sin on account of this abandonment, then it was she who would bear the burden for his sins: "So afraid was I lest you should stumble into the pitfalls to which you were exposed that I formed a pact with God that I might pay the price for your sins in this life."[19] She was no more responsive to her son's accusations in 1654 than she was in 1633 when she left him to enter the convent. She reserved for last the one reason that could finally have convinced her to write to him about her inner life: "And lastly, that if I granted you this consolation you would help me to bless Him who has given me such a large share of His graces and heavenly favors. I must confess that the latter reason moved me."[20] She agreed to share the secrets of her bliss with him only if he joined her in thanking God, thereby accepting that her abandonment of him was justified and thus leaving him no cause for complaint.

The only bond she agreed to have with him, which rendered possible the disclosure of her commerce with God, is that of a companion on her spiritual journey, of an equal, of a mystical rather than a natural son: "Having lost you by choice, I found you again in the bosom of a loving God through the holy vocation which we have both followed."[21]

She had wanted her son to become a priest even before he was born, and he had done so; she had wanted him to follow her in the mystical path, and he was to follow her. If he could cherish the same wishes as she, then she no longer needed to blame herself for abandoning him. For his part, he lost the right to protest, for the abandonment reunited them more closely than could mere physical presence: "Although close to God, I never leave you. Let us dwell on this vast ocean and live this life in anticipation of eternity when we shall see each other truly. Farewell."[22] She only agreed, therefore, to reveal the richness of her spiritual life, for which she had abandoned him, on condition that he desist from demands for reparation and accountability on her part. Finally, in 1656 her gamble seemed to have paid off: "With regards to our position, I am glad that you now approve of our decision to stay in Canada."[23] She even succeeded in turning the tables, so that at the end of his mother's life, Claude Martin would come to ask her forgiveness for having been an obstacle to her vocation. In a letter of 1668 she replied: "Why do you ask me to forgive what you call your youthful outbursts?"[24] In one of his frequent additions to the text of Marie de l'Incarnation's *La Vie*, Claude Martin himself excused his mother's abandonment: "She did not leave him out of inconsideration, nor out of hardness, nor to get rid of him. . . . Whatever love she had for him, she had infinitely more for Him, who commanded her to leave him."[25]

With the exception of the first missive, the tone of Marie de l'Incarnation's letters to her son is friendly and protective, like that of a spiritual director, increasing in intimacy while remaining friendly, as Claude advanced in the mystical way and as his grudge vanished. This stands in sharp contrast to the loving or erotic tone that she used with God and that she eventually let her son read in a letter: "You are the most beautiful of all the sons of men, oh my beloved! You are handsome, my dearest love . . . and you transport my spirit in an indescribable vision."[26] While the son yearned to be the sole object of his mother's desire, indeed to take God's place, she continually encouraged him to become a mystic, to abandon the idea of being the object of her desire and, instead, to adopt as his own her desire for God. Her response to her son's desire to monopolize his mother as the object of his fantasies takes the form of establishing herself as the subject of her own desire. By finally acceding to his desire and writing to him of the delights of her relationship with God in the spiritual account he had requested, she made him a witness to her subjectivity; he became the third party to a loving couple, which did not include him, which required that he fade as a subject. In this perspective, Freud's statement, which assumes that the son constitutes the mother's only object of desire and thus denies her subjective status, appears to be a fantasy on the part of the sons (Freud and Marie de l'Incarnation's apologists included) and evokes the insistent demands made by the son of Marie de l'Incarnation.

The Clerical Injunction to Write

Mystical experience is not always linked to writing, but it seems that for many mystics writing and ecstasy share common characteristics and stem from an inner compulsion. Indeed, while many female mystics may maintain that, since the ecstatic state is ineffable, words fail to render it faithfully, they seem no less compelled to write of themselves and of their experiences. Despite the expressed opinion of Teresa of Avila that when in ecstasy one cannot describe it, even less record it in writing, many female mystics tended to do both at once. Marie de l'Incarnation often repeated that she felt forced, from inside, to write.

In a letter of 1661, Marie de l'Incarnation linked the phenomenon of ecstasy with that of writing: "[W]hile I was in a state of extraordinary transport in our house in Tours one day, I had a vision of the superiority and sublimity of that twofold beauty of the twin natures of Jesus Christ. In this state of transport, I picked up my pen and wrote down visions in accordance with the sufferings of my spirit."[27]

The link between ecstasy and writing excuses female mystics' scriptorial act, but they still have to reinforce this excuse with statements clearly showing that their writing is divinely inspired, without reflection, style, or corrections, and that the female mystics thus are not authors or literati. In the letter of 1647 in which she agreed to send her son a brief piece of work written after her illness, Marie de l'Incarnation evoked once more her internal need to write, adding the theme of her total lack of reflection: "[A] light filled my spirit with the twofold beauty of God, and my heart had to unburden itself through my pen without conscious thought, for the spirit did not allow it."[28] In 1653, she sent him a brief index of the states of orison and explained to him how she wrote it: "Therefore, without thinking of what use it could be, I took some paper and immediately wrote a list or summary which I placed in my portfolio."[29] She insisted that because it was born of divine inspiration, her writing was not a literary work upon which she had been reflecting:

> I have simply laid bare my feelings without method or politeness, but as the pure expression of my spirit and heart. Had I wished to draw comparisons and use rhetoric to make myself understood, this would have prolonged matters, and I would have stifled the purity of spirit of the things which I have written which do not bear adulteration.[30]

Yet, despite the profusion of writings produced by the current of female mysticism, the authorization to write was not axiomatic

for the female mystic.[31] Her personal need to write of her religious
experience came into conflict with the social and religious interdictions dictating that a woman should not teach, preach, pretend to
know more about God than the church hierarchy, or think of herself, a nun, as an author. The cloister or the scrutiny of the clergy
was meant to keep her in a state of eternal oblivion from the world
and from herself. Authorization to write, for female mystics, was
linked to problems of ecclesiastical rule and with the recognition by
the latter of the charismatic authority of the mystic. In order to
receive the authorization to write, female mystics first had to persuade the church authorities to recognize their divine mandate.
Having obtained this recognition, they could venture to write on
the condition that they were required to do so by a member of the
clergy. Only then could female mystics circumvent the many prohibitions that condemned them to assume a passive, humble, and
silent role, without feeling responsible and guilty or being accused
of pride and indecorum. By means of obedience to a clergyman,
they could assert themselves without posing a threat to the stabil-
ity of the established order. Thus, the clerical injunction to write,
which was originally intended to prescribe and supervise the spiritual activity of female mystics, allowed them to break into the public arena by obeying the very clerics who issued that interdiction.
The male religious authority who ordered the mystic to write about
her experience often also allowed the publication and disclosure of
her secrets and her promotion to the rank of saint or of a cult figure, thus conferring a legitimacy to her teaching. Without this recognition on the part of the ecclesiastical authorities, the female
mystic was consigned to heresy, dereliction, criminality, or delu-
sion.

Thus the clerical injunction to write is nonliterary in origin, in
that mystical confession was an attempt to satisfy the insatiable
demand of the clergy. This demand was motivated either by the
ecclesiastical hierarchy's distrust of all forms of religious experience and practice that fell outside its control or by a member of the
clergy who was convinced by the charismatic authority of the mystic and who held the power to have her recognized as a saint. The
clerical command to write could become a dictate but also a safeguard, allowing the mystic to bring her experiences into line with
orthodox thinking and to avoid any accusation of heresy. It was

common for a member of the clergy who had listened to or read the experiences of the woman under his spiritual guidance to give her a mystical text in which she "recognized" her own experiences, hence the rather repetitive character of the genre.

The female mystic who laid claim to a knowledge and power as coming directly from God threatened the strictly masculine ecclesiastical hierarchy, which wanted to regulate all commerce between the individual and God through the sacraments, the distribution of which was the exclusive domain of the clergy. Thus the position of the female mystic who wished to remain within the bounds of orthodoxy and to be legitimized by those in power was akin to that of the tightrope walker. If she wished to have her divine mandate accepted by the religious powers she had continually to reassure the hierarchy of her obedience to the clergy and of her need for the sacraments. She also had to refute the type of accusations normally directed at every female mystic, namely her presumptuousness to preach the truth, her audacity to meddle in the teaching of men, her pretentiousness in claiming to know more than her spiritual director, and her departure from the enforced feminine humility and restricted world of the cloister, imposed upon her by the church. In short, she had continually to deny or moderate what she claimed on the basis of her divine mandate— that God spoke directly to her as a woman, that He filled her with knowledge of the truth, and that He gave her the mission of transmitting it to others without operating through the hierarchy of the church. The thread that linked her to orthodoxy was tenuous, and the deviation that could emerge from her discourse was subjected to close clerical scrutiny, making the threat of exclusion always present. In fact, the female mystic lived in a constant double bind, with all that this existential situation implies for the balance of the psyche. The only exception to this pattern of tightrope walking is Marguerite Porète who was burnt at the stake in 1310, not for any proven heretical writings but surely for her refusal to compromise with the institution.[32]

As a consequence of this problem, mystical texts written by women proliferate with protestations of humility regarding the act of writing. When Dom Claude Martin published the first of his mother's writings in 1677, he felt obliged in his preface to excuse the very fact that she recorded her spiritual experiences in writing:

"It is unusual for someone to write about her life herself and to publish the inner graces and secrets with which God has enriched her; one of the first effects of grace is to hide grace itself."[33] One of the marks of "true" grace is that it remains concealed, thus highlighting one of the obstacles to writing that the female mystics had to overcome. He adds, however, that "it is not always forbidden to reveal the gifts of grace" if it is done for the glory of God, and that "it was these other motives which led Mother Marie de l'Incarnation to reveal part of that which was most secret within her."[34] In order to further legitimate his mother's act of writing, Claude Martin invoked the clerical injunction to write: "[S]he wrote nothing of her own volition, but on the instruction of her Superior who ordered her to do so."[35]

It is true that Marie de l'Incarnation's correspondence with her son before 1654 is full of protestations of humility and reticence concerning her mystical experience. We must note, however, that this reticence does not apply to her writings on the colony, the work of the Ursulines, or the Indians, but only to the spiritual writing. It is also true that the clerical injunction to write is to be found in all of her autobiographical accounts. In 1633 she had written a spiritual account at the request of Father de la Haye, which corresponded to the conventional motif of the clerical command to write. She had asked him to guide her, and in order to understand her better, he had pressed her to write the story of her inner life. Père de la Haye destroyed the part concerning her sins, for these fell under the seal of the confessional. Claude Martin was in possession of what remained when he began to edit the works of Marie de l'Incarnation. In 1636 she wrote another account, also at the request of her spiritual director, Father Dinet, in order to convince him of the genuineness of her vocation to go to Canada. Claude Martin reproduced the *Relation* of 1636 in its entirety. The account she wrote for her son in 1654 also displays the conventional topos that refers to her then spiritual director, Father Lalemant: "Since God's earthly representative . . . asked me to write."[36]

Yet, her correspondence reveals another image behind that of the institutional female mystic she presented in her autobiographies. The image chosen by her son as an institutional mystic was also the one favored and approved of by the ecclesiastical hierarchy and by her twentieth-century editors and apologists from the abbey of Solesme. Many clues in her letters, however, lead us to believe that her seemingly humble protests to the effect that she either did not write on the subject of her mystical experiences or that she had destroyed what she had written, as well as her demands that her son swear never to let others set eyes on and to destroy whatever she finally sent him at his request, might have other motives than humility. Similarly, the use of the clerical injunction to write, when she finally consented to send him her spiritual autobiography, might have another function than that of obedience to the clerical demand. While in the autobiographies the claims to be following a clerical injunction to write and her accompanying protestation of humility concerning writing are traditional clichés, in the correspondence they are linked to the topos of the abandonment of the child and reveal a different motive. Their combined function is to reveal the mother's desire and to subvert the need for clerical authorization altogether.

If for ten years Marie de l'Incarnation resisted her son's request for total confidence, it was not out of humility. She probably did so because she did not feel he was ready for such revelations, and also perhaps because she did not feel confident that he was an ally. His reproaches to her for having abandoned him, his questioning of the validity of the Ursulines' presence in the New World, and his demanding to know how she was so sure that her mission was divinely ordained could certainly justify her discretion. Before 1654, she only responded to his query by giving him the kind of advice that did not reveal her inner life. If, on occasion, she did talk to him about her inner life, she did so only indirectly, and always implying that she was not producing any writing on her mystical experiences. On one occasion she told him that she burned several writings about her inner life before leaving Tours and therefore had nothing to send him. She did add that this act of excessive humility incurred the censure of the Mother Superior, for indeed every mystic who was recognized and approved by the ecclesiastical authorities brought fame to her convent, and with it not only prestige but also donations. This proves that she wrote a good deal on the subject, at least before she departed from France. In the letter of the summer of 1647, she replied: "As for my papers, what papers? I have very few, my dearest son, for I do not stop to write about the subjects which you imagine."[37] Yet in the letter she wrote to him on September 1, 1643, she referred to her son's question about her spiritual writings: "Note well, my dearest son, that if you outlive me you will know more since you wish me to give you my papers, and if obedience allows it at that time, I am willing to do so in order that you may know the excessive divine goodness granted to me, as well as to you."[38] She therefore intimated to him that these writings on her inner life did exist and that she was willing to reveal her passion to him, but not before her death. When he insisted, she made vague promises: "If God is willing, I shall send you what you ask me for one day, or others will do it for me; and I shall write down what you desire after I have fulfilled pressing obligations so that it is ready to be sent to you when divine Providence decrees it."[39] But little by little she sent him short pieces as a reward for his advances along the mystical path she wanted him to tread. In the letter of the summer of 1647, after many requests from her son, she agreed to send him a short piece she had written in a moment of divine inspiration, and she told him that she was acceding to his demand because they were both committed to the religious life: "In truth, it seems to me that I *owe* this to a son who has consecrated himself to the service of my divine Master and with whom I feel spiritually united."[40] In 1648, in her delight at his beginning to show an inclination for the inner life, she expressed a wish that this should be the justification for their correspondence: "It gives me inexpressible comfort to see such religious inclinations in you and I agree with your feeling that our exchanges should lead to the end to which we aspire."[41]

In 1651, her convent was destroyed by fire. In the letter in which she related the event to her son, she said that she had deliberately allowed several documents concerning her spiritual life to burn, as well as an account she had begun, which was destined for him:

> Everything met the same fate, for I left my papers and all that I had for my own private use. These papers were those which you had requested and which I had written recently in obedience (to Father Lalemant). Were it not for this accident it was my intention to send them to you since I had undertaken to satisfy you on condition that you burned them after reading them. It occurred to me to throw them out of the win-

dow, but such was my fear that they might fall into some-
body's hands that I willingly abandoned them to the flames.
. . . After all these thoughts, I chanced to lay my hand upon
them, and I felt moved by an inner feeling to leave them. . . .
[I]t is done now, dearest son, and you must not think about it
any more.[42]

As the son did not desist in his wish to receive her spiritual
writings, in the letter of August 9, 1654, she told him that since he
had expressed his desire for her to edify him by recounting her
spiritual states, she had "felt *compelled* to discuss several aspects
of her spiritual life with him in her letters."[43] In the same letter,
she added that on seeing that what she said in her letters did not
satisfy him, she had resolved to overcome her reluctance and to
write an account of her spiritual life especially for him. By the
same token, it is evident that in order to write the *Relation* of 1654
for her son, she used many documents and memoirs she had already written and that must have survived the fire of 1651, even
though she had told him that everything had been burnt and that
he should thus no longer insist.[44] After 1654, she more freely
shared with him her inner life. Thus, the rhetoric of protestation
regarding the act of writing about one's own spiritual experience,
characteristic of female mystical writing and so manifest in Marie
de l'Incarnation's letters to her son, was not designed to claim humility but rather to test his trustworthiness.
    In the letter of the same year in which she finally sent him her
autobiographical account, she told her son that she had clerical approval. To be sure to avoid any error, in fact, she had consulted her
spiritual director, who not only allowed her to send the spiritual
account to her son, but also renewed his command to write it, as he
had done on a number of previous occasions. She said, however,
that she had felt unable to comply earlier: "I had deferred obeying
for more than five years. I was so very reluctant that the order had
to be repeated three times."[45] It was not the authority of her spiritual director's clerical injunction to write that pushed her, for she
let the reader know in this letter that she only responded to the
director when, satisfied with her son, she had decided to comply
with his request. She did not forget to add, however, that neither
her son nor her confessor was the source of inspiration:

At that time, my Superior and spiritual director, Père Lalemant, had instructed me to ask Our Lord that if He desired
something from me before my death which could contribute to
His glory, He should reveal it to me. After praying in a spirit
of obedience, I had only two visions: the first was to offer myself as a sacrifice to the divine Majesty to be consumed for
this desolate land in whatever fashion He might order; the
second was to record in writing the conduct which He had
imposed on me since the time He called me to the inner life.[46]

Dom Claude Martin finally did what Marie de l'Incarnation
claimed to fear, or perhaps to desire above all else, and which a
priest alone could do: that is, to make her known as an author and
as a mystic. In his publication of her writings, the son as a priest
fulfilled the role traditionally assumed by the mystic's spiritual director. The contract established between the mystic and the institution was respected. Indeed, Marie de l'Incarnation wrote down
her deepest intuitions at the request of her son who, in his role as a
man of the church, was to become the apologist and editor through
whom she is known to modern readers. Armed with all the documents that established him as his mother's spiritual heir, he had
no difficulty in also obtaining the diverse documents written at the
request of her confessor (Father Dinet), which she had left behind
in Tours when she departed and whose existence she herself had
revealed to him in 1653.[47] When it became known that Claude Martin was undertaking the writing of a biography of Marie de l'Incarnation, the Ursulines in Paris spontaneously sent him her autobiography of 1633, which another, previous spiritual director (Father
de la Haye) had entrusted to them. And still today the contract
holds. The Benedictines of Solesmes have recently reedited the entire works of Marie de l'Incarnation, precisely because her son belonged to the religious community of Saint-Maur of which the
Benedictines are heirs. The authority of the priestly figure was in
fact subverted once again, however, since her son was not actually
her superior. Although he was a priest, she was not obliged to obey
him; rather, she granted him a favor by entrusting her inner life to
him, and she only communicated her spiritual writings to him
when she felt he was ready and personally committed to both the
mystical life and to her. She quite undoubtedly established herself

from the outset as his spiritual director, adopting a position of clerical rather than maternal authority in relation to him, and she remained in this role until her death.

At the end of her life, when her son finally relinquished his fantasy of holding power over her, she told him that she would have chosen him as her spiritual director if they had been able to see each other more often.[48] Notwithstanding the irony of this statement, as it was certainly she who was his spiritual director, she did not acknowledge her son's fantasy, or the authority of his priesthood, but rather approved of and rewarded his role as an excluded witness who had relinquished his wish to be the object of her desire. It is at this point that the son and the spiritual director become one, proving that her writing arose not in response to a request from her son or to a clerical mandate, but that the spiritual director and son were the necessary witnesses to the theater of her desire, in which her resistance was enacted.

Despite frequent mention of the theme of abandonment and regret, Marie de l'Incarnation evaded the social claims of motherhood by refusing to play into her son's desire. In regard to the need for the clerical injunction to write, she resisted the obedience expected of the female mystic by the ecclesiastical hierarchy, despite her reiterated lip service to it. Finally, in spite of her repeated desire for secrecy, all her writings were in fact published. It is as if, reinterpreting the masculine creation myth in which woman is born of man, Marie de l'Incarnation gave birth to her interlocutor, reader, and publisher, as surely as she had given birth to her son.

For this to be possible, it was imperative that she maintain the distance separating France from New France and son from mother. Failing to make her return to France, Claude Martin told his mother that he, too, was thinking of becoming a missionary in Canada, a project she received with unmotherly sympathy:

> You say that you would want one day to come to Canada and say mass in the land of the unfaithful. If God bestowed that honor upon you, I would have the joy that you expect. How happy I would be if it was reported to me that my son was martyred for God. Saint Simphorose could not have been happier than I would be. This is the extent of my love for you: that you be worthy of spilling your blood for Jesus Christ.[49]

Claude Martin had only said that he wanted to say mass in Canada, whereas she offered him as a holocaust. It is hardly surprising that any mention of his wish disappeared from subsequent correspondence.

Chapter Four

The Double Bind
The Invisible Historical Subject as Historiographer

ad she entered a contemplative order shut off from the world, Marie de l'Incarnation would certainly have been known as a mystic, and undoubtedly would also have authored autobiographical and spiritual writings of acceptable orthodoxy but, I suspect, of little originality. Her decision to join a new order that was more open to the world at large subsequently facilitated her setting out for the New World. This decision not only gave a new turn to her spiritual writings but it also put her in a set of circumstances that demanded that she write history. Although not traditionally included within discussions of female historical writers of the *ancien régime*, because such works have focused on women memorialists of the aristocracy close to the court and the salons, Marie de l'Incarnation, alone of her sex, did contribute to the rich corpus of historical publications produced by travelers, missionaries, and explorers on the beginnings of New France and on the inhabitants of this part of the New World.[1] Even though she was from a different cultural and social milieu than the seventeenth-century women memorialists, her historiographical endeavors attest to Faith E. Beasley's claim that women of that period were keenly interested in history, particularly when they participated in it as agents.[2] Marie de l'Incarnation was indeed most interested in the history in the making, both as witness and active participant.

Her historical writings, covering 1639 to 1672, constitute an important source of information for historians of New France and of the American Indians of the Northeast.[3] Moreover, they provide a great number of details about the Indians and the colony that are not in *The Jesuit Relations*, a yearly publication from 1610 to 1791, which represents the most prolific and important source of information about New France.[4] Furthermore, Marie de l'Incarnation's letters and memoirs also depict the world and the work of women in the colony that had been ignored by other historical writings on the history of New France, such as *The Jesuit Relations* or Du Creux's *Historiae Canadensis*.[5] In this chapter I will focus on her representation of women.

Like the Jesuits, Marie de l'Incarnation functioned as a historian, a chronicler, and a propagandist for the Ursuline Mission in New France, with the alleged purpose of benefitting Indian and French girls and women. As the founder of the first convent for women on mission soil, she was in charge of educating, Christianizing, and Gallicizing the Indians, and instructing the French girls. She also was responsible for advertising the work of the Ursulines in order to encourage donations, as the Ursuline mission was in great need of financial help.

Unlike the Jesuits, however, Marie de l'Incarnation also wrote history for specifically self-serving reasons. As discussed in the previous chapter, the desire to legitimize her divine election to the mission in Canada undergirded her stance toward the role of the body, both in her piety and in her rhetoric of health. The same desire can be read behind her historiographical enterprise. In fact, this desire intertwines her triple vocation of mystic, missionary, and historiographer in the New World. The privileged relationship of the mystic with God singled her out as the person especially capable of successfully conducting missionary work with the Indians. On the other hand, as a historian whose writings celebrated the success of the woman missionary and that of the colony, she also actively demonstrated the necessity of the Ursulines in New France. In turn, the success of the mission reaffirmed the legitimacy of her divine election for carrying out missionary work. Thus, Marie de l'Incarnation had a triple agenda in her historiographic project: to obtain gifts and support from France; to defend the work and the necessity of the Ursulines' presence in New France; and through the flourishing of her mission, to prove to her contemporaries that her election as missionary was indeed decreed by God.

Historiography and Gender Politics

Writing history, however, was not self-evident for her as a woman and a nun. Joan Wallach Scott, feminist historian, has shown how the production of the invisibility of women in all areas by a phallocentric symbolic and by patriarchal politics has been reproduced by the writing of history.[6] Furthermore, she has explained how history, as a discipline, participates in the reproduction of sexual difference, as it has been created and maintained by the male-dominated system. Her research corroborates the formulations of postmodern feminist theorists, who suggest that the conflation of women with the feminine as a social and symbolic construction serves as a negative counterpoint, as other, both to the construction of a positive, masculine identity and to the preservation of a patriarchal representation of sexual difference. This feminist reflection on the writing of history has made visible that which had to be suppressed so that the omnipotence of the representation of universal Man could be maintained. It has become evident that the invisibility (rather than absence) of women from historical discourse is not owing to negligence; instead it is a sine qua non condition of the preservation of gender politics. What has become clear as a result of this research and these reflections is that in order to redress the balance and include women in the writing of history, it is not enough simply to produce new data without first analyzing how sexual hierarchies have been constructed, legitimized, and preserved.

As the Jesuit enterprise went hand in hand with that of the

Ursulines, it is particularly illuminating to compare the Jesuits' and Marie de l'Incarnation's different positionings regarding the privilege of writing history. The fact that Jesuits and Ursulines had very close ties and common interests in New France makes their disparity on certain points all the more significant. Furthermore, because Marie de l'Incarnation found herself in the position to record the same period of history as that recorded by the Jesuits, the history of New France provides a unique opportunity to witness the occultation of women in the official historical discourse of the Jesuits and to see it as the product of the presiding sexual politics regarding the writing of history as such.

Although Marie de l'Incarnation's official motives for writing history were sanctioned by her religious institution, her historiographic undertakings ran into enormous difficulties. Nuns were certainly allowed to write chronicles of their order and hagiographies of their religious sisters, but these pious works were not read outside the convents and addressed mostly the restricted history of a particular order. Marie de l'Incarnation did practice these two genres, following their rules to the letter.[7] But, the history she was writing in New France was of a vaster scope, and she was aware that it engaged not only the prestige of the kingdom of France, but more importantly for her that of the kingdom of God. She was, however, indeed in an economic and political position very different from that of the Jesuits when she set out to undertake her historiographic work.

First, the Jesuits were wealthy and had at their disposal established publication sources and distribution channels in France. The Ursulines in Quebec were poor and completely dependent upon the goodwill of the Jesuits to inform the general public of the results of their work. It was in the interest of the Jesuits that the mission of the Ursulines, as well as their own, was thought well of in France. But it was also in their interest that the Ursulines not be allowed to take center stage. To that end, they mentioned the Ursulines from time to time and occasionally included in their *Relations* some excerpts issuing from the pen of Marie de l'Incarnation, but they did so only sparingly. In other words, they conspicuously exercised their control of the writing of history.

Second, martyrdom was the Jesuits' trademark; and, since it was considered by their readers in France as the most glorious act that could be accomplished by any missionary, it was likely to stir interest and increase funding for the mission.[8] The Ursulines, however, like all women, were forbidden by the Jesuits to go on missions outside the established colony, and they could not, therefore, participate in this act of Christian heroism.[9] Thus, in addition to her often-mentioned regrets at not having personal access to martyrdom, Marie de l'Incarnation did not have at her disposal tales of any other Ursulines' martyrdom with which to stir the imagination and the purse of her readers. It is even more likely that such an event, if it had occurred, far from winning glory for the Ursulines, would have won them a quick and forced return to France.

Third, the Jesuits were well educated, knowing how to use literary allusions to embellish their stories and please their audience. They could write their history of Canada in Latin in order to stimulate interest in their undertaking among the intelligentsia and scholars.[10] For although they were written by educated, capable men, and even though they were well read in France, the *Relations* did not attract the attention of the literary circles as the Jesuits had anticipated. In order to remedy this, the Jesuits decided to publish a version of their *Relations* in Latin, which could be addressed to a chosen public and thus exercise a more prestigious influence. The Jesuit Du Creux was singled out for the task, and he worked on it under the direction and censure of his superiors. His work says more about what the Jesuits in Paris wanted to be known of their mission than it does about the realities of the Indians and the life of the colony. Even more restrictive than the *Relations*, the *Historiae Canadensis* of Du Creux focuses on the facts and deeds of the Jesuits alone. By comparison, the Ursulines did not, by far, receive the same education as the Jesuits. As for Marie de l'Incarnation, her education had been that of a girl from the artisan class. She had learned to write and count, and she had read a few love novels in her youth, followed by many religious texts during her adult life.

Fourth, she was dependent upon the Jesuits not only for the publication of her pieces of propaganda but also as a source for her own letters and memoirs. She wrote her letters once every year before the annual departure of the ships for France, and the Jesuits let her take from their reports whatever she considered useful for her own propaganda. The choices that she made from among their accounts and the changes that she forced these accounts to undergo are the most interesting aspect of these pieces. But *The Jesuit Relations* were not her only source of information. Marie de l'Incarnation was indeed cloistered, but this does not mean that she was not kept informed about what was happening in New France; quite the opposite, in fact, occurred.[11] Her prestige was such that the world of the Indians, the mission, and the colony came to her. The Jesuits from the three closest residences (Sillery, Quebec, and Notre Dame des Anges) came often to the monastery for spiritual conferences, for the preaching given at retreats, and for the affairs of the Indians.[12] The secular world also came to Marie de l'Incarnation; it is documented that she was the temporal and spiritual advisor of several governors of New France, in particular the governor d'Argenson and the marquis de Tracy, lieutenant general of the King for French America.[13] The Indians constantly occupied the parlor of the Ursulines, and by 1641 their visits increased up to eight hundred per year.[14]

Finally, an even greater difficulty existed for Marie de l'Incarnation, which affected the very possibility for her to produce historical writing as well as to inscribe women into history. The prohibition against writing to which women were traditionally subjected was rapidly weakening in the seventeenth century, among aristocratic and upper-class women. Yet, partly, no doubt, because she was from an artisan milieu, but most probably because of the added demand of humility for nuns, the pressure against women writing is still very much at work in her historiographical writing. As a mystic, however, Marie de l'Incarnation could circumvent such prohibitions by having recourse to divine inspiration and thereby authorize herself with the clerical injunction to write. As a historian desiring to write about women's and her own contribution to history, she could not have found any insitutional authorization.

In contrast, neither the Jesuits nor the Sulpicians, both of whom wrote the first histories of French Canada, needed excuses in order to refer to their own deeds and actions in the first person. But a nun was disallowed from taking it upon herself to become an author, believing that the work of a woman writing about women was of any great interest, or proposing that it offered a significant contribution to humanity. In fact, quite often Marie de l'Incarnation played into the requirement imposed by men that women be humble, as evidenced when she qualified her work as "small tasks" or "minor services."[15] When the Jesuits inserted some of her texts into their *Relations*, they did not refute the diminutive epithets used by their fellow missionary, although they never referred to their own work in such a way. Christian humility was above all a woman's affair, and for Marie de l'Incarnation, was in sharp contradiction with a work of propaganda or of historiography, which required speaking of oneself and one's colleagues' creative work in the colony and the mission.

In turn, it was to Marie de l'Incarnation's own personal advantage, as well as to her mission's, that her stories be published in *The Jesuit Relations* or in Father Du Creux's *Historiae Canadensis*. When the Jesuits asked to see her work, however, she felt obliged to be reticent; when they used her work without asking her for it, she manifested bashfulness. In 1669, Father Le Jeune included her hagiography of Mother Marie de Saint Joseph in the *Relation* without her knowledge.[16] She did not fail to remark on this in a letter to her son:

> I was very surprised to learn that one of our friends, who suspected that I was sending this account to our Mothers, opened my package and handed [my account] over to the Reverend Father Le Jeune, procurer of the missions, who had for a long time been his director in this country, and [Father Le Jeune] put it in the *Relation*, after having had it printed.[17]

Le Jeune also mentioned in the *Relation* that this had been done without her knowledge, thus exonerating her from talking about herself and her order in eulogistic terms. The topos that a private piece of writing fell into the publisher's hand, and thus was published without the author's knowledge or desire, was commonly used by both men and women in the seventeenth century. In this case, however, the Ursuline used it, while the male missionaries did not.

On another occasion in the refectory, as Marie was reading the *Relation* aloud to her sisters, she fell upon the same passage she had written and that Father Le Jeune had borrowed without her knowledge. The Christian humility required of a woman made her react with appropriate modesty:

I had given orders that a copy of the account that I had made to our Mothers, about the life and death of our dear defunct, should be sent to you. I was informed that this has not yet been done because this piece of writing has fallen into the hands of R. Father Le Jeune. This good Father has taken from it that which he wanted to put into the *Relation*, without my asking him to do so. It pleased me that he published it, but it gave me a greater pleasure not having my name appear. I, who knew nothing of all this, being reader at the refectory, found myself precisely reading my own story. I was embarrassed and I stopped reading, leaving to have it read by another.[18]

In 1660, Du Creux, who knew that Marie de l'Incarnation had written an autobiographical memoir for the information of her son (proof that the activity was not as secret and private as she had said it was), asked the son to let him have several extracts for his *Historiae Canadensis*. The son refused; when he informed his mother of the request, he received the following reply from her:

You have pleased me not to communicate our writings to be included in the work of this good Father who writes the history of Canada. For more than ten years he has been pressing me to give him something similar; I have always declined. I do not know if Father Lalemant has given him some memoirs; he could have done so if he so wanted, because he is the one man in the world who knows me the best. If he has done this it is without consulting me.[19]

This demand that she succumb to female humility spurred her to utilize this rhetorical stance as a strategy. In a letter of 1642, in which she responded to an invitation from Father Vimont to write something about her mission for the *Relation* of that year, we find her answering with her superb rhetoric, which allowed her to appear humble and yet, at the same time, to say what she wanted to make known: "My Reverend Father, I send you a few short remarks to obey your requests."[20] This first sentence gives us the impression that she only gives him the material out of a sense of duty, and that, moreover, there is not much to say about the work of the Ursulines. But a second sentence gives a different sense to "short remarks" and "obedience": "I had difficulty in making up my mind, for if one wanted to say everything which would reflect the actions of our girls, this would never be finished."[21] In other words, the remarks are short and it was difficult for her to obey his order, because it is impossible to recount in detail the considerable success of the Ursuline mission. The following sentence, of course, contradicts her boasts: "[W]e are little satisfied with what we do, being nothing but useless servants, myself in particular. It is for this reason that I would like you to not make any mention of us: it is enough that God who is our Father knows with what love we serve our Neophytes."[22]

Notwithstanding this contradiction, she offers a hyperbolic description of the effect of the Ursulines' education upon their students, who thus receive in turn great benefits. Although Marie de l'Incarnation had not been schooled in the subject, she knew how to use rhetoric to her advantage. Despite her reticence and her protestations to the contrary, we know that over the years she wrote several accounts especially for the *Relations*, and that she prepared material for the *Historiae Canadensis* of Father Du Creux. In 1668, she wrote to a nun from Tours: "The Reverend Father du Creux, who wrote the history of Canada, asks me every year for news he can insert; I sent him many things from this dear mother [a nun who had died] which he has printed."[23]

Be that as it may, Marie de l'Incarnation's historical pieces, whether they appeared in *The Jesuit Relations* or in the *Historiae Canadensis* of Father du Creux, were usually abridged. They are not the most interesting pieces and appear only infrequently. They are marked by the most restrictive self-censure, concerned, for the most part, with optimistic and edifying reports (a genre practiced just as frequently by the Jesuits) on the conversion and sincerity of the young Indians placed in the charge of the Ursulines. The image of Marie de l'Incarnation, of the Ursulines, and of their work, which emerges from the history written and published by the Jesuits, is one of humble women performing "minor tasks" in the obscurity of the cloister which are necessary but not very glorious. In the official history, Marie de l'Incarnation, when talking about herself and about the work of the Ursulines, is forced to render the women of the mission invisible by dint of devalorization. If the annals of history had left only the short pieces of her historical writing that found a place in the official version, they would be of little interest. What is reproduced in the official version of the history of New France is the invisibility of the female missionary, which reproduces the wordly invisibility of the nuns—an invisibility ensured by the cloister and ordained by the church. The Jesuits represented Marie de l'Incarnation as they wanted women to be: obscure, serving, humble, and silent. And when writing for the *Relations*, Marie de l'Incarnation complied with their desire.

Self-Representation in Unofficial Historical Writings

Marie de l'Incarnation compensated for the lack of access to publication with many handwritten letters and copious memoranda. She wrote letters to her son, to women's convents, to other nuns, to ladies of the aristocracy who were likely to be interested in a woman's mission for women and hence to make donations. The Ursuline Convents served her as networks of diffusion.[24] It is certain that this mode of communication reached far fewer people than *The Jesuits Relations*, and that it also demanded a great effort of her. She often complained about the large number of letters she had to write. In a letter to her son in 1666 she takes leave of him by saying: "I beg you to accept in good spirit that I finish in order to rest a little, being very tired due to the great number of letters I have written. I have no more than forty more to write, which I hope to send by the last vessel."[25] In another letter in 1667 she remarked: "For four months I have been continually writing letters and memoirs concerning our affairs in France."[26] It is certain that access to publication would have greatly spared her pen and her energies. But, given the quasi-total control that the Jesuits had on the production of the history of New France and the encounter with its inhabitants, publication at the time she was writing would certainly have deprived us of many interesting details, of the positive image that she gave of herself, and of an alternative history in which women had a central place. Marie de l'Incarnation was conscious of writing for posterity and of the contradictions carried by her status as a nun historian writing about women and herself. She was also aware that the obstacles to the publication and the circulation of her historical writings constituted a danger for the Ursuline mission, and for the credibility of her own personal mission as well. Finally, although the Jesuits neglected her, she talked about them at great length because she was their tributary in many respects, and it was in her interest to stay on good terms with them. In these texts, which were not intended for the official channels but rather for women of her network, as well as for her son who was part of that network, she revealed a portrait of herself completely different from that given in *The Jesuit Relations*.

Although she usually managed to respect the rules of feminine humility and deference to the Jesuits, she let her anger and frustration explode in 1668 in a letter addressed to her son, apparently in response to rumors—that he probably had brought to her attention—that suggested that the Ursulines would be sent back to France because they were thought useless in the New World:

> If it is said that we are useless here, because the *Relations* does not mention us, it should also be said that Monseigneur the Prélat is useless, that his seminary is useless, that the seminary of the Reverend Fathers is useless, that *Messieurs les Ecclésiastiques* of Montreal are useless, and that finally the *Hospitalières* Mothers are useless, because the *Relations* say nothing at all about any of this. And yet it is this which constitutes the support, the force, and the very honor of the country. If the *Relations* say nothing about us nor about the Companies or Seminaries of which I just spoke, it is because they only make mention of the progress of the gospel and those things related to it; and what is more, when copies of *The Jesuit Relations* are sent from here, a lot of things are cut out of it in France . . . . M.C. who prints the *Relations* and likes the *Hospitalières* from this area very much added to it, of his own accord, a letter that the superior had written to him, and that caused a great interest in France.[27]

She excused the Jesuits by emphasizing the fact that the aim of *The Jesuit Relations* was to talk about the Jesuits, and that therefore it was not surprising if many things occurring in the colony were not recorded in it. She also excused them by stating that the Superior of Paris edited and cut their accounts. Despite these excuses, she did not fail to show her frustration against the authors and publishers of the *Relations*. For example, by saying that when the *Relations* did condescend to talk about the *Hospitalières*, France became interested in them, she insinuated that there would be as much interest in the Ursulines if the *Relations* were to talk about them. Nor did she fail to suggest that those things unaddressed in the *Relations*, specifically her own mission, figure no less among that "which constitutes the support, the force, and the very honor of the country." The editor of the *Correspondance* tells the reader that the rumors suggesting that the Ursulines were useless led Father Mercier to mention them in the *Relation* of that year. This mention consists of a single page and repeats the banalities already said about the Ursuline mission:

> One cannot value enough the good fortune of Canada which has had there for almost thirty years the two Religious Houses of the Ursulines and the *Hospitalières*, who were necessary to that place and who perform, with worthiness and holiness, that which God and men could expect from them, each one of them in their tasks to which the divine providence had destined them. The Ursuline Mothers were so successful in the instruction of the girls who were put in their care, either boarders or students from outside who attended their classes, that in seeing the households of Canada and each house in particular one can very easily distinguish there, by the Christian education of the children, those among the mothers of the families who were educated by the Ursulines from those who did not have this opportunity.[28]

This is not the way she portrayed her work. Although she sometimes referred to her work as "small works," the way she talked about it to her son belies the diminutive: "I assure you that I need more courage than a man to bear the crosses which abound in our private affairs and the affairs of the country, where everything is lined with thorns, among which we must proceed in darkness."[29] Likewise, in a letter to her son in 1641, which she wrote at the beginning of her stay in New France, she described her work in the following manner:

The work is so pleasant and easy to manage that I am experiencing what the Lord has said: "My yoke is easy and my burden is light." My efforts have not gone wasted in the learning of a new language which comes now so easily to me that I have no difficulties teaching the saintly mysteries to our neophytes, of whom we have a great number this year; more than 50 seminarists, over 700 visits from savages male and female, all of whom received our spiritual and temporal assistance. Being in the saintly employ of God gives me such joy that it erases all the pain of daily chores.[30]

In 1668, two years before her death, she described her missionary work with the same enthusiasm:

From the beginning of Lent to Ascension Day, I have written a large Algonquin book of sacred history and saintly matters, together with a dictionary and an Iroquoian catechism which is a real treasure. Last year I wrote a large Algonquin dictionary in the French alphabet; I have another one in the savage alphabet.[31]

But she still had to make excuses:

I am telling you this to show how the Divine Goodness gives me strength in my weakness to enable my sisters to work toward His salvation of the souls . . . but after we have done everything in our power, we must think of ourselves as useless servants, small grains of sand at the very bottom of this new church's structure.[32]

Marie de l'Incarnation was convinced of the importance of her and her sisters' work as educators and of their lasting contribution to the very social fiber of the colony. There was not a single French girl in Quebec from any social class who did not come into contact with her: "We take great care here to educate the French girls; and I can assure you that without the Ursulines, their salvation would constantly be in jeopardy."[33] She believed that the Ursulines accomplished useful and necessary work, the kind of work the Jesuits could not do: "French girls would be veritable beasts without the education we provide for them, which they need even more than the savages. The Reverend Fathers can take care of the savage [men], but they cannot take care of the women for the reasons you can imagine."[34]

In spite of her confinement, her intense participation in the life of the colony cannot be denied; she was not even a stranger to war. When the Iroquois became more aggressive, the Ursulines and their boarders took refuge elsewhere, except for Marie de l'Incarnation, who supervised the defense of the convent: "I watched over all of this, for even though I was shut up in our dormitory, my ears were pricked all night for fear of an alarm and in order to be always ready to give our soldiers the munitions required in the event of an attack."[35]

To be sure, the perception of the female sex, even in the writings of Marie de l'Incarnation that were not intended for the official channels, is at times marked by the prejudices of her period. For example, in a letter addressed to her son in which she talks about her acquiring the knowledge of Indian languages, she said: "I see that this study is harsh on people, particularly in people of my sex and of my station."[36] She added: "You know that, at last, divine Providence has organized things such that over these recent years our blessed order has moved into these countries of Canada so that, according to the small capacity of our sex, we can work there in applying the blood of Jesus Christ to the souls that barbarity and ignorance would have otherwise excluded from salvation."[37] Further, she made a double-edged compliment about a book authored by a woman, which her son had sent to her and which she admired. This compliment reveals at once not only her pleasure and her pride that a woman had written such a good book, but also her surprise that a woman had been able to write such a good book:

I thank you again for your delightful book, *Année Bénédictine*. If you had not assured me that it is the work of a woman, I would never have believed it, nor would my sisters any more than myself. This noble Mother is well enlightened, and the spirit of God has worked with her knowledge. I admire this work, and we are greatly indebted to you for having offered us such a delightful gift. Once again, how I love this generous woman, and how I wish her well! If you know her and if she is in Paris, I beg you to visit her on my behalf and assure her of the esteem in which I hold her; for, in truth one can rank her among the illustrious people of our sex.[38]

Nevertheless, under other circumstances she was not afraid to take great liberty and to disagree quite stongly with the sexist prejudices of her culture. When her son confided in her the carnal temptation (which lasted for nine or ten years) that he felt in the presence of one of his charges, a girl of sixteen whose purity and intentions were, however, never in question, Marie de l'Incarnation reported:

> As regards that which you propose to me and which concerns you in particular, do not be distressed and do not desist from offering charity to this good Lady. It is the novelty of this task which causes this anxiety; when experience will have cured you, it will not be the same. But, even if it be difficult all of your life, you should not stop being charitable.[39]

As a challenge to the prevailing misogyny, which turns upon woman the temptation felt by man, Marie de l' Incarnation suggested to her son that his temptation belonged to him and that he did not have the right to refuse assistance to a woman because of his own weaknesses. This is all the more remarkable at a time when more and more frequently preachers and confessors represented women as agents of the devil and warned men against their ruses.

The disparity between Marie de l'Incarnation's image as it appeared in the Jesuits' history (whether she or they have written it) and the self-image that appeared in the unofficial version of history that she wrote herself indicates how the work of women was taken for granted by the Jesuits and society at large. This comparison also sheds light on the difference between the prescriptive images of women, as found in many texts written by men and women, and the actual social practices of women. While the Jesuits prescribed how she ought to be, Marie de l'Incarnation demonstrated herself to be a woman with many strengths who refused invisibility and who demanded recognition, despite the many contradictions and institutional compliance she manifested.

Newsworthy History

The New World and Europe's imperialist and missionary passion offered women of seventeenth-century France the opportunity to expand their field of action, and the most intrepid among them did not miss the chance to distinguish themselves in the construction of this new society.[40] However, the history of New France, written in the seventeenth century by Jesuit missionaries, offers as little information about the women of the colony as about the Ursulines.

Marie de l'Incarnation was interested in all aspects of the colony and the mission. With her good business sense she realized that evangelization and colonization went hand in hand with commerce, and she never lost sight of temporal affairs. If the war with the Iroquois continues, she said,

> Commerce will not be able to continue; without commerce, there will be no more ships; without ships, all things necessary to life will be unavailable, like fabric, linen, most provisions, like lard and flour which the garrison and the religious houses cannot do without. . . . If commerce is lacking due to the continuation of the war, the savages who only stop here in order to trade will disappear into the woods. Thus we will not need a bull anymore, there being nothing left for us to do here, being here only in order to bring them faith and to win them over to God.[41]

She discussed the affairs of the state, the religious hierarchy, the mission, the Indians, the war, and the English advances. In 1670, she wrote:

> As for temporal affairs, the King is spending a lot of money here, and he has again sent 150 girls and a large number of soldiers and officers with horses, sheep and goats in order to populate. . . . He has commanded that hemp, cloth and serge be made; this has begun and will increase little by little. He has had a brewery and a tannery built in Quebec because of the large number of animals that there are in the country.[42]

But she did not forget that the work and contribution of women to the colony also fit into this history, and she gave their work adequate attention.[43] That Marie de l'Incarnation wrote about women is not exceptional. According to Natalie Davis, "all [women historical writers of the *ancien régime*] were conscious of the relation of their sex to their work; and all of them somehow took up women as subject."[44] And yet Marie de l'Incarnation was innovative because she spoke of women of the laboring class as well. As an artisan herself who was on her way up the social ladder but was also an expert in matters of business and all sorts of procedures, Marie de l'Incarnation did indeed take an active interest in the work of women of all social classes.

In 1668, she expressed her esteem for the work of women of the laboring class in a letter to her son: "We no longer want to ask for anyone but village girls suitable for work like men. Experience makes one see that those who have not been raised in this way are not right for here, where they find themselves in a state of inescapable need."[45] This remark underlines how the colony depended on the production, as much as the reproduction, of women. The Ursulines participated in this work by teaching not only catechism, reading, writing, and arithmetic, but also by offering women training in skills useful to the economy of the colony: "Women and girls are urged as strongly as possible to learn to spin. We are encouraged to teach it to our Seminarists both French and savage alike, and materials are provided for this."[46] In 1669, she wrote a hagiographic text about Anne Bataille de Saint Laurent, a lay sister from her convent; she did not fail to highlight, amid other clichés of the hagiographic genre, her hard labor on the Ursulines' farm and in their convent, which Anne had undertaken alone, having been the only lay sister of the monastery for several years:

And the good thing is that she was silent, burying herself in her work without respite, not only for whole days, months and years, but she did it her whole life, her courage being tireless. Although she felt her body was becoming more and more weak under the weight of work and great illness caused by the efforts that she had made under the strain of her condition that she had undergone all alone, there not being any other lay Sister than she in the space of several years. . . . Notwithstanding all these troubles, she did not spare herself, and she strove to obtain, like the most precious graces, the

most laborious obediences and those which are the most re-
pugnant to nature. . . . Sick as she was, for nearly three years
she took charge of the bakery and the care of washing the
linen (which are very difficult during the winter in this country) as well as the care of a pack of pigs which she fed and
fattened with as much fatigue as thrift.[47]

Through this homage to the lay sister, Marie de l'Incarnation
also renders homage to all the peasant women who, each on her
own farm, did the same work, providing the indispensable support
for the familial and social fabric that the historians of work have
neglected for a long time. Moreover, Marie de l'Incarnation did not
forget to underline an aspect of Anne Bataille's activity that did not
fit comfortably under the rubric of work or social production, but
which, nonetheless, has its importance in human societies and
which we would translate today as psychotherapy: "Her charity
was universal, consoling the Sisters, God having given her a particular gift for consoling the distressed and strengthening the weak ."[48]
It is interesting to note that *The Jesuit Relations*, which devote a
good number of pages to the hagiography of Mother Marie de Saint
Joseph, who was of noble origin, say absolutely nothing about the
lay sister. Her work and her position as lay sister probably did not
contribute anything to the glory of the Jesuits; she thus had no
right to receive any mention, as was the case with many other
women of the colony whose work did not directly concern the mission of the order.

Marie de l'Incarnation also talked about the work done by
women of the Quebec elite: the care of orphans and the sick, the
assistance to the poor, the consolation of prisoners, and so on.
These activities had been traditionally the work of pious women.
But Marie de l'Incarnation presents them rather as an integral
part of the social workings of colonial society. About one of these
ladies, she writes:

As for Madame Bourdon, she would very much like to see you.
This woman is an example of piety and of charity throughout
the country. She and Madame Dailleboust got together to visit
prisoners, to help criminals, and even to take them in a cart
out of the prison to bury them. She of whom I speak as the

most active and supportive, is continuously occupied with these good works, and with collecting funds for the poor, which she does with success. In short she is the mother of the destitute and the example of all sorts of good works.[49]

Marie de l'Incarnation championed the domestic ingenuity of the women of the colony. She described how the women prepared the fruit and vegetables picked in the country and how they experimented with them. She explains the use Iroquois women make of wild plums and pumpkins, whose seeds she sent to her son:

They are prepared in different ways; in soup with milk, and fried. They are also cooked in the oven, like apples, or under the embers like pears, and this way it is true they taste like green apples. . . . Plums are not cooked in the oven because only a nut covered with skin is left; but they are used to make marmalade with sugar, which is excellent. We make ours with honey, and this seasoning suits us for ourselves and our children. . . . Green currants are preserved, as is piminan also, which is a wild fruit that is made pleasant by the addition of sugar.[50]

Also, she does not hesitate to let it be known to others that the New World demanded new customs, even among religious women. The Ursulines preached to and taught Indian men, whereas in Europe it was strictly forbidden for women, even for nuns, to teach or preach to men. Speaking of an Indian man who came to see her and who repented of his sins, Marie de l'Incarnation said:

When I had reprimanded him, I consoled him for the decision which he had made, which was genuine, for he spoke of his sins aloud in front of another savage and accepted my reproaches with such humility that nobody present could fail to be moved. I must confess, dear sister, that such inclinations are pleasing.[51]

Similarly, in the hagiographic essay she wrote about Mother Marie de Saint Joseph, she told how this Mother preached in her parlor, surrounded by a troop of Indians:

Our Lord had endowed her with a special grace for winning the hearts not only of girls, but of the men and women of both of these two nations. . . . I acted as her companion in this work and was delighted to hear her and see around her forty or fifty Hurons, as many men as women and girls, listening to her with unbelievable eagerness.[52]

In a letter of 1643 to a sister at the convent of the Visitation in Tours, Marie de l'Incarnation even spoke of a female apostle: "This year a very elderly woman called Angélique assumed the office of Apostle to the Attimak in order to strengthen their faith, to teach prayers to those who did not know them, and to prevent those who knew them from forgetting them."[53] The liberty Marie de l'Incarnation took in reporting this bending of the church's ban that had prevented women from teaching or preaching to men can be interpreted in two ways: either the new church needed new rules that afforded women a more active and substantial role, or Indian men were not really considered to be men, but rather children, so that even women could preach the Word to them.[54]

On occasion, when Marie de l'Incarnation did not agree with the Jesuits, she did not hesitate to correct their stories. In 1642, hardly two years after her arrival, she wrote a letter to the Mother Superior of Tours in which she boldly condemned the conduct of a Jesuit, taking sides with a young Indian woman who, in her view, had been unjustly punished by them.[55] What follows is my summary of the story that Marie de l'Incarnation related.[56]

A young Indian woman was sought out by an Indian man who was already married, and according to pre-Christianized Indian customs, she consented to marry him if her family agreed. Her family, who was converted, wanted to hear nothing of it and wanted to force her to break all ties with him and to become a Christian.[57] To this effect, Father de Quen put her in the charge of the Ursulines, warning them that she surely would give them trouble. Instead, according to Marie de l'Incarnation, the Indian woman, after two or three days of sadness, declared, of her own accord, that she wanted to become a Christian. Her family took her back in order to test her decision, but at this moment the Indian man tried to see her, tracked her down, and she ended up going into hiding. She recounted the event to her family, but they did not believe her, accusing her of having arranged to meet her suitor.

The converted Indians decided to punish her; some said that she deserved death, others opted for a public whipping in order to set an example for other women. They were referred to Father de Quen who, without knowing exactly what had happened nor just how far things would go, agreed to the public whipping. They took action and she was given three violent lashes of the whip, at which point Father de Quen intervened and put a stop to the incident.[58] The docile and resigned young Indian woman asked Father de Quen to baptise her. According to Marie de l'Incarnation, the priest, believing she was guilty without even questioning her, refused her and proceeded to recount the episode to the Ursulines.

Marie de l'Incarnation's account differs from that of the *Relation* on important points. The *Relation* presumes that the Indian woman is guilty, while Marie de l'Incarnation believes she is sincere and innocent. The *Relation* does not mention the dubious role of Father de Quen, although Marie de l'Incarnation accuses him of having acted without giving the matter due consideration and without having inquired into the facts. Her version of the story is not flattering for the Jesuit, and she ends her account by expressing clearly her resentment toward him:

I must confess to you, my dearest Mother, that I am angry with him for having let this poor innocent woman be whipped without stopping the excessive fervor of the savages. But finally as everything happened innocently on both sides, I should laugh at the simplicity of the savages and remain edified by the patience of the woman.[59]

The anecdote tells us a good deal about the methods used by the Jesuits in order to change a "savage" femininity into a "civilized" one, and about the condescension of the French toward the Indians. Father de Quen was more inclined to make a public example of an innocent woman in order to breed fear among Indian women than to inquire into the truth. It cannot be said that, as a matter of policy, Marie de l'Incarnation disapproved of the Jesuits' methods; but she nevertheless dared to suggest that a Jesuit (her superior) was wrong, to show her anger against him, and to spread an alternative version of the story.

On another occasion she reported a story that is imbedded in her relation of the French campaign against the Iroquois; although the event was of considerable importance, it was not mentioned at all in *The Jesuit Relation*.[60] At one point during General de Tracy's campaign against the Iroquois, the French army was searching for certain Iroquoian villages:

> But fortunately there was a young Algonquian woman in our group of Algonquins who had been prisoner of the Iroquois in her youth and recaptured by her nation in another encounter. She told our Governor, Monsieur de Courcelles, that there were four of them [villages], which spurred him on, together with Monsieur le Chevalier de Chaumont. It was nearly dark when the third one was taken so that it seemed impossible to move onto the fourth, especially for those who did not know the paths. However, this woman took a pistol in one hand and led Monsieur de Courcelles by the other, and she said to him: "Come with me, I shall take you straight there." She did in fact lead them there without danger.[61]

It is surprising that those responsible for *The Jesuit Relation* overlooked this detail, which Marie de l'Incarnation very probably obtained from de Courcelles himself. But, publishing the story in the widely read *Relation* would have made public the fact that the French owed their victory to a "savage" and, what is more, to a woman. This might have marred the national image. Marie de l'Incarnation's account, however, championed the Algonquian woman and ascribed to her the primary role in the success of the French campaign against the Iroquois, and she did not hesitate to let it be known, or to record it for posterity.

The difference between the official and the semiprivate texts of Marie de l'Incarnation, concerning the presence or absence of women, their valorization, or their abasement reveals the mechanisms that dictate the relevance or the insignificance of facts or of recorded events in the writing of history.

The Memory of History

Her intellectual and spiritual strength placed Marie de l'Incarnation far ahead of most pious women of French society who, encouraged by the church, opted for adventure and larger horizons in the

New World. Yet, after her death, she received merely seven pages of hagiography in *The Jesuit Relation*, as compared to thirty-four pages for Madame de la Peltrie who died in the same year and forty-nine pages for the other Ursuline, Mother Marie de Saint Joseph, who died in 1653. How should one interpret this distribution of pages and this discrimination in the passing of historical memory to posterity? Who are the women worthy to be remembered in history that is written by men?

I would suggest that Madame de la Peltrie was given more pages than Marie de l'Incarnation because she dedicated her fortune to the founding of the Ursulines of Quebec; thus she indirectly supported the enterprise of the Jesuits who had requested their presence in New France. She was also of noble descent, as was true of many Jesuits, which certainly aided her reputation. Further, she could serve as a model for other wealthy, noble women. Marie de Saint Joseph, also of noble origin, was an exemplary nun. Unlike Marie de l'Incarnation, she had dedicated her life to the mission in total obscurity. At her death she was the object of a cult that the Jesuits tried to exploit.

I believe that Marie de l'Incarnation was afforded seven short pages for reasons other than her social origin. It was rather owing to her reputation as a mystic, as a chronicler, and as a woman of strong will and presence, with whom even the Bishop had to reckon. It was also, quite probably, owing to her reputation as a teacher of considerable spiritual influence that *The Jesuit Relations* silenced her memory. Her personality and her accomplishments could certainly overshadow the feats of missionary martyrs, or at the very least compete with them in the minds of the French public. The fact that the Jesuits did not publish her writings after her death, although this task was incumbent upon them as spiritual directors of the Ursulines and as their partners in the missionary enterprise, further contributes to my suspicion that they were unwilling to share the limelight with her. It is certain, in any case, that in their eyes her strong personality could not serve as a model for other women.

Chapter Five

The Confrontation between "Civilized" and "Savage" Femininity in the New World

The encounter between Europeans and American Indians produced a geographic and anthropological decentering in the European consciousness at the dawn of the modern world. This encounter deeply stirred the European imagination, producing a voluminous literature which, for the most part, was written by men (travelers, explorers, missionaries). In this context, the historical writings of Marie de l'Incarnation are unprecedented and invaluable because they constitute a testimony to the meeting of a Western woman with the inhabitants of the New World, and most particularly with women. Her testimony is the only one in New France to stage the encounter of two versions of femininity and to give an idea of what this encounter meant for both parties. Her representation of Indian women sharply contrasts, at times, with that by men, especially as recorded in *The Jesuit Relations*.[1]

Undoubtedly Marie de l'Incarnation shared with the Jesuits several anthropological assumptions.[2] Stephen Greenblatt identi-

101

fies several visions of the American Indians in ethnographic accounts of encounter and historical scholarship on the subject.[3] One is the "vision of the victor," according to which Europeans had a mission to civilize and Christianize the indigenous populations encountered in the lands they colonized. It is certain that, in many ways, both the Jesuits' and Marie de l'Incarnation's position fit into this well-documented category.[4] For Ursuline and Jesuit missionaries alike, the misery of the "savage" and her/his "depraved" moral state stemmed from original sin, from which she/he had not had the grace to be freed through baptism and Christian teaching. According to this vision, the Indians were waiting for one thing alone: to be Christianized.

The "vision of the victors" reverberated in the missionary vision of the Catholic Reformation as well as in the desire for political expansion on the part of the king of France. Indeed, Marie de l'Incarnation's departure for New France in 1639 in order to found a convent for women, to educate French girls, and to Christianize and civilize American Indian women, was part of the Catholic Reformation movement, which sought to establish in the New World the religious purity that allegedly characterized the Primitive Church.[5] This three-pronged agenda found agreement in Richelieu's expansionist decree of 1626, which demanded the creation of a colonizing society whose three aims were to exploit the country, to populate the area with French people, Gallicize, civilize, and convert the Indians in order to produce a mixed population.

In contrast to the "vision of the victor," Marie de l'Incarnation equally shared with the Jesuits another position also identified by Greenblatt, which has become the focus of recent scholarship of encounter literature from Europe and the Americas.[6] This position neither eulogizes nor views with total cynicism Europeans' encounter with the native populations. In reading encounter literature, this recent scholarship attempts, on the one hand, to reconstruct the meaning of the indigeous populations' response to Europeans and, on the other, to capture the ways in which Europeans' ideological code was unsettled by the encounter. This reading of encounter literature reveals at times "someone who has engaged in a complex and often desperate negotiation with values he could have neither securely manipulated nor comfortably embraced."[7] Although this epistemological and ideological destabilization did not achieve better communication and understanding, it nevertheless attests to an attempt to register the presence of otherness. It shows that the "vision of the victor" was not monolithic and that the encounter with new lands and different people provoked fissures and displacements in their values.

I will focus, in this chapter, on the epistemological and ideological destabilization at work in Marie de l'Incarnation's texts regarding Indian women, processes that have not been noted heretofore in her writings and that are not present in the Jesuits' texts.

Another Other

From the late sixteenth century to the beginning of the nineteenth, the American "savage" became one of the privileged representations of the "other." The European imagination produced an array of representations of the American Indian, entwining reality and fiction and ranging from the benign to the outrageous. Europeans who had dealings with the American Indians disseminated highly contradictory myths: the myth of the noble savage, the depraved barbarian, the cruel brute, the hirsute man-beast roaming the forests, and the diabolical monster.[8] It has been said, with some justification, that America was not discovered, but invented by sixteenth-century Europeans.[9]

Indian women did not escape this conflicting representation. Their representation was, however, complicated by two additional factors. First, as women, they already occupied the position of the "other" in Western epistemology. Second, their position in their own society, which differed considerably from the position held by women in European society, threw Western men's preconceptions of gender-based distinctions into utter confusion. Writers of the period, at times, represented the Indian woman as an all-powerful, terrifying matriarch, every bit as cruel, bellicose, and licentious as a native man. At other times, they represented her as a docile, poor creature, deprived of all rights, overburdened with work, and scorned by Indian men who stood around smoking as they watched women work, indifferent to their hard labor. This dualistic representation of Indian women was in keeping with a Western, dualistic representation of the other in general, be it men of another civilization or women of their own culture. As their constant and closest other, European women were represented as either idealized, chaste creatures who interceded between God and men (e.g., the female mystics) or as temptresses, whores, incarnations of wickedness of the flesh, who needed constant surveillance and containment in order not to contaminate men. These contradictory representations of Indian women are ubiquitous in *The Jesuit Relations*. The Jesuits scandalized their contemporaries with their tolerance for cultural difference.[10] Their capacity, however, to accept difference did not extend to women, whether from their own culture or from different ones.

The following quotation from *The Jesuit Relations* encapsulates the traditional polarity in the notion of femininity, as it is characterized in the Christian West: "You would have seen these frenzied, shouting, bawling women burning [the] pudenda of their [victims], stabbing them with stakes, biting them heartily like furies, cleaving their flesh with knives; in short carrying out every act that frenzy could suggest to a woman."[11] The Jesuits seized upon a dualistic conclusion that claimed that Indian women did not behave as women should (according to their idealization of them) and that their behavior was very feminine (according to the abasement they ascribed to them).

Furthermore, the Jesuits could not understand the status of Indian women in their society and were surprised that they seemed to be both "mistresses and servants," "mistress" being understood here as the feminine of master. They saw them as mistresses because they carried undeniable authority in their society, because the birth of a daughter was preferable to the birth of a son, because the price demanded from the enemy for a female murder victim was higher than that for a man, and because women had jurisdiction over the children.[12] By contrast, the Jesuits also saw them as merely servants because women were perceived as doing all the work. According to historians, men's contribution to the work of the community was less visible to the Europeans because it involved clearing the field, bartering and negotiating with other tribes, hunting and fishing: all activities that were not visible when Europeans visited Indian villages or met them for negotiation.

These differences, and what was perceived as an unnatural division of labor and authority between the sexes, troubled European patriarchs who viewed the decrees they imposed on women as natural or God given. Formed by Antiquity, medieval Christianity,

and the Renaissance, which often relied on misogynist views of
women, Europeans could either not discern or, if they did, not accept the fundamental differences between their own conceptions of
the relationship between the sexes and those of American Indian
society; accordingly, if they understood the Indian women's strong
position, they thought of it as "unnatural" and they sought to
change it. One thing is sure, that many male writers dwelled on
the privileged status of Indian women as compared to that of European women. One century after the arrival of the Europeans, the
Jesuit Joseph-François Lafiteau, who, according to de Certeau,[13]
founded anthropology as an autonomous science with his *Moeurs
des sauvages amériquains comparées aux moeurs des premiers
temps (1724)*, wrote:

> Nothing, however, is truer than this superiority of the women.
> They constitute the nation; and it is through them that no-
> bility of blood, race and family are perpetuated. It is they who
> hold the true power. Everything belongs to them, the land, the
> fields, the harvests. . . . The children are their property, and
> the line of succession is transmitted by their blood.[14]

Since the Jesuits of the seventeenth century did not think well of
women's power among the Indians, they sought to establish patriarchal rule according to their own view of the natural order of
things.[15] In *The Jesuit Relation* of 1632, the author wrote that
when he asked an Indian to give him his two sons to raise in the
French fashion, the Indian replied that he could not do so because
his wife would not permit it. Hearing his response, the Jesuit com-
mented: "Women hold great power here: if a man promises you
something and does not keep his promise, he feels that he is excused if he tells you that his wife does not want it. I therefore tell
him that he is the master and that in France women do not give
orders to their husbands."[16]

Another Femininity

Although Marie de l'Incarnation no doubt participated in the European fantasmatic representations of the other/Indian and the
other/woman, and even though her writings at times echo those of

the Jesuits, she nevertheless entertained with the other/Indian woman a more complex relationship, which went beyond the dualism found in most male accounts. Often, but not always, she drew her sources from *The Jesuit Relations*, and she revised their representation of Indian women. Even though the freedom, independence, and power of Indian women represented for Marie de l'Incarnation an obstacle to their becoming "civilized" or even Christianized, they were for her, nevertheless, an object of fascination she wished to share with her female readers in France. In her writings, Indian women stand out as epic heroines whose courage is untinged by self-sacrifice. Indian women, she believed, affirm their strength, their freedom, and their courage without excuse or equivocation, and their daring is in sharp contrast to the self-effacement, humility, and constraint required of European women, although she does not herself overtly make this comparison. Her account of Indian women produced an important option for femininity that has no place in *The Jesuit Relations*.

When peace negotiations and the exchange of hostages with the Iroquois allowed closer contact with the French, certain novel aspects of Iroquoian social interactions became evident for the first time. Europeans became aware of the existence of a model for the relationship between the sexes quite alien to European society.[17] Because Iroquoian society was sedentary and more tightly knit than other Indian societies known to the French, the favorable position women held in their community was dramatically revealed. Iroquoian women enjoyed moral, social, economic, and political prestige, which was transmitted through the matriarchal line; moreover, their religion spoke of a goddess who created the world and humanity.[18] Marie de l'Incarnation noted the eminent role of these women in a letter to her son in 1654:

> In the peace treaty we suggested to the Iroquois that they should bring us some of their girls, and Reverend Father le Moine was to bring us five daughters of their female chieftains when he returned from their country, but the time was not right. These female chieftains are women of standing amongst the savages, and they have a deciding vote in the councils. They make decisions there like the men, and it is even they who delegated the first ambassadors to discuss peace.[19]

In a letter of 1661, she slipped another reference to Iroquoian women into a piece of Christian propaganda: "They say that when the priests left the land, the women, who have the deciding vote in the councils, or at least those among them who are chosen to do so, cried for seven whole days over their loss and the children did the same."[20] In another letter dating from the beginning of her stay in Canada, around 1640, she had already referred to the rights Indian women had over their children: "[I]t is the custom in this country when married couples separate for the wife to take the children."[21] In contrast, the authors of *The Jesuit Relations* interpreted the matriarchal line in Indian society according to a patriarchal logic that they defended most vehemently:

> Since these people are familiar with this form of corruption [a degree of sexual licence], they would rather take their sisters' or brothers' children as their heirs than their own, casting doubt on the fidelity of their wives. Since they do not doubt that their nephews are of their own blood, among the Hurons, for example, a chief will choose a nephew as his successor, rather than his own son.[22]

Another striking example of how Marie de l'Incarnation interpreted the relationship between the sexes in Indian societies differently from European men is when she described rape. When her son and her superiors persisted in trying to make her return to France because they feared the aggression of the Iroquois, she pointed out that she and her sisters were less at risk from the Iroquois than women in France were from French soldiers who were combing the country owing to civil unrest. In fact, it is true that rape was an unknown phenomenon in American Indian societies of the Northeast until the arrival of the Europeans. On this subject she wrote most eloquently:

> Some people consider this country to be utterly forsaken, yet I see no cause for apprehension such as that experienced, according to my news from France, by those of our sex and position at the hands of French soldiers. What I hear makes me shudder. The Iroquois may well be barbarians, but they do not commit acts of indecency against our sex like those which I hear are perpetrated by the French. Those who have lived

among them have assured me that they do not use violence [against women] and that they free those [women] who do not want to comply [with sexual demands].[23]

By contrast, the Jesuits and other men attributed the fact that Indian men did not force women into sex to the cold nature of these native men, whom they likened to women, or to their immaturity, which they saw as childlike because Indians had no beard. Jaenen provides an example of this, which he takes from a book written in the eighteenth century and which echoes texts written in the sixteenth or seventeenth centuries: "The savage is weak and his reproduction organs are small; he has no body hair and no beard, nor any desires for females."[24]

Tales of Four Women

In the *Correspondance* there are four narratives of escape achieved by Indian women demonstrating great courage and boldness. Three of these are drawn from *The Jesuit Relations*. When the two versions of these accounts are examined in tandem, however, they reveal important differences. The last one does not figure in the *Relations*.

Marie de l'Incarnation's rendering of the three episodes that she draws from *The Jesuit Relations* differs not in content but in tone. Her first account of Indian women's courage is taken from *The Jesuit Relation* of 1647.[25] The *Relation* devotes chapter 2 to the escape of four Algonquian women held prisoner by the Iroquois who reached a safe haven thanks to their strength and will to survive. Of these four stories, Marie de l'Incarnation chose to tell the story of a woman who was the most clearly heroic among them, owing to her ingenuity as a survivor. This woman not only saved her own life as did the other women, but in the process she turned nature to her advantage. She reached the French quarters after two months of hard traveling, not broken in health like the three other women whose story Marie de l'Incarnation did not retell, but rather with a surfeit of provisions.

The circumstances of the story are related by Marie de l'Incarnation and the Jesuits as follows. The Indian woman escaped and found herself 100 leagues from her own home as well as from the

French. If she were found by the Iroquois, as a fugitive she would have been first tortured, then slowly burned and consumed alive. If she had hid in the woods, she would have had to endure famine, the intense cold, and wild animals. She decided instead to commit suicide by hanging herself by her belt, and after three unsuccessful attempts, she decided that God surely did not want her to die. *The Jesuit Relation* says of her attempted suicide: "It is an error for which a poor savage woman can be forgiven,"[26] attributing her "error" to her savage status and to her sex. Marie de l'Incarnation says that it was "the error of a savage," omitting all reference to sex. In *The Jesuit Relation*, the epithets "poor women," "poor savage women," "poor creatures," and "poor unfortunates" recur frequently. By contrast, Marie de l'Incarnation does not use such epithets, expressing pity in her accounts of the escapes of Indian women. Furthermore, it is interesting to note that by privileging the qualities of a healthy body, abundance of food, self-reliance, success, and triumph of earthly life, Marie de l'Incarnation privileged precisely those qualitites that are contrary to those valued by female mystics.

Here is how Marie de l'Incarnation renders the story.

God, who never forsakes those who trust in Him in times of need, allowed her to find an axe in a place in which the Iroquois had made camp. This tool saved her life. First she had the idea of making a tinder-box with which she could light a fire at night and extinguish it at dawn for fear of being betrayed by the smoke. She then found little tortoises of which she collected a supply. She lived off this small store of food for several days; for in the evening after she had said her prayers, she spent the night eating, warming herself and sleeping, and she spent all day walking and praying to God. She came across some Iroquois who were setting out to hunt, but they did not see her. They had left a canoe on the riverbank, intending to collect it when they returned: she hurled herself into it and set off, and from that moment on she could enjoy herself since the worry of being found by her enemies and the uncertainty about where she was had disappeared. She eventually reached the great St. Lawrence River, going from island to island where she found large quantities of birds' eggs, which she ate as often as she needed. She made a long wooden spear and burned the end to harden it, and she used this tool to catch sturgeon five or six feet long. She killed a number of deer and beavers. She chased them into the water and then set off in pursuit in her canoe. When she reached them, she killed them with her axe, and when they were in their death throes, she pulled them on board and took as much meat as she needed, so that when she arrived in Montreal, she still had a fairly good store of provisions.[27]

In contrast to Marie de l'Incarnation's account, *The Jesuit Relation* offers as a motive for the Indian women's escape the power of attraction the motherland exerted over the barbarians, even though this country was far less beautiful than that in which they were detained. The author supports his argument by referring to the authority of the ancients:

What could be more splendid in former times than the city of Rome? Or more harsh than the cold and ice of Scythia? And yet the barbarians fled from this great city to return to the rigors of the snow. The land of our birth has a certain indescribable charm which makes it impossible for men to forget it. The Algonquin's country has been a place of death and sickness for several years, and yet the women released by the Iroquois in their country, in order to marry their sons, nevertheless had such a great longing and fondness for their homeland that several braved awful dangers and horrifying pains and toil in order to see it again. Here are several examples.[28]

The Jesuit Relation suggests that the Algonquian women should have been happier among the Iroquois than in their own country and that it was the appeal of the motherland that gave them the courage to face human and natural dangers. By collapsing different time periods, cultures, and the sexes of the escapees, the Jesuits' references to antiquity trivialize the exploits of the Indian women and thus detract from the reasons these women risked escape through extraordinary acts of self-determination. Marie de l'Incarnation, on the other hand, does not ascribe any motive to the Indian women. Their desire to escape, when they are detained by force by the Iroquois, seems to her to speak for itself and thus does not require any justification for her seventeenth-century female readers. Although the author of *The Jesuit Relation* states that the Iroquois preferred marrying prisoners to women of their own nation because prisoners were more docile, he remains silent or blind to the issue of the prisoners' desire to escape. He also does not comment on the fact that when men in their family were killed in war, Iroquoian women also had the right to choose their replacements from among the prisoners.

In the second tale of female courage, an Indian woman who was dragged for ten days by the Iroquois and was tied up at night to four stakes in the shape of a cross managed to untie herself, found an axe, and, overcome by rage, drove it into the skull of the nearest Iroquois, whereupon she fled.[29] Marie de l'Incarnation describes her escape through the woods. It lasted thirty-five days, during which time the woman displayed as much ingenuity and courage as the woman in the previous account. Marie de l'Incarnation also drew this story from *The Jesuit Relation* of 1647.[30] She, however, omits saying that the woman arrived emaciated and in ill health, and she does not call her "poor creature." Nor does she employ the *Relation*'s commentary, which devalues the woman's sufferings while regretting that they were endured for the love of life rather than of Jesus: "O God, what suffering! Is man such a lover of life?"[31] Furthermore, while the *Relation* calls this woman an "Amazon," a qualifier which, according to the *Dictionnaire du dix-septième siècle* from Trévoux, was applied to courageous and bellicose women or girls, Marie de l'Incarnation simply says she is a woman, thereby deflecting a widespread view that argues that the exceptional case of a great or courageous woman indicates not her feminine courage but her virility. Louis Montrose writes that "the matriarchal, gynocratic Amazons are the radical Other figured but not fully contained by the collective imagination of European patriarchy," and sixteenth- and seventeenth-century travel narratives often recreate the ancient Amazons of Scythia in Africa or America.[32] In this particular case it seems that, on the contrary, the use of the word *Amazon* mythifies Indian women and contains them within patriarchal imagination, while Marie de l'Incarnation's account, remaining grounded in the historical present, does not distract attention from the Indian women's actions and offers the possibility of apprehending these women as agents.

The third story of female heroism, which Marie de l'Incarnation draws from *The Jesuit Relation* of 1655, differs only in one important detail:

> When an Algonquian woman had been abducted by the Iroquois along with her entire family, her husband, who was firmly bound told her that if she wanted to she could save them all. She understood clearly what this meant and therefore she bided her time in order to seize an axe, and with unparalleled courage, she cleaved the Chief's head in two, cut another's throat and behaved with such frenzy that all the rest fled. She untied her husband and children, and they withdrew unharmed to a place of safety.[33]

The *Relation* simply says that she untied her husband, whereas Marie de l'Incarnation clearly states that she untied her husband and children and thereby saved them all. By its lack of precision, the *Relation* highlights the violence of the Indian woman's act, rather than the fact that it aided others.

The fourth story is brief:

> One of the two [Algonquian women prisoners of the Iroquois] was so brave that she slit the belly of her Iroquois with his knife. His companions were so afraid that they fled, leaving behind their arms, baggage, women and the children which they were holding. Thus the women captives were released and took their booty, which they placed at the Governor's feet.[34]

The twentieth-century editor of the *Correspondance* states that this was the incident recorded in the *Journal of the Jesuits* of 18 July 1658. In fact, however, the *Journal of the Jesuits*, edited by Thwaites, only mentions the following sketchy details: "A Montagnais woman was killed by the Iroquois in Monsieur de Repentigni's field. Two other Algonquin women were injured and two little girls escaped."[35] This proves that Marie de l'Incarnation did not use these accounts simply because they figured in *The Jesuit Relations*. She chose them and retold them according to what was significant about them for her, and she drew them from other sources as well.

As we know, Marie de l'Incarnation's letters concerning the Indians, the mission, and the colony of New France were written to be read by a network of religious and lay individuals, possible benefactors of the mission. This applies even to the letters addressed to her son on the subject, for she often asked him to try to interest his friends in the fate of the Ursuline mission. The bulk of the benefactors of the Ursuline convent were in fact women. She therefore consciously chose to propagate these accounts of Indian women who roamed the woods, defended themselves as fiercely as men, and braved untamed nature and its dangers. Neither demonized nor made into victims, Indian women in Marie de l'Incarnation's text lose the transparency of allegory they have in the Jesuits' texts. In turn, Marie de l'Incarnation loses her own transparency as an exceptional yet compliant European woman, who subscribes to the gender ideology of her society and who is ready to impose on Indian women an idealized femininity, incompatible with that which she obviously admired in them. Her accounts of their heroism paint a positive portrait of Indian femininity which, however unassimilable and unacceptable it might have been to European sexual anthropology, is nevertheless as present in her texts as it is absent from those of the Jesuits.

While Marie de l'Incarnation undeniably favored, and even admired, the Indian women, her admiration was certainly discrete. Her observations on the rights of Indian women, which were denied to European women, were done without making any comparisons between them nor constructing a moral argument, as the Jesuits did. Nor did she attempt, in presenting her portraits of Indian women, to translate the practices of this alien femininity into the practices of femininity in her own culture, as she, along with the Jesuits, had done for other cultural elements. She merely presented her representation of a radically different femininity to her readers in France. More than a silence, this lack of attempt at assimilating the other in her texts constitutes a hiatus or a syncope in the rhythm of her narrative. Her restraint is all the more astounding, since on other occasions she does not hesitate to give her opinion on a variety of matters. We may wonder why she resisted at this point "the subtle, powerful, insidious human desire to craft a dramatically satisfying and coherent story out of fragmentary and ambiguous experience."[36] I argue that this rupture in the rhythm of her narrative attests to attempts to register the challenge of radical otherness. It points to the opening of a space that engaged her in utterly competing values with no possibility of reconciliation. The syncope in the thought process, in this case, would constitute a safeguard against the fear of chaos that could have been brought about had she been willing to draw the consequences of the femininity she was representing—a chaos that would negate her very existence. It may also, simultaneously, have another significance and another function for her.

Imagining Freedom

This unusual suspension of judgment on her part may attest also to the fact that the encounter with a radically different femininity provided her with an imaginary escape, or a safe haven, from the contradictions inherent in her own status, which she could not overtly expose but which tyrannized her existence. Furthermore, it was these very contradictions in her status that allowed her to see, conjure up, imagine a different femininity, even though it sharply contradicted not only her own position as a woman in Western patriarchy, and all the more so as a woman in a religious order, but also the very work she had come to accomplish in America; namely, to tame Indian women. In this case, the space the encounter created, inhabited by the radically different femininity, could function as the mystical space which, according to de Certeau, escapes language, allowing for deep resistance to alienation and the emergence of the unknown. Just like the silence of the mystical meditation is supposed to allow the encounter with the Other (God), the syncope in her text would attest to the transformative violence of the encounter with the other (human).[37]

Of course, her favorable representation of Indian women was not just a figment of her imagination but reflected a social reality that she looked upon with awe and admiration. The New World, indeed, gave her the opportunity to witness societies in which women had rights and privileges unheard of in the Old World, in which the relationship between the sexes was set according to rules that established a far greater balance of power than in her own, and finally, in which the division of labor did not conform to what was thought of as the natural order in her society. Recent research into American Indians in the seventeenth century indeed reveals a society in which the strict division of labor between men and women entailed neither scorn nor the devaluation of women; nor did it mean male supremacy.[38] This objective reality alone does not suffice to explain why she was able to see such a difference without attempting to reduce it to familiar patterns by passing a moral judgement on it. In order to understand this, we must appreciate the contradictory intersection of gender, power, and mysticism that interacted to generate Marie de l'Incarnation's authorship of a different vision of femininity, even though that model was never an option for herself.

The European gender system positioned Marie de l'Incarnation quite differently from the Jesuits, with regard to the "civilization" of Indian women. A first contradiction is present in the concept, the metaphor, and the actual object of *clausura*, when applied to a mission in foreign lands.[39] In Quebec, *clausura* constituted for Marie de l'Incarnation an obstacle to the mission with which she had been entrusted. In the very beginning of her stay in Canada she related to her son the Indians' amazement and puzzlement when they saw the concealment of the Ursulines from the public eye: "Several of them arrived from a far away nation and on seeing us they were distressed by our way of life. They asked me why we covered our heads and why we could only be seen through holes, as they called our grill."[40] In fact, she repeated to him on more than one occasion, but always in veiled terms, that *clausura* represented and symbolized a lack of freedom and thus was the major obstacle to the assimilation of Indian women. This forced enclosure meant that Indian girls and women could be reached by the Ursulines only within the restrictive confines of the convent. She lamented that this was hardly feasible, and reported that many of the Indian girls entrusted to the Ursulines behaved like Marie Négabamat, who was the first to flee into the woods after tearing from her body the French-style dress she had been given by the nuns. If, on the other hand, they were too docile to succumb to the call of the woods, they were afflicted instead by melancholy:

Others . . . only stay until they become sad, which is unbearable for the savage temperament: as soon as they become sad their parents take them away lest they should die. . . . Others leave on a whim or when the fancy takes them; they climb our fence which is as high as a wall like squirrels and go off to roam in the woods.[41]

The little Indian girls could not get used to being constrained:

I do not know how all this will end, for, to be totally frank, it seems impossible to me. In all the years in which we have been in this country, we have only civilized seven or eight, who were Gallicized; All the others have returned to their families, albeit as good Christians. The savage life holds such charm for them on account of its freedom, that it is miraculous if one can interest them in French ways which they see as beneath their dignity.[42]

On another occasion she reiterates her misgivings: "We have had experience of savage girls; they cannot survive claustration, they are naturally melancholic, and their habit of roaming freely wherever they wish persists and increases their melancholy."[43]

Despite the docility which, in her letters, she sometimes attributes to Indian girls, she acknowledges also that they resort to lies, flight, nostalgia, or even death, in order to escape from the confinement and discipline that had been imposed on them. Their escape from what they saw as the stifling enclosure of the Ursuline convent, despite, Marie de l'Incarnation says, the concessions made to native practices like dancing and food preparation, was an escape from Christianity and from "civilization." In fact, the *clausura* of the Ursulines, with all that it symbolized for European femininity, became in the texts of Marie de l'Incarnation a metaphor for all that separated the "civilized" from the "savage" woman.

At first, the Christianization of the Indians had been for the missionaries, above all, interdependent with their project to Gallicize and civilize them. When this effort proved to be a failure, Marie de l'Incarnation believed that if the "savages" were not amenable to civilization they could nonetheless be Christianized; and, in this view, she sided with the Jesuits against the authorities in France who were uneasy about the separation of civilization from Christianization. *Clausura* still meant that the Ursulines were dependent on the Jesuits' mission to bring the Indian women to them, and thus to place them within the enclosure of the convent in order to convert them. So when the Indian neophytes disappeared because of epidemics and of the wars with the Iroquois, Marie de l'Incarnation's status as a missionary was threatened, for she could not, like the Jesuits, go far away into the forest to attempt to find new converts.[44] She confided to her son her longing for the outward missions and her imaginary participation in them:

> It is true that while *clausura* does not allow us to follow the bearers of the Gospel into the new Nations being discovered every day, since I am incorporated into the new Church to which Our Lord has done me the honor of calling me, He unites my mind so strongly with theirs that it feels as though I follow them everywhere and that I work with them in such rich and noble conquests.[45]

She indirectly admitted her desire to set out on a mission and the impediment *clausura* constituted to her missionary vocation:

> I am well aware that I shall never go out, but I have a consuming interest in the gaining of souls for God, while waiting for matters to reach the desired conclusion. I can say that I shall not go because the time is not right, and it is not in keeping with my position; but these missions will provide us with girls.[46]

Clausura profoundly contradicted the aims and the work of a missionary, as vividly illustrated by the Saint Sulpice missionaries (the founders of Montreal) who recognized the limitations and the difficulties of missions run by cloistered women. They, therefore, requested that Montreal be sent secular women who were free to go out among the Indians.[47]

For Marie de l'Incarnation to admit explicitly that *clausura* was an impediment to the civilization and Christianization of Indian women was to admit implicitly one of two things: either that she was obsolete as a missionary because she was required to remain in *clausura* while there were no more Indians near her convent (a conclusion that obviously she could not have agreed with, for she firmly reiterated that she would rather die than leave Canada and the mission) or that it was *clausura* itself that was obsolete. This was, however, much too dangerous for her to say openly. To have called into question the practice of *clausura*, which had been firmly established for religious women by the Council of Trent, would have been considered scandalous and would certainly have been perceived as an attack on the authority of the church. This scandal would have seriously endangered her mission and would have raised doubts about the necessity of the Ursuline presence in Canada.

Marie de l'Incarnation's already contradictory position vis-à-vis her mission to civilize and Christianize Indian women was complicated by yet another factor. Within the context of European femininity, she was an exception. She had chosen to resist, within the limits allowed, the prescribed definition of femininity placed upon her by European culture. Drawing on her visions, her prophecies, her powers of persuasion, and her tenacity, she convinced the ecclesiastical hierarchy to let her become the founder of the first women's convent in missionary territory. She faced a multitude of challenging physical conditions, yet she refused to return to France and to admit defeat in the face of the Iroquoian threat and the destruction of her convent by fire in 1650. She learned four Indian languages and wrote Huron, Algonquian, and Montagnais dictionaries and catechisms. She wrote hundreds of letters and autobiographical and spiritual writings, she taught, looked after, and supervised groups of one hundred people at a time. Yet as a woman in the religious life, she was cloistered and was obedient to the male hierarchy of the church, that is, to her confessor, her spiritual director, and her bishop, however shortsighted or irrational the church's views may have been. It is known that many mystics, Marie de l'Incarnation included, were not short of tactics to employ in order to obtain what they wanted. Whether conscious or not, their strategies and manipulative techniques enabled these women to circumvent the repressive prohibitions placed on them, without subverting or destroying the strict code of behavior. Consequently, these strategies and manipulations, despite their aims, often resulted paradoxically in the consolidation of the very repressive system these women were seeking to circumvent. So despite her stature as a strong woman, Marie de l'Incarnation arrived in "savage" territory with a feminine ideal strongly colored by her culture and by the demands of her religion. Aided by her mysticism, she had been able to forge a destiny for herself that had little in common with the norm prescribed for women in her century. She neverthe- less offered Indian women the traditional feminine ideal of Euro- pean society, an ideal imbued with self-sacrifice, which accepted a patriarchal order and for which *clausura* constituted the actual and metaphorical limits.

The model of femininity that the European woman, convinced of its benefits and assets, wanted to impose on the Indian woman, was incomprehensible to the latter. It is noteworthy that when the Indians were decimated through epidemics and wars with the Iro- quois, this in turn exhausted Indian women's resistance to Chris- tianization, and some of the converted women acted in a manner similar to European female mystics. Jaenen reports that Jesuits were disturbed that Micmac women had taken on a spiritual role in the "new religion," a role that was not denied to them in their traditional religion: "These [women] in usurping the quality and name of *religieuses*, say certain prayers in their own fashion and affect a manner of living more reserved than that of the common- ality of Natives, who allow themselves to be dazzled by the glam- our of a false and ridiculous devotion."[48] The Jesuits might not have liked it, but these women were honored by their peers, male and female alike: "One woman in particular was honoured among the Abenakis. She was 114 years old and said her prayers on unstrung beads of rosary which she gave out as relics, saying they had fallen from heaven into her hand."[49] So it seems that Indian women, like their European counterparts, had caught the patriarchal clergy at their own game. But just as for the Europeans, the game could turn against them:

Indeed, the excessive fervour of some converts, mockingly called "Marians" by the pagans, gave rise to misgivings and unease. At Tadoussac in 1645 the Jesuits had to intervene to terminate scenes of spontaneous public penance accompanied by bloody self-flagellation. In 1672 the converts at Lorette vil- lage were reported to have desired "to mingle their blood with their tears" during the Good Friday observances. Claude Chauchetière reported excess of zeal in the early 1680s as near-hysterical women threw themselves, or dipped their infants, into icy streams in mid-winter.[50]

This shows how encounter affected both sides: Indian women, under the pressure for assimilating, acted as mystics, while the mystic Marie de l'Incarnation was fascinated by Indian women's freedom and power, even though she was intent in assimilating them.

A third contradiction inherent in Marie de l'Incarnation's mission to civilize and Christianize Indian women lies in the fact that what for her constituted a gain of power (access to the New World and missionary work with Indian women) constituted a loss of power for the Indian woman (the acceptance of a patriarchal order). If the Jesuits had requested religious women to come to the New World and thus presented them with a means and an excuse for expansion, it was because the mission had cherished the hope that Indian women and girls would be a key to the conversion of the Indians. Wanting to reach the adult population through their children, they arranged for the raising of young Indian girls among the Ursulines. In this scheme, European women were given much importance. Hence, women's mission was not just an appendage to the men's mission but became, paradoxically, its most important building block. This, as we have seen, is reflected in the pride with which Marie de l'Incarnation describes woman's missionary work in her letters. So, ironically, this granting of importance to European women was motivated by a desire to better impose a patriarchal order on Indian women. On the other hand, by overturning one of the oldest and strictest rules of the church that prohibited women from preaching, and allowing the Indian women to preach in their tribes, the Jesuits hoped to break down Indian resistance to Christianization and to counter resistant Indian women's harangues against the Jesuits.[51] Accordingly, if Indian women were valued, it was for the purpose of contributing to their own demise.

The hopes of the missionaries were dashed, however. In fact, along with the Indian sorcerers, it was the Indian women who resisted most vigorously the attempt at cultural assimilation carried out by the missionaries.[52] This resistance is easy to understand when one considers that Indian women enjoyed a social and political prestige inconceivable to Europeans in their own society.[53] According to Jaenen:

They believed that their persons and their social roles were objects of a two-fold attack on the part of the missionaries, first as women and second as natives. Among the nomadic bands the proscription of polygamy, if adhered to, would have greatly increased a woman's workload. Among the sedentary agricultural tribes the women, especially the "grandmothers" as the Jesuits called the matrons, refused to give up their children to be educated at Quebec. The men as hunters, traders, and warriors might be more amenable to conversion as a means of consolidating their relationship with the French, but the women saw few immediate advantages. What right had the missionary to undermine a woman's authority in the clan or to assign a man to women's agricultural work? More than one matron drove the converted son-in-law from the longhouse.[54]

Furthermore, the missionaries who were sensitive to the issue of morals wanted Indian women to give up their sexual independence and, worse still, wanted to impose family structures that established masculine authority, female fidelity, and forbade divorce.[55] Finally, although American Indian women were very attached to their children, the missionaries insisted on separating them, in order to force the children into seminaries where they would be indoctrinated.

When reflecting upon the reasons for the failure of the civilizing enterprise, Marie de l'Incarnation hesitates. She could not acknowledge, of course, nor even perhaps conceive of the idea that the Indians were not interested in Christianity or that they considered their social and religious structures to be superior to those of the French.[56] Nor could she see that if they consorted with the French and seemed sometimes even to have been converted, it was for reasons that escaped European rationale and because the fur trade they desired was inseparable from religion for the Jesuits, who could facilitate or block the trade. She could not admit or conceive that the Indians who consented to convert and to live on the reservations founded by the Jesuits did so for motives that differed from those of the French who encouraged them. Marie de l'Incarnation's questioning could only result in tautology. The Indian women could not be "civilized" because they were "savages."[57] This tautology, rather than duplicating the Manichean vision of the opposition between civilized and savage (viz., the "vision of the victors"), in fact, conceals an antithesis, which appears in her texts but which is never explicitly articulated nor resolved. The civilized woman is confined, like the Ursulines who were trying to civilize Indian women; the native woman roams freely in the woods and "paddles a canoe like the men."[58] To such a chiasm she could only respond with the silence of a syncope.

Part Two

𝔐adame 𝔊uyon
(1648–1717)

𝕵 eanne-Marie Bouvier de la Mothe was born in Montargis to a
well respected, although not wealthy aristocratic family, on
April 13, 1648.[1] Her father was Claude Bouvier, Seigneur de
la Mothe-Vergonville, and her mother was Jeanne Le Mais-
tre de la Maisonfort. Jeanne-Marie was the second child of this
marriage, preceded by her brother Jacques and followed by
Guillaume. As her parents were both widowed when they married,
Jeanne-Marie also had a number of half-brothers and half-sisters
from both sides of the family. Neglected by her mother, she said,
she was left to the care of women servants and raised in a number
of different convents in the region. Although standards of aristocratic education rose in the seventeenth century, her education
does not seem to have been carefully planned, as was the case for
other women of the period.[2] Most of her learning was of an auto-
didactic nature. While at home, she benefited indirectly from the
lessons of a preceptor who had been hired for her brother; it is in

this way that she learned to debate moral issues.[3] Similarly, at a young age, on the occasion of an illness in which she had been left alone for fear of contagion, she read the entire Bible. This acquaintance with both the Old and the New Testaments, rare at the time for a Catholic woman whether lay or religious, had an impact on her writings.

She was married without her prior consent at the age of sixteen, on February 18, 1664, to a rich man of the region, Jacques Guyon (1630–1676), Seigneur du Chesnoy, son of one of the constructors of the Briare canal. He was eighteen years her senior and emotionally dependent on his domineering mother. Their marriage lasted only twelve years and was characterized by exceedingly neurotic, familial relationships and by profound despair, aggravated by five births and several deaths of people close to her. Her despair was relieved only for a few years by the humane spiritual direction of Mother Granger, Prioress of the monastery of Montargis from 1649 to 1674. In 1674, she learned Latin from a preceptor who had been sent to her for her son. In 1676, she became a widow at the age of twenty-eight and remained in Montargis for an additional five years. She was very well off, receiving an annual income of 70,000 *livres*.

Up to the point of becoming a widow her life followed a common pattern for girls of the noble and upper bourgeois class. Like many other girls of her social group, she did not have the opportunity to decide her own fate. The rest of her life, however, was not so typical. As a young and rich widow with religious inclination, she had three options. The first of these was to remarry—an option her wealth and beauty would have facilitated. Second, she could go to Paris, where she would have access to an influential devout coterie and where she would lead a worldly yet private and pious life. Third, she could found a convent or lead one of the religious congregations that were flourishing at the time. She did not choose any of these available options. Instead, possessed by an apostolic mission she could not as yet define, she searched for her own path, which did not seem to adhere to any of the existing lay roles permitted to women nor to any of the roles that the church reserved for rich widows in the late seventeenth century.

This search sent her on a meandering trajectory for the next five years, from 1681 to 1686. First, she went to Gex in Savoy with the intention of working in the *Nouvelles Catholiques*, an institution first established in Paris in 1634 and dedicated to the forced conversion of protestant girls and women. Repulsed by the means with which this institution attempted to convert protestants, she retracted her support. The Bishop of Geneva, Jean d'Arenthon d'Alex, fearing that the institution might be deprived of her fortune and good will, offered her the prospect of becoming the prioress of the *Nouvelles Catholiques* and thus pressured Father La Combe, her confessor, to force her to accept his proposal and to give up her fortune to the institutution. La Combe's refusal to put pressure on her, combined with Guyon's resistance to the scheme, was the beginning of a campaign of calumnies directed against both of them. Meanwhile, her family, afraid that she might give her fortune to the church, devised a means of securing her inheritance by forcing her to give up the guardianship of her children. In March of 1682, she agreed to sign a convention that deprived her of this guardianship but left her, nevertheless, with a handsome annual pension of 15,000 *livres*.

In the summer of 1682, while she was in Thonon to attend a retreat with La Combe, the Bishop of Geneva expulsed La Combe from Thonon for failing to comply with his urgings to put pressure on Guyon and "invited" Guyon to leave the territory that was under his jurisdiction. It was while she was in Thonon that Madame Guyon wrote her first work, *Les Torrents spirituels*.

In October 1683, she was invited by the Marquise de Prunay to come and stay with her in Turin. And in April 1684, La Combe persuaded her to comply with her family's wishes to return to Paris so that they could keep an eye on her and thus accompanied her to Grenoble. During the time she spent in Grenoble in 1684–85, she wrote her *Explication et réflexions sur la Bible*.

Upon arriving in Grenoble, she was greeted by the calumnies the Bishop of Geneva had already spread against her. On March 7, 1685, her *Moyen Court* was nevertheless published in Grenoble, owing to the initiative of Giraud, an admirer, and a counselor in the local parliament. During her stay in Grenoble, she also wrote *Examen de l'Ecriture Sainte*, a meditative interpretation of the Bible. At the same time, false rumors of witchcraft and counterfeit were circulating about her. Thus, on the advice of the Bishop of Grenoble, Etienne Le Camus, who also wanted to get rid of her, she left for Marseille in March 1685, where she was welcomed by Bishop Etienne de Pujet who introduced her to the great mystic,

Malaval. Pressured once again by the controversy thickening around her, she left for Turin and joined La Combe in Verceil. In June 1685 she wrote to Bishop d'Arenthon d'Alex, asking him for his permission to live in the St-Gervais district of Geneva, which he refused to grant her. Between February and March of 1686, she returned to Paris by way of Chambéry, Grenoble, Lyon, and Dijon, accompanied by La Combe who had been transferred to Paris. She arrived in Paris on July 21, 1686, and lived in the cloister of Notre Dame.

Persecutions reached her there as well. The origin of these new troubles is obscure, but it involves a family jealousy on the part of her half-brother, the Barnabite Dominique La Mothe, who coveted a sum of money that Guyon had promised to give as a dowry to a woman in Gex who was about to become a nun. Apparently he also wanted her to give him a pension from the money she had secured for herself. In her autobiography, Guyon also mentions a jealousy between the Parisian Barnabites and the Barnabites from Savoy, the former finding it humiliating to have a Savoyard for a superior.[4] Unfortunately, Dominique La Mothe, a Parisian Barnabite, was also the superior of Father La Combe, confessor of Madame Guyon, and a Savoyard Barnabite. This tells much about the covetousness by which rich widows were beset, both by relatives who were anxious to see family money stay within the family and by the clergy who wanted their money for the church when not for their own use. In this case, the half-brother was also a member of the clergy. As Father la Mothe could not obtain what he wanted from either Guyon or La Combe, the latter was accused of quietist doctrine and was imprisoned on October 3, 1687.

Very soon, however, the accusations crystallized against Madame Guyon. In November 1687, a pastoral letter condemning Guyon's *Moyen Court* was published. It was written by Bishop d'Arenthon d'Alex of Geneva, who was in league with Father La Mothe. Accused by the zealous Archbishop of Paris, François Harlay de Champvallon, of preaching heretical notions on prayer, Guyon was sequestered in the convent of the *Visitation Sainte Marie* of Rue Saint Antoine in Paris on January 29, 1688. Her adversaries focused on her *Moyen Court*, judging it heretical, even though it had been published with due approbations, and they intended to prove that her heresy was attributable to La Combe's influence. She strongly assumed sole responsibility for the doctrine contained in the book and proved to her accusers that La Combe could not have influenced it. Thus began a series of interrogations, which, in the end, could not prove heretical thinking on her part. Meanwhile, her *Commentaire du Cantique des Cantiques* was published in Lyon in 1687. Archbishop de Champvallon of Paris, who had obtained a *lettre de cachet* from the king ordering Guyon to be locked up in the convent of the *Visitation Sainte Marie*, proposed the following transaction to her: she would be released if she agreed to marry her daughter to his own nephew. Her fortune was once again at stake with the church or with members of the church, who used official power for their own advancement or to further their private interests, as is clear in this case. She categorically refused. Not being able to convict her either on charges of heretical doctrine or on her moral conduct, the Archbishop of Paris circulated still more calumnies about her, this time insinuating that she had held secret meetings and was therefore a political schemer.

It seems that a certain Jansenist faction was also allied with her half-brother La Mothe.[5] Rather than be sequestered for only ten days in the *Visitation* as she had expected, she remained seven long months, although nothing was ever proven against her. It was then that she adopted the attitude she maintained in all her future trials: she was willing to correct certain expressions in her writing that might be erroneously interpreted, but she refused to admit, as her diverse adversaries wanted, that she had consciously maintained or propagated doctrinal errors or heretical beliefs.

Madame de Maintenon (the wife of King Louis XIV), solicited by influential women (Mme de Miramion, a friend of Guyon, and Madame de La Maisonfort, her cousin), obtained a letter from the king to liberate her. Thus, despite the ruling of the Archishop de Champvallon of Paris, Madame Guyon was set free on September 13, 1688. The papers that relate to her interrogation at the *Visitation* have not survived and were no doubt destroyed on the order of Harlay de Champvallon himself.

Guyon lived for ten months with Madame de Miramion, who was the prioress of a community of pious women, neither cloistered nor bound by any solemn vows, who received ladies wishing to do retreats. Madame Guyon then lived for two years with her daughter, who had recently married. During this time, she had access to a pious milieu who held the favor of the court (the Ducs and Duchesses de Beauvilliers and de Chevreuse, and Fénelon himself) and which Madame de Maintenon liked to frequent. In October 1688, she met Fénelon, who eventually became her disciple, at her friend's the Duchesse de Béthune-Charost. On August 16, 1889, Fénelon was named Preceptor to the Duc de Bourgogne, grandson of King Louis the XIV. The little group of *dévots* to which she belonged had formed a society calling themselves the *Confrérie de l'amour pur*. Madame Guyon was probably aware of the mystical and political hopes that Fénelon placed in the Duc de Bourgogne as he might eventually inherit the throne, but nothing in her own behavior proves that she shared his hopes.

Her cousin, Madame de la Maisonfort, invited Guyon to the Maison Royale of Saint-Cyr, where she was well received by Madame de Maintenon. Originally Saint-Cyr was a school for impoverished girls from the nobility, and it was founded by Madame de Maintenon in 1686. Eventually, Maintenon forced the teachers to become nuns (the *Dames de Saint Louis*), and, in 1694 at her own instigation, she was named superior for life. Then in 1693, Madame de Maintenon, who, until then, had been a follower of Madame Guyon and a member of the devout coterie that had adopted Guyon as a spiritual teacher, turned against her. Perhaps Maintenon did this because she was frightened that Archbishop de Champvallon, who was ready to launch a second offensive against Guyon, would seek revenge on her for making a fool of him when she freed Guyon from his harrassment. Guyon's preaching had made many followers at Saint-Cyr and, no doubt, had been misunderstood (or perhaps only too well understood?) by certain pupils as a license for following their own intuitions and for disobeying the rules of the house. Mme de Maintenon, who feared the disapproval of the king because of the current antimystic sentiments and religious quarrels, asked Guyon, on May 2, 1693, not to return to Saint-Cyr at any time. To support her action and to dissociate herself from her previous support of Guyon, she found the accusation of quietism handy, perhaps even necessary. One must not forget that such an accusation during these years was tantamount not only to an accusation of heresy but also to one of debauchery and tartufferie. In the summer of 1693, ill advised and misjudging the doctrinal position of the Jansenists as well as their influence,

Guyon, wary of accusations of heresy, had her work examined by the Jansenists Nicole and Boileau. Finally, on the advice of Fénelon, who also misjudged Bossuet's doctrinal position in regard to mysticism as well as his Jansenist sympathies, Madame Guyon had Bossuet himself review her work. Thinking she could trust Bossuet, she supplied him with several of her unpublished writings as well, including her autobiography. Although Nicole, Boileau, and Bossuet were at first favorable to her, they later turned against her. Nicole wrote a refutation of the *Moyen Court* in which he misquoted Guyon.[6] The Jansenist Boileau stooped so low as to use forgers to ruin her. Bossuet, who had at one time supported Guyon, was solicited by Maintenon to go against her as early as September 1693. In order to avoid any scandal, Maintenon engaged the help of Bossuet, and to "save" Fénelon who was known as being close to Guyon, she ordered Bossuet quietly to get rid of Guyon. Maintenon had not counted on the resistance, the intelligence, the strength, and the courage of Madame Guyon, nor on the integrity of Fénelon. Bossuet and Maintenon utilized all measures—slander, forgery of documents, insinuations, lies, subterfuge, imprisonment, psychological brutalization—to ruin Guyon and subdue Fénelon. It was of the utmost importance for Maintenon and Bossuet that Guyon be found a heretic and guilty of all charges and that Fénelon be forced to abandon her. They were greatly helped in their efforts by several factions, which for familial, political, or doctrinal reasons wanted Guyon condemned. One of these factions included the Chartreux Innocent Le Masson. Le Masson wrote a biography of Jean d'Arenthon d'Alex—the Bishop of Geneva who had first welcomed Guyon, then barred her from his diocese. In his biography of the Bishop of Geneva, Le Masson insinuated that he was in possession of memoirs that incriminated Guyon's relationship with her confessor La Combe and revealed her "immodesties."[7] When solicited by Bossuet, however, he was unable to produce these memoirs; his testimony was nevertheless retained as valid against Guyon.

On June 10, 1694, Guyon asked Maintenon to hold a trial in order to examine her moral conduct. Maintenon refused; she undoubtedly felt that calumnies were sufficient for dealing with the question of Guyon's moral reputation. So as to appear as one of Guyon's accusers rather than as someone who had at one time supported a heretic, Maintenon organized a doctrinal trial at Issy, outside of Paris; this took place from July to September 1694, with Bossuet, Bishop of Meaux, Noailles, Bishop of Châlon, Tronson, General Superior of Saint-Sulpice, and Fénelon as examiners. Guyon acted as her own lawyer and requested that all questions and answers be written down. Bossuet refused. During the summer and autumn of 1694, Guyon wrote her *Justifications*. In this work she gathered a great number of quotations from authorized mystics of the tradition and inscribed her writing and teaching within this tradition to prove that she was not a "new," therefore, heretical mystic.

Bossuet, sure that certain intimate details of her autobiography would weaken her case, broke the secrecy of confession and showed the manuscript of this autobiography to the three other members of the Issy Commission. On the other hand, he did not give them her *Justifications* to read, for he suspected rightly that this document would help her cause.

Meanwhile, the zealous Bishop of Paris, Harlay de Champvallon, seeking revenge on Guyon and jealous that the examinations at Issy excluded him, especially because they were held in a territory under his jurisdiction, anticipated and went beyond the Commission of Issy. He publicly condemned Guyon's *Moyen Court* and her interpretation of the *Canticles* on October 16, 1694. To avoid further persecutions, Guyon asked Bossuet to receive her in his diocese of Meaux, arriving there on January 13, 1695. She understood it as a refuge; he understood it more or less as an incarceration. On February 4, 1695, Fénelon was named Archbishop of Cambrai by King Louis XIV. On March 10, 1695, the thirty Articles of Issy, prepared by Bossuet, Noailles, and Tronson, then revised into thirty-four articles by Fénelon, were signed; these articles in no way indicted Guyon as a heretic nor accused Fénelon as having supported a woman whose doctrine was dangerous to the church. Nevertheless, both Bossuet and Noailles wrote pastoral letters condemning the *Moyen Court*, on April 16 and 26, 1695, respectively. Fénelon refused to do the same for his diocese of Cambrai. Furious, Bossuet used all possible means to win, even if his arguments were contradictory. He publicly asserted that Fénelon had been actively agreeing with the Commission of Issy and that he was now perjuring himself, thus making Fénelon appear as an equal partner among the members of the Commission. He also publicly asserted that Fénelon had not been allowed to be an active member of the Commission and had obediently submitted to signing the document as would a child under the command of an authoritative father, and that he was once more rebellious.

The Articles of Issy did not constitute any official proof of Guyon's heterodoxy, despite what Bossuet wanted his readers to believe. Bossuet, probably pushed by Mme de Maintenon, sought further a signature from Guyon admitting that she embraced heretical ideas. He went to see her at the *Visitation* of Meaux and, in order to obtain what he wanted, he used intimidation, ruse, threats, and psychological brutalization. Although he had the power, he could not win because Guyon was perfectly coherent in her explanations. She signed nothing against her conscience. Momentarily defeated, Bossuet gave her a certificate of orthodoxy. The last paragraph of this document specified that she had nothing to do with the quietist abomination of Molinos, and thus he let her leave Meaux with his blessings. But a few days later, regretting this gesture, he wrote another certificate withholding the last paragraph that had been for Guyon the most important safeguard, and he insisted that she give back the first certificate. She, of course, refused and subsequently left the *Visitation* of Meaux. Caught in his own contradictions, he spread rumors that she had escaped the *Visitation* of Meaux by jumping over the wall at night. To this new accusation Guyon responded, not without humor, that not only was she poor at jumping, but that all the nuns in Meaux could certify that she left through the door in broad daylight. Fearing Bossuet's ill-intentioned maneuvers and understanding that she was at the mercy of an arbitrary justice, Guyon tried to hide in the outskirts of Paris, in different lodgings and under different names. However on December 27, 1695, Madame Guyon was arrested at Popaincourt, and on the 29th, imprisoned at Vincennes, where she remained eight and a half months. On October 1696, she was transferred to a small convent of the Sisters of Saint Thomas at Villeneuve. Two years later she was in the Bastille, where she remained from June 4, 1698, to March 24, 1703. One of her servants was locked up at Vincennes, the other remained twelve years in the Donjon at the Bastille.[8] During the entire period of her incarceration, she was put through no less than eighty interrogations, each lasting eight to ten hours, all about her personal life, her friends, her relationship with La Combe and Fénelon.[9] The purpose of these interrogations was evidently to trip her up and get her to sign incriminatory declarations. Even false letters from La Combe claiming that he had had an illicit relationship with her were forged. When the supposed letter of La Combe was read to her, she responded that either this letter had indeed been written by him and therefore he must have gone mad, or it was a false letter, which was tantamount to her accusing the prelates of France of forgery. She asked to see the original letter but her request was never granted. Harrassed, psychologically brutalized, made to understand that all her family and friends had abandoned her, she stood firm despite her ill health, and she never lost her coherence or her dignity. Always lucid, she refused to denigrate La Combe or to sign any retractions. She reiterated, again and again, that if she made mistakes in her writing, it was out of ignorance, but that her intentions were nevertheless irreproachable. Nothing could be proven against her, and she withstood it all. She remained seven years in prison without ever receiving a final judgment.

During the time she was in prison, from 1695 to 1698, Fénelon and Bossuet engaged in a doctrinal and literary duel in which Fénelon defended his own doctrine and refused to denigrate Guyon, while Bossuet tried to destroy them both. The end of the story is known. Bossuet and the antimystics won. The papal brief *Cum Alias* that condemned Fénelon's *Explication sur les maximes des saints* was extorted by King Louis XIV from the reluctant Pope Innocent XII on March 12, 1699.[10] What was condemned in Fénelon's *Maximes* was the notion of "pure love," which was defined by an absence of fear of God or of His punishment and also by an absence of desire for rewards. What was unacceptable to the antimystics was the notion that, in the state of saintly indifference, even the desire for one's own salvation disappears because all desires are considered selfish and therefore not oriented toward God.

Fénelon submitted and was exiled to his diocese in Cambrai, his friends and family banished from the court. Guyon remained in the Bastille until Bossuet's death in 1703, despite the fact that no ground for prosecution was ever found against her, and even though the case was eventually dismissed in 1700.

Finally, Noailles, who had become Archbishop of Paris upon the death of Harlay de Champvalon, was struck by remorse for the role he had played in Guyon's fate. He thus encouraged her family to ask for her liberation. On March 24, 1703, she obtained permission to leave the Bastille and went to Blois to live close to her son, in whose guard she had been entrusted. A few years later she moved into a house of her own, and for twelve years, until her death, she at last pursued, undisturbed, her spiritual mission as she had always understood it.

Chapter Six

A Figure of Transition

Madame Guyon between the Female Mystical Tradition and the Emergence of a New Era

This chapter aims to situate Madame Guyon in the different, sometimes conflicting currents she participated in or was implicated in, so as to subsequently better understand her originality, her contradictions, the reasons why she was persecuted by her contemporaries and debased by eighteenth- and nineteenth-century historians. She found herself in the midst of the epistemological conflict described by de Certeau, the outcome of which was the decline of Western mysticism. The tensions provoked by this conflict are recorded in her writings, as well as in the Quietist Affair, in which she was one of the three main catalysts.

The innumerable and very real persecutions and acts of defamation Madame Guyon suffered in her lifetime, together with the dishonest conduct of several high-ranking clerics in her many trials, were obscured or denied by historians for two centuries following her death.[1] As late as 1910, even, Henri Brémond was still able to write: "We do not know the names of all the conspirators, nor the precise object of the conspiracy, nor still the nature of their alliance, whether conscious or not, but we know a few of these characters."[2]

The task of reopening the Quietist Affair and of unraveling its complicated intrigues was undertaken in this century by such historians as the above-mentioned Brémond (1910),[3] Louis Cognet (1958),[4] and Jean Orcibal (1951–1975).[5] The work of Georges Gusdorf added a European dimension to the significance and influence of Guyon's writing.[6] Very recently, the thorough and inspiring work of Marie-Louise Gondal on the life and spirituality of Madame Guyon, as well as her publication of several unpublished documents written by Guyon, give her indeed a new profile.[7] Dispeling the shroud of ignominy and mystery surrounding Madame Guyon, these diverse studies recognize her influence on the thought and spirituality of Fénelon. Thanks to these new works, not only does Guyon emerge cleansed of over two centuries of calumnies, but she also stands out as a powerful spiritual teacher and writer, a woman of courage, intelligence, and determination who did not let herself be intimidated by the institution of the church and the unjust punishment she was made to suffer. Finally, these new historical and critical works allow us to measure the extent to which her work was involved in the articulation of Pietist thought, which left its marks on German philosophy in subsequent centuries.

Most importantly, these historians depict Madame Guyon in one of her most important facets, as a healer of minds. It is important to note that besides the usual claims of legitimacy invoked by the mystics (conformity to the tradition, orthodoxy, the performance of miracles), Madame Guyon also argued that she possessed a beneficial and pacifying power on others. She had the gift of bringing peace to scrupulous minds tormented by the ever-growing intrusion of confessors in the conscience of the faithful.[8] She had herself suffered greatly from tormenting scruples and regrets as a young woman,[9] but she had learned to free herself from them and advised others: "Do not rehash the past; go to confession only when you really feel you need it, and not because you cannot stop rehashing."[10] In a time when Jansenism exerted a powerful influence on the minds of the faithful, with its emphasis on guilt, original sin, and fear of a hidden God, she conveyed the possibility that a friendly and benevolent relationship might exist with the divine, therefore minimizing guilt. She taught the existence of a spiritual path leading to inner peace, where there are no more accusers.[11] These teachings no doubt provided one of the reasons why some Jansenists were particularly adamant in persecuting her.

Yet, some ideas about Guyon invented in the past two centuries die hard. Historians of the twentieth century who have honestly worked to establish the truth about her, notwithstanding the fact that this truth shattered the previous images of Bossuet and Fénelon, are not altogether free of prejudice. For example, according to them, the reason Fénelon did not betray Guyon was owing to the chivalrous feelings characteristic of his cast, rather than because of his honesty and gratitude to her.[12] Clinging to this idea, they ignore Fénelon's own declaration on the subject: "The second reason why I support Guyon is that by refusing to contribute to her defamation, I wanted to avoid soiling myself."[13] Or, taking at face value Fénelon's statement to Madame de Maintenon, according to which "he had no taste for Guyon's person," the revisionist historians hold on to the notion, also dear to previous historians, that although Fénelon was attracted to Guyon's spiritual teaching, he did not like her personally.[14] To explain this statement, which can be invalidated by his lifelong relation with Guyon, they ignore the very fact they themselves underline; namely, that Madame de Maintenon was powerful and held Fénelon's career in her hands. Fénelon, therefore, might have had a moment of weakness, fully compensated by his subsequent unwavering support of Guyon. Further, lest Fénelon's letters to Guyon testify to the contrary, Orcibal, in his publication of Fénelon's entire correspondence, appends a note each time Fénelon writes something to Guyon that has an accent of genuine friendship. His notes give a reference to Fénelon's letters to other women in which he had used similar expressions. This practice seems to be designed to prove that what might be taken for expressions of a rare and genuine friendship are rather expressions of general politeness.[15] We could reverse the argument and say that Fénelon used such expressions each time he addressed a genuine friend. Masson had proceeded in a likewise manner when he published the correspondence between Fénelon and Guyon some seventy years earlier, but judging from his full acknowledgment of Guyon's importance for Fénelon, we can presume that his intention was different from Orcibal's.[16]

Likewise, historians still repeat that Guyon's *Justifications* owed much to Fénelon, and they insinuate that he wrote it himself. This traditional disclaimer of women's authorship needs no further comment, other than to recall that during her lifetime her adversaries also wanted her to confess that her *Moyen court* owed everything to Father La Combe, an accusation she deftly disproved. As a schooled member of the clergy, Fénelon might have provided Guyon with a bibliography, books to read, and even quotations written in his own hand that might help bolster her argument. We have no reason, however, to attribute Guyon's *Justifications* to him. Despite historians' desire to represent Guyon as a woman who feels, and Fénelon as a man who thinks, Guyon's own judicious teaching addressed to Fénelon in their correspondence, as well as her perspicacious judgment of his personality, demonstrates that she was perfectly equipped to experience, think, and teach on her own. As for Fénelon's claim that he had not read Guyon's work, it should be attributed to Fénelon's bad faith and not be proffered as truth, as Orcibal persisted in doing. On the contrary, Fénelon's letters to Guyon contain numerous statements proving that he was sincerely interested in her writings.[17]

Finally, I would like to dispel another prevalent cliché concerning Madame Guyon. Like all female mystics, Madame Guyon needed to defend herself against the accusation of writing out of a desire to be admired as an author. Consequently she had to insist on the fact that she did not reflect on what she was writing, nor correct or rewrite her texts. But her claim was taken at face value by historians, who chose to see in her a rare case of automatic writing. This interpretation went along with the image of Guyon as a hysteric, conjured up in the nineteenth century. But with Marie-Louise Gondal's discovery of two additional manuscript copies of Guyon's autobiography, which present variants and corrections in the author's hand, proof now exists that Madame Guyon was neither solely writing spontaneously, as she claimed, nor writing automatically, as historians have asserted.

Guyon and the Female Mystical Tradition

Jeanne-Marie Bouvier de la Mothe-Guyon (1648–1717) belongs to the fourth generation of female mystics inspired by the Catholic

Reformation and thus comes after Mme Acarie (1566–1618),[18] Jeanne de Chantal (1572–1641),[19] and Marie de l'Incarnation (1599–1671). On the theological and spiritual level, Madame Guyon, like Acarie, de Chantal, and Marie de l'Incarnation, is anchored in the tradition of negative theology, which was initiated by the Beguines and the Nonnenmystic, respectively, in Flemish countries and in Germany in the thirteenth century. Although an autodidact, Guyon knew this tradition very well, as her *Justifications* testify,[20] even though like other female mystics, she denied any claim to learning. I agree with Brémond that Guyon's *Justifications* is a work as erudite as it is intelligent and subtle. Furthermore, Guyon's explanation of the negative theology of John of the Cross is considered exemplary in the French language,[21] and I agree with Henri Delacroix who has judged her own mystical theology as the purest expression of negative mysticism.[22]

Also, Guyon shared with female mystics of previous centuries a body traversed by divine communications, which she thought God expected her to relay to others.[23] Like many other charismatic women, Guyon claimed to possess divinely inspired knowledge,[24] and to "at once feel as strong as God and as weak as a child."[25] Moreover, illness had a central place in her life, and Hildegard of Bingen's statement, according to which God loves to inhabit sickly bodies, suits her well.[26] Indeed her autobiography is punctuated with illnesses, which she said were sent by God to exercise her patience or to give her joy, since suffering for God means joy.[27] Illness was also for her the occasion to experience total dependence on God, paralleling the state of Jesus as a baby.[28] Frequent miraculous healings accompanied her illnesses.[29]

Furthermore, she practiced literary genres peculiar to the mystical tradition: spiritual autobiography, commentary on the Song of Songs and on the Scriptures in general, justifications, methods of meditation, and letters of spiritual advice. Finally, she shared with previous female mystics the problem of insisting, as a woman, that she, too, had an apostolic mission to accomplish.

Within the framework of the female mystical tradition, Madame Guyon most especially resembles the French Beguine Marguerite Porète.[30] What sets them sharply apart from other female mystics is not the alleged heterodoxy of their doctrine, but rather their refusal to compromise their beliefs and to conform to the institution of the church or to a preexisting model of female sainthood. It is true that many of the critiques on points of doctrine leveled against Porète were also leveled against Guyon, but so were they against Teresa of Avila, Eckhart, or John of the Cross and therefore cannot be taken as proofs of heterodoxy. What distinguishes Porète and Guyon from other female mystics, however, is their strong critique of the church of their time and their clear message that the entire church hierarchy should be put into abeyance, arguing that the institution itself had little to do with salvation. It is true that many saints and mystics had admonished the church and worked for reforms. But Guyon's and Porète's originality in that regard results from their belief that no amount of reform could ever achieve the purity they sought. Like other mystics, they implicitly invalidated the role of the hierarchy in spiritual matters; unlike most mystics, they sometimes did it quite explicitly.

Porète and Guyon are strikingly alike also on several other points. Although both Porète and Guyon may have sought and obtained the approval of theologians for the publication of their work, once arrested and crushed by the inquisitorial machine of the church, neither woman internalized her judges' accusations, and, consequently, neither fell prey to fear, compromise, or psychic disorientation. Indeed, Marguerite Porète did nothing to alleviate the violence of the confrontation. In her *Miroir*, a book stating her spiritual doctrine, she had written that the noble and perfectly free soul had no need to answer the peasants of Reason (theologians), and she remained silent throughout the period of her imprisonment and trial. Guyon was more diplomatic, but no less adamant in the defense of her doctrine and her spiritual freedom in her critique of the institution of the church and in her denunciation of the limitations of most clerics in matters of spirituality. The idea of keeping silent throughout her trial occurred as well to Guyon, but her fate was linked to that of several high-ranking aristocrats of the court, and she decided to defend herself in order to save them. Like Marguerite Porète before her, Madame Guyon was guilty of having broken off the contract between cleric and female mystic that had existed since the thirteenth century: the clerics demanded humility, obedience, and orthodoxy, and they exerted strict control over the female mystic, all in exchange for an official recognition of her charismatic call and a specific place for her in the church. Madame Guyon gave the clerics the orthodoxy they required, but, like

Porète, she refused to submit to abject humility and obedience. At this point it is important to stress again that Guyon, like Porète, did not owe her persecution to a lack of orthodoxy or to the fact that the implications of her doctrine were different from those of accepted mystics, but rather to her refusal to cower to institutional authority. Porète's overt questioning of the authority of the church was a radical position, and the outcome of her choice was death at the stake in 1310. By the end of the seventeenth century, however, things had changed in such a way that Guyon was not put to death, nor could she be silenced. It is this difference that I analyze further.

Indeed, because she lived at the end of the seventeenth century, Guyon, in many ways, is different from mystics of the tradition, whether they be thought orthodox or heretical. In previous centuries, women whose apostolic missions and charismatic dispositions could not be muted were nevertheless forced into convents, put under strict clerical supervision, or simply eliminated. In any case, they had to considerably tone down any claim to apostleship. By contrast, Guyon, who claimed to be divinely called to apostolic work outside the convent and even the hierarchy of the church, managed to outsmart the clerics who pressed her to enter a convent or some other religious congregation by invoking the very principles of the Council of Trent. To the Bishop of Geneva, Jean d'Arenthon d'Alex, who wanted to force her to become prioress of the congregation of the *Nouvelles Catholiques* in Gex in order to appropriate her fortune for the foundation he sponsored, she responded that by so doing he abused his authority as a bishop:

> He insisted I return to Gex and become superior of the order. I responded that no one could be superior without having been a novice first, that I had told him in Paris and in Gex that my vocation was not for the convent; that I spoke to him in his capacity as a bishop, who held God's place; that he should be careful to only consider divine concerns in what he was asking me; that if he told me to become superior, in his capacity as a bishop, I would comply. He was surprised and told me: "After your warnings, I cannot advise you to do it. It does not behoove bishops to go against vocations, but, please, be generous to this foundation."[31]

According to Brémond, had Guyon entered a convent after her widowhood, the Quietist Affair would not have occurred. With Guyon safely guarded within *clausura*, mysticism would have fizzled out with a whimper, rather than end as it did in a big bang with the Quietist Affair. In a convent, she would have been controlled, her writings would have been severely edited, she would not have preached, she would not have had disciples, and she would not have been able to teach meditation of silence to all, a practice the church reluctantly reserved to a few. Had she caused trouble, the worst of prisons, a convent cell, would have taken care of her, and indeed posterity would hardly have known of her existence.

There is some truth to Brémond's argument. One should keep in mind that while Madame Guyon, as mystic and woman, was being publicly ridiculed by antimystics for her comparatively sober, extraordinary manifestations, the convents were full of obscure nuns who experienced, unabated, the extraordinary sensory mysticism of medieval saints.[32] Moreover, unlike most mystics of the past and of her own time as well, Guyon did not play the institution of the church against the institution of the family in order to obtain a modicum of self-determination. She refused both, for neither one satisfied her desire. In fact the two institutions that she shunned banded against her, reaffirming, above their sometimes diverging interests, their common goal: the control of women.

Not only did Guyon manage to escape *maritus aut murus*, the stake or life imprisonment, but her conception of an apostolic mission made it impossible for any institution to co-opt her energy, her intelligence, or her talents. Marie de l'Incarnation's apostolic desire, by comparison, coincided with the needs of the Jesuits, those of Cardinal Richelieu, and those of the Crown. The same can be said of Hildegard of Bingen, who supported the Gregorian Reform, or Teresa of Avila, who endorsed the projects of the Catholic Reformation. By contrast, Guyon's apostolic desire fitted no existing, established institutions. She understood her mission as the teaching to everyone of the "interior path," either through silent communication or through her writings.[33] Her mission, as she understood it, was to help bring about the inner transformation of the individual. Finally, Guyon had read both the Old and New Testaments, and, in this again, she escaped clerical control and differed from most female religious.

Guyon, Quietism, and Antimysticism

The word *quietism,* which the antimystics used to defame the mystics (who refused the label) is often confusing because it is applied to two very different things.[34] In one sense, quietism is synonymous with negative mysticism. This spiritual path is characterized by a form of mental practice, called "orison" in the seventeenth century, in order to differentiate it from Ignacian meditation or from any other kind of mental practice that advocates using the faculties of the mind to focus on an object of meditation. Contrary to these practices, orison aims at the abandonment of cognition, representation, conceptualization, the memory of God and of oneself. In this dark and silent path of negative mysticism, a quieting of reason and of discursive thought is achieved in order to reach new insights. For mystics of this school, the use of discourses, thoughts, or operations of the mind adhered to by other forms of meditation, prevents the operation of the divine.

In the seventeenth century, the French school of mysticism to which Madame Guyon belonged followed the tradition of orison and preached the spiritual practice of simple presence of God, the annihilation of the self in God's essence, and acquisition of knowledge without images or representations. Through this practice, followers of this school tended to go beyond both the humanity of Christ and his divine attributes. These mystics considered any desire, any demand, or any regret an imperfection. This total lack of self-interest and detachment was called pure love, and it leaned, at least in theory, toward the disappearance of the subject, together with that of the objects of worship. Finally, these mystics claimed that the ultimate and perfect union with God could not be undone and could be achieved in one's lifetime.

The term *quietism* also collectively designates the errors to which, in the church's view, this negative mystical theology and practice would or could lead. The argument of the antimystics within the church itself, through the centuries, was that the mystics' claims of charismatic election and their valorization of the individual experience of God led to their dismissal of both the sacraments and the hierarchy of the church and its dogma as superfluous. Mysticism could also, according to these antimystics, render useless good actions and works of charity carried out in the pursuit of salvation. Finally, the antimystics alleged that the mystics who claimed to have reached perfection also stated that they could indulge in vice and crime without sinning, on the premise that their perfect state excused them from common rules of morality.[35] The church no doubt also feared that the practice of negative mysticism, through the dissolution of the logos and of duality, language, and representation, would incapacitate the church's control over its practioners. The church further objected to the doctrine of pure love, on the ground that it would disarm fear as a means to living virtuously. Indeed, pure love advocated the love of God for His own sake, rather than out of fear of punishment or hope for rewards. Throughout the centuries, many mystics, and among them some who were later canonized, had to face similar accusations.

In the seventeenth century, the church's fear of new and potential schisms encouraged a paranoid suspicion of any deviation from the common rule. During this period in France, antimystic agitations multiplied, fueled by the novel notion that mystics were introducing an unfamiliar element into spirituality. It was as if the antimystics within the church had forgotten, or denied, that the church had sanctioned mysticism since the late Middle Ages, while at the same time, the accusations that they hurled at the "new mystics," as they called them, rehashed previous charges waged against the Beguines, Marguerite Porète, Eckhart, Teresa of Avila, or John of the Cross.[36]

The reports of antimystic agitations in other nations were widely publicized in France. In 1623, the so-called Alumbrados in Seville were eliminated, and, in the following year, the acts of their condemnation were translated into French. In 1635 a certain number of people presumed to be "Illuminés" were persecuted in Picardy, and a prequietist affair took place in France in 1639, the Jesuit Antoine Sirmond accusing Jean-Pierre Camus (beloved disciple of François de Sales) of quietism. This particular quarrel, unlike the Quietist Affair, resulted in the reaffirmation of the mystical experience and of the notion of pure love.

In 1657, the Carme Chéron published his *Examen de la théologie mystique* in which he took to task the Jesuit mystic Jean-Joseph Surin; in 1679, Pierre Nicole wrote his *Traité de l'Oraison*, which became a best seller among French antimystics in 1695. This *Traité* was a warning against the mystics Guilloré, Bernières, and Barcos, whom he reproached for spreading an orison void of distinct thought, lacking any explicit consideration regarding faith and bearing no mention of prayers asking for God's grace or thanking Him for it. Even Bérulle, one of the founders of the French school of mysticism, had to defend himself against accusations of heresy.[37] Closer to the Quietist Affair, in 1687, the Jesuit Miguel de Molinos was condemned in Rome for his *Guia espiritual*, which had been translated into many languages and summarized the century's mystical spirituality. Neither the efforts of his friends nor the sympathy of Pope Innocent XI was able to avert his condemnation, all the more so as the Gallican antimystics denounced the pope as a defender of suspicious mysticism.[38]

The sixty-eight propositions of the *Coelestis Pastor*, which condemned Molinos's book, summarized all the errors denounced rightly or wrongly in certain mystics since the Middle Ages, and they became a catalogue against which seventeenth-century antimystics scrutinized the work of their contemporaries. These propositions were widely publicized in France. Around 1681 and 1682, "meditation" and "orison" had already become factional slogans. Meditation referred to a mental exercise involving the imagination, feelings, and reasoning, and it was advocated by antimystics, while orison, the practice of silence and detachment, was advocated by the promystics. In the wake of the Molinos trial, several mystic writers were placed on the index of forbidden books: Antoinette Bourignon (1687), Malaval, Falconi, Bourdon, La Combe (1688), Benoît de Canfield, Mme Guyon, Bernières (1689).[39] After 1687, accusations of quietism multiplied everywhere in a collective hysteria, making it impossible to distinguish facts from fiction.

The Quietist Affair, which involved Madame Guyon, Fénelon, and Bossuet from 1693 to 1698, was the last stone in the wall whose construction had started much earlier in the century. It relegated mysticism with its claims to a different way of knowing to a past era. The Affair culminated with Bossuet's polemical and satirical *Relation sur le quiétisme* in 1697, the condemnation by Rome of Fénelon's *Explication des maximes des saints* in 1698, and the imprisonment of Madame Guyon from 1695 to 1703. Collapsing negative mysticism, bodily manifestations of piety, extraordinary graces, and error into the word *quietism*, Catholicism evacuated its own mystical tradition in the seventeenth century.[40] After the Quietist Affair, mysticism was increasingly relegated to monastic institutions, and especially to female cloisters.[41]

Guyon and a New Era

According to several historians and theologians, Guyon's mysticism was outmoded and at odds with her era, which was opening to the rationality and positivism of the modern world. I argue that although steeped in the mystical tradition, paradoxically, it is through the very practices of negative mysticism that Madame Guyon found a viable philosophy for this time of transition. Together with a certain intellectual avant garde, she took inspiration in medieval mysticism while participating in the shaping of a new philosophy with new claims for the individual. This paradox can help to explain why Guyon was persecuted and maligned equally by antimystics and promystics, respectively for her traditional mysticism and for the protomodern elements in her teachings and thought.

Antimystic feelings fueled by this epistemological change were also buttressed by a tendency of all established churches toward authority, often in alliance with secular power. Although the tendency for dogmatism and conformist piety was most strident within the Catholic Church, it also existed in other established Christian denominations. We find religious dogmatism allied with political power in England in 1619, as well as in the reformed Synod of Dordrecht in the United Provinces, which favored orthodoxies in the debate on predestination.[42] Furthermore, antiquietism was to be found not only in the Catholic realm, but also in the Lutheran.[43] Even more than ever before, heresy—for the Catholic or Reformed churches—meant whatever or whoever opposed authority and institution. With this rigid attitude, the established churches excluded any aspects of religious practice that were not institutional.

Against the dogmatic tyranny of the established churches and their demand for a conformist piety, and against the claims of reason in matters of faith, a new religious conscience emerged in Europe at the end of the seventeenth century. This new spirit understood religion in terms of individual conscience and lived experience for all people, rather than for only a few. Religious aspirations turned to the future and launched the basis of modern Western philosophy. For subscribers to this new religious spirit, the hierarchical church ceased to be conceived as a structure allowing a communication between heaven and earth, and collective adherence came to be replaced by individual conscience. The idea arose that religion could no longer be identified with a particular confession, whether Catholic or Protestant. It is because this new religious spirit escaped confessional barriers, that, according to Georges Gusdorf, not only its internationalism but its very existence has escaped historians who, instead, attempt to seize the shift of religious feelings in the seventeenth and eighteenth centuries exclusively within confessional demarcations. A common religious inspiration and a common philosophical reflection brought together Christians from a variety of traditions. This movement was manifested in the Quietist Movement within Catholicism, in the Pietist Movement in the Lutheran Church, and in the movement eventually leading to the foundation of the Methodist Church, as separate from the Anglican Church in England and Scotland.[44] Bracketing their national and confessional barriers, these individuals, sharing a commonality of spirit, found a religious "internationale." For the lack of a better term, I will follow Georges Gusdorf's example and name this religious movement "Pietism," although strictly speaking Pietism belongs to the Germanic domain alone. It is from this "Pietist" movement, taken in its widest application, that European Romanticism was born.

Far from remaining within the religious sphere, this new spirit had ramifications in the cultural sphere at large. In Catholicism, the condemnation of Galileo in 1633 declared a divorce between scientific and philosophical enquiries on the one hand and Christian ideology on the other, forcing the former enquiries into clandestinity and atheism until the end of the eighteenth century. Such was not the case in the Protestant realm. According to Gusdorf, both Newton and Locke, who inspired the physical, mathematical, and human sciences, belong also to the history of religious thought.[45] It is interesting to note, for example, that Newton called the attention of the poet Cowper to the poems of Madame Guyon.[46] Also, in Germany, Emanuel Hirsche anticipated the future of all Western philosophical thought in his history of modern evangelical theology.[47] A similar meeting of scientific, philosophical, and spiritual concerns is unthinkable in the thought of Descartes, Malebranche, or Voltaire.

This new religious spirit, which prevailed in the eighteenth century, marked a desire to return to an experiential spiritual life, as opposed to piety understood either as conformism or as theology, that is, as a discourse on the divinity as object of discourses.[48] Although involved in philosophical preoccupations of their period, these Pietists reaffirmed a demand of direct address to the divine, which had been constant throughout Christianity but which also had been disciplined and interfered with constantly by the church. Indeed, beyond the dogmatism of the churches and their demand for conformity, the Pietists sought inspiration in the Catholic mystics of all centuries. This international Pietism was rooted in the apophatic mysticism of Eckhart, Ruysbroeck, and Tauler, who themselves were inspired by the thirteenth-century Beguines. Echoing the mystics of the thirteenth century, the religious drama for the Pietists took place in the soul and spread to society at large. The historical difference between the medieval mystic movement and the Pietists was that at the end of the seventeenth century, thanks to the schism within the church, those whose religious aspirations were no longer satisfied through the established churches could find a measure of safety away from the stake, the prisons, compromise, or silence. The Pietists understood apostleship not as a conversion of others or of oneself to a specific confession, but as the cure of the soul, one's own and that of others.

Gusdorf presents the argument that an avant-garde seventeenth- and eighteenth-century European religious and philosophical movement found its roots and inspiration in late medieval apophatic mysticism, and it eventually led to European Romanticism and to modern philosophy. This thesis helps explain facets of Guyon's thought and its impact, facets that had remained invisible in French history, whether lay or Catholic. Gusdorf's thesis also helps to explain the fact that Guyon's work has been translated into English and German and has been widely available in England, Scotland, the Netherlands, Switzerland, Germany, and in the United States. It also sheds light on why we find traces of Guyon in the writings of Schopenhauer and Kierkegaard, as both of them, according to Gusdorf, have their source in the German Pietist movement. Above all, this perspective permits us to understand how Guyon, who was a product of the Catholic Reformation and an heir to Western mysticism, emerged into the new era.

While steeped in negative mysticism, Guyon also emerged into the modern debate concerning freethinking and antiauthoritarianism, tolerance, and the right to pursue happiness, while at the same time the focus of her position was not, as for freethinkers of the time, a rejection of formal religion as incompatible with reason.

In relation, on the one hand, to the exclusionary practices of the new epistemology, and, on the other, to the conformism demanded by the church, Madame Guyon appears as a truly *free* thinker who took a measure of liberty both from rational, secular wisdom and from rigidified church institutions and dogma. Much has been said about the anti-intellectualism of Guyon and of mystics in general. But it must not be forgotten that negative mysticism is anti-intellectual only insofar as it does not limit cognition to the realm of reason or consciousness. In contrast, the antimystics are intellectual only insofar as they attribute to reason and to the faculties of the mind the capacity for cognition. This does not mean that Guyon or the mystics were negating the usefulness of reason, but rather that they were delimiting its power and acknowledging it as but one of the possibilities of the psyche, and a limited one at that; another reality, for them, lay beyond words and duality. Bayle's struggles against the abuses of dogmatic and theological reason, as well as those of Pascal, must be understood according to these principles.

Far from conceiving reason and mysticism as antagonistic, the mystics themselves asserted that the practice of silence did not imply a renouncement of the mind's capacities after the period of orison, but, on the contrary, that their spiritual practice enhanced and sharpened those faculties which, as a result, became unencumbered. Guyon claimed that her mental practice of silence liberated her from her constant fears,[49] allowing her the necessary freedom to utilize uninhibitedly her strong intellectual faculties in her own defense:

My mind, which I thought I had lost in a strange stupidity, was given back to me with inconceivable advantages. I was myself astounded, as I saw that nothing was too complicated for me, or that there was nothing I could not solve. . . . I knew,

I understood, I conceived, I could do everything, and I did not
know where this mind, this knowledge, this intelligence, this
strength, this facility had come from.[50]

Indeed, what is striking in Guyon's defense and stance throughout her trials is precisely an unshakable and surprising boldness,
independance of mind, and inner freedom. According to Brémond,
it is only owing to a miracle of intelligence, energy, and virtue that
Madame Guyon could have saved her honor.[51] As it was precisely
her honor Bossuet wanted to tarnish, he interpreted her coherence,
intelligence, and lucidity as arrogance, stupidity, and obstinacy. It
is true that Guyon indefatigably and lucidly explained her arguments, defended herself, opposed reasons with reasons, secured papers proving her innocence, and avoided the traps laid for her by
her jailers, all with as much courage as subtlety. But not only did
she save her honor, she also saved her sanity as well. Madame
Guyon was not alone in her century to have been accused of quietism (a charge regarded as dishonorable by the church) and to
have been ostracized for it. She did not share the fate of Father La
Combe, her confessor, who was first to be interned in a convent,
then transferred to the Bastille, and subsequently sent to the
prison of Lourdes. Eventually, having gone mad, he was transferred to the insane asylum of Charenton, where he died in 1715,
never having undergone an official trial.[52] La Combe, undoubtedly,
internalized the false accusations leveled against him; Guyon did
not. Although Guyon suffered, was often sick, somatized, and was
excruciatingly tormented by her adversaries, she did not psychically fragment. This strength of character in the face of a hostile
majority may have much to do with her own mental practice
of silence, which deemphasized guilt, stressed detachment, and
brought her much-needed equanimity. In her own eyes she was not
guilty, and she claimed that the inner freedom created by her mental practice allowed her full resistance. During her persecutions,
trials, and imprisonment, she indeed seems to have genuinely
practiced what she wrote and preached to others.

It is important to keep an open mind and an unprejudiced ear
to Guyon's claims about the effect of her practice on her clarity of
mind. Although it is not fashionable in Western intellectual or academic circles to suggest that one may be freed from the "prison

house of language," or even worse, to appear to give credence to the claims of those called mystics in Western or Oriental tradition, I suggest we listen to them.[53] These traditions, which advocate a mental practice of silence, assert that one's mind may be set free from ego formations and identifications, be they individual or collective, and from the discursive chattering that conditions the mind and therefore the actions of individuals. According to the mystics, in the space that is thereby created, limitless freedom, fearlessness, clearmindedness, and joy abound.

It may indeed be true that because Guyon was protected by a psychic space not ruled by language and created through the practice of inner silence, she never internalized the standard images of the heretic, hysteric, insane person, or criminal, as dictated to her by the church, state, and the court. This form of spirituality may indeed have afforded Guyon the means to escape severe intimidation and clerical control, to ward off the straitjacket of received ideas and the dialectic of reason that bound the individual in dogmatic fetters.[54]

This practice of silence by a woman must not be confused with the imposed silence traditionally demanded of women. Guyon's mother-in-law and her husband demanded, for example, that she conform to the female ideal of silence and that she never speak her mind. She was much too vivacious to ever comply with their demand, which she found unjust. She wrote: "One day outraged with sorrow (I had been married for six months), I took a knife, as I was alone, in order to cut my own tongue out so that I would not be forced to speak to people who made me talk only in order to shut me up with anger."[55] Bossuet later also demanded that she keep an eternal silence, which he believed was befitting to a woman.

Those who demanded that she comply to such patriarchal norms understood that her orison of silence was a subversion of their control. When she started her practice, family and church alike worried that she had escaped them. Guyon reports that her husband and his mother kept watch over her, for they were in league with her confessor:

My confessor tried to prevent me from the practice of orison and from seeing Mother Granger. And as he was in agreement with my mother-in-law and my husband, they kept watch on me constantly from morning to evening. I did not dare leave the bedroom of my mother-in-law or the bedstead of my sick huband. Sometimes I sat next to the window under the pretext of better seeing my work, so that I might have a moment of respite; but they came to verify that I actually was working rather than in deep orison.[56]

Whereas the patriarchal ideal of female silence imprisoned the mind, the meditative practice of silence, on the contrary, was meant to free the mind.

A dual position of outer conformity and inner freedom is common to female mystics, but it is more noticeable in the case of Guyon because she was not conformist in her claims for spiritual freedom and because antimystics' attacks forced her to systematize her position. After her trials, she was relegated to the dual margins of the Catholic Church and of her own society. Yet her mystical discourse remained unreproachably orthodox in the theological or symbolic meaning she gave to her experience, much to the chagrin of her adversaries who were unable to obtain a condemnation on these grounds alone. Theological and symbolic meanings, such as the Eucharist or the Trinity, are, however, so relativized in her doctrine as to sometimes appear as simple props or appeasements to conformity; spiritual life for Madame Guyon happened elsewhere than in theology. This, again, supports my argument against Bynum, who sees in theology the causal factor of female mystics' behavior.

Guyon's escape from the mind control of the church affords a more adequate explanation for the persecutions she underwent than does the content of her teaching. We must not forget that although she was punished and imprisoned as a criminal on charges of disobedience, she was never formally convicted of heresy, nor of any civic, moral, political, or even ecclesiastical violations. She was censured in her public writings by five episcopal ordinances, and although she was forbidden to speak and to direct others, she never was excommunicated.[57] One incident, which happened on the occasion of her second incarceration in 1696, serves as a vivid example of this kind of escape from mind control. In order to satisfy the Archbishop of Paris, Guyon was asked to sign the following text: "She was contrite because she had caused scandal and troubles through her writings and her books, and was resolved to practice the Apostle's order that 'woman must learn in silence.'"[58] She signed the document but she added in her own handwriting: "I submit to everything *he* thinks God demands of me."[59] Madame Guyon had much humor, and thus I cannot help wondering if "*he*" referred not only to the Archbishop of Paris but also to the Apostle himself. In any case, this example proves that the silence assigned to her by the hierarchy and power of church, state, and family was not the fertile and liberating silence of the mind she was preaching and practicing.

Guyon's rare inner freedom and independence of thought led her to adopt an equally rare stance vis-à-vis the respect of individual conscience and tolerance. There has always existed within the church a tradition of conscientious objectors to ecclesiastical imperialism, ranging from the heretics of the early church to the Franciscans, the Brothers of Free Spirit, and the Brothers of Common Life. According to Gusdorf, Luther's revolt is not different from these movements.[60] Madame Guyon squarely fits into this tradition. The difference, however, is that she did not conceive of a need either to separate from the church or to found a new one, or even to found a new order within the institution. As far as she was concerned, any church institution would do, because deep spiritual transformation occurred elsewhere. This may explain how she could conform to orthodox theology while at the same time preserve her inner freedom, as the kind of freedom she was practicing was precisely beyond words and representations. The difference between Guyon and earlier advocates of religious freedom is that, unlike many schismatics who demanded the respect of their individual conscience but did not extend the same respect to others, Guyon did both. She is known to have professed that she "would rather die than to distance herself in the least from the Spirit of the Church."[61] She also repeatedly demonstrated by her actions as well as by her words and writings that she would rather endure prison or even die on the scaffold than act against her conscience or sign a document in order to avoid trouble.[62] In her categorical refusal to compromise, and owing to her constancy in opposing totalitarianism, whether legal, religious, or theological, she did not display the fanaticism often characteristic of resisters who oppose one belief in favor of another. To the contrary, Guyon, along with the

new religious movement delimited by Gusdorf, advocated an unprecedented openmindedness and conceived of faith beyond confessional demarcations. Her fundamental position was to resist dualistic oppositions and simplistic categorization.

The idea of tolerance was not new in the seventeenth century.
It already had been affirmed in the reflections of a few noted Renaissance philosophers: Nicolas de Cusa, Guillaume Postel, Jean
Bodin. And yet, there is no clearcut discourse of tolerance in
France in the sixteenth century.[63] The freedom of individual conscience among the Calvinists cannot be equated with tolerance, as
they recognized this freedom only for themselves. Of course Marot,
Rabelais, Bonaventure Des Périers, and Montaigne can be invoked
on the general subject of religious tolerance, but nothing precise
can be quoted from them. La Boétie, in his *Mémoires sur la pacif-
ication des troubles*, writes about the necessity of tolerating the
Calvinists in France and is against the label of "heretics" given to
Protestants. But this idea is expressed in a few lines buried in a
treatise of over fifty pages. Furthermore, the reasons he invokes for
not labeling Protestants as heretics are pragmatic rather than eth-
ical. Both Marot, in a long poem about the death of a Protestant
friend at the stake, and Bonaventure Des Périers, in a piece attributed to him entitled *Cymbalum Mundi*, point to the horrors of religious intolerance. But they take infinite precautions, and their
point is lost in literary metaphors.[64]

In the French seventeenth century before Guyon, Cyrano de
Bergerac's *Voyage dans la lune* and *L'Histoire comique des états et
empires du soleil* are the only works in which tolerance can be in-
ferred from the author's relativistic position. Only at the end of the
century does a debate relative to tolerance finally enter the public
arena. On the side of secular thinking, the French Protestant
Pierre Bayle was at the heart of a debate among thinkers of the
time because he tried to conceive of a social cohesion that would
not depend on the fear of God. He even went so far as to contem-
plate the possibility of a religion without God.[65] The two contemporary attitudes regarding tolerance or the lack thereof are illustrated in the dialogue between Leibnitz and Bossuet, in which the
German thinker upheld the necessity of a pluralism of confessions
and of respect for individual conscience, while Bossuet was relent-
less in maintaining the immutable divinity of Catholic dogma.[66]

The issue of tolerance, however, did not neatly pit the reactionary Catholics against the liberal Protestants. The Pietists' attitude toward tolerance cannot be attributed to the Protestant Reformation. The Reformation, it is true, had relativized Christianity by pluralizing it, but the reformed religion could not avoid institutionalization and therefore new dogmatism, which, in turn, led to the need from within the congregation of the faithful to create a new distance from others. Nor had tolerance been traditionally a quality displayed by mystics, male or female. It is sufficient to recall Hildegard of Bingen's raving against the Cathar Heresy;[67] Teresa of Avila's ranting against the Protestant heretics; Marie de l'Incarnation's harsh words against the "heretical" English and her acquiescence to a politic of total annihilation of the "heathen" Iroquois, under the pretext that they constituted an obstacle to the spread of the Catholic faith; Marguerite-Marie Alacoque's Eucharistic piety, which was inspired and used as an argument against the Protestants, whom she called infidels;[68] or, finally the cripple Madame Acarie's exclamation: "Ah! If I held in my hands the last heretic, and he refused to convert, I would destroy him with my crutch."[69]

On the issue of tolerance or conciliation with the Protestants, Bossuet was guilty of the most exclusionary position, particularly after 1685. And, notwithstanding the fact that the eighteenth century made him into a liberal individualist and the nineteenth century saw him as a forerunner of the French Revolution, Fénelon was, in fact, Superior of the *Nouvelles Catholiques* and the *Nouveaux Catholiques* for ten years, from 1679 to 1689. He was surely aware of, and agreed to, the forceful and deceitful methods used by these institutions to convert the Protestants. Jacques Le Brun mentions Fénelon's passion for converting Protestants and Libertines, his vindication of the infallibility of the church, his ardor in combatting Jansenism, and his role in the preparation of the *Unigenitus Bull*.[70] It is certain that the idea of tolerance preached and practiced by Guyon was foreign to both Bossuet, her enemy, and Fénelon, her friend. For Fénelon as for Bossuet, who also upheld monarchy by divine right, the fight for Catholicism was confused with the fight for the state. Even Richard Simon, the most enlightened of priests, stated that "[a]ny religion which is not the state religion is againt the common right of the kingdom, and consequently against the State. Therefore it can only exist by special privilege."[71]

Fénelon, who later attracted several of the same Protestant disciples as Guyon, retained to the end of his life the need to convert them to Catholicism. This is not the case with Guyon. Toward the end of her life, apropos the conversion by Fénelon of André-Michel de Ramsey, her disciple and secretary in Blois, Guyon is reported to have said that Fénelon converted too much.[72] Her practice of negative mysticism led her beyond duality and the hierarchical discrimination of difference. It allowed her to escape the wars of opinion and religious dogma, as well as the general hostility that the different denominations harbored toward each other. She was convinced of the obsolescence and the futility of conversion. Thus, within the Catholic context, Guyon appears as unique on the issue and practice of tolerance.

The first confrontation between Guyon and the church occurred at the very beginning of her missionary career, precisely on the issue of conversion and tolerance. She had had premonitions that her mission pointed in the direction of Geneva. After having consulted the Bishop of Geneva in Paris about this premonition, he convinced her that it meant she ought to work for the *Nouvelles Catholiques*, who were undergoing at that time full expansion. Guyon was not aware of their methods of conversion when she agreed to work with them. Thus, despite hesitations, she signed on July 6, 1681, a contract of association of 6,000 *livres* with the community of the *Nouvelles Catholiques*. She had also received encouragement from the Benedictine, Claude Martin, the son of Marie de l'Incarnation, Jacques Bertot, disciple of the mystic Bernières, and François La Combe, her confessor, all three of whom were promystic.[73] In 1681, leaving her two sons in the care of their paternal family and taking her daughter with her, she left for Gex, in Savoy, with the nuns in charge of founding a new institute of the *Nouvelles Catholiques* close to Geneva. Soon after, she was profoundly disappointed and even repulsed by the methods of forceful persuasion and outright violence applied by them in the "conversion" of Protestant girls. Thus Guyon disengaged herself from the enterprise although she continued to fund them. Too frank or perhaps not artful enough to hide her feelings, she imprudently confided them to the Mother Superior of the institute:

As I am very honest . . . I even told her that the manners of
the *Nouvelles Catholiques* held no attraction for me and that
besides [these institutions] were involved in too many intrigues. I added that many of the abjurations and the roundabout ways by which they were achieved were displeasing to
me, for I wanted sincerity in all things; consequently my refusal to sign the abjurations, which I deemed were not done in
full faith, somewhat shocked them.[74]

For her, the existential taste for God and conversion of the heart
were more important than confessional demarcation or outward
conversion. This is an attitude to which she remained faithful for
the rest of her life. Coherently following the line of negative mysticism and pushing its refusal of duality further than anyone else,
she bracketed *any* religious institution or *any* dogma, and she thus
rendered conversion, apostasy, or even atheism irrelevant.

Guyon fully realized her spiritual ideal after her liberation
from the Bastille. Close to his death, Bossuet renounced his opposition to her liberation. She finally was left in peace although assigned to residence in Blois. The commotion made by the Quietist
Affair and her imprisonment in the Bastille had spread Guyon's
name and her books throughout Pietist circles all over Western Europe. A new and different generation of disciples formed around
the house she occupied in Blois, starting in 1704.[75] Pierre Poiret, a
French publisher living in the Netherlands, first discovered her.
Then new friends, attracted by her spirituality and her works,
came to her from other confessions than Catholicism and from
other countries than France: Holland, England, Germany, Switzerland.[76] While she was in Blois she cautiously exchanged letters
with her new disciples, who also were in contact with Fénelon.
There are many reasons to believe that the correspondence between Guyon and Fénelon was resumed after she left the Bastille.[77]
Her letters were copied and discreetly circulated among the members of the group.[78] It is in this way that Madame Guyon entered
into an international spirituality whose underpinning political
agenda had nothing to do with her. Nonetheless, her influence facilitated international relations among her Scottish, Dutch, and
German disciples, all of whom became personal friends. In England, her work was enthusiastically read by a Scottish group of

the Episcopal Church, which was paradoxically enamoured with science and marked by political engagement. They were Jacobites faithful to the pretendant James III, who was living in exile in Saint Germain-en-Laye. Through one of the Jacobites, George Garden, the influence of Guyon spread to a member of the High Church, John Wesley, founder of the Methodist Church.[79] Guyon was the only woman, the only unschooled member, and one of the few Catholics in this international spiritual network. Her disciples were all men whose religious beliefs and education were formed outside of Catholicism. They sought to articulate a modern philosophy that would take the spiritual life into account. Through this network, she entered into a new era in which spirituality did not disappear but rather was transformed, influencing the development of philosophy. What these men were seeking in her teaching was something they could find neither in established churches, nor in a Cartesian rationality pushed to its extremes, nor in a simple return to the mystics of the past. Those who came to her belonged to the future, and for them, her teaching spoke to that future. Guyonian echoes, which one finds in Pietism and consequently in its offshoot, German Romanticism, indicate the importance and significance of her message for these Christians. Modern epistemology and the rigid institutionalism of the established churches left them bereft of spirituality.[80] Madame Guyon freely welcomed her guests and never tried to convert them; in return, what they sought from her was beyond specific confessions. She and her group acted in an authentic, ecumenical manner.

Madame Guyon's tolerance and antiauthoritarian stance in spiritual matters led her to the democratization of the pursuit of individual happiness. To be sure, the teaching of the church had always been universalist in its promised salvation for any believers, regardless of their perceived depth of piety or understanding, on the condition that they submit to authority and to the direction of the clergy. It was on this universalist ground that Bossuet based his opposition to Guyon and other mystics' teachings, insisting that there had always been one, unique path recognized by the church for those who sought salvation.[81] In a sense, Bossuet was accusing mysticism of being elitist because mystics believed there was another path toward union with the divine, one not so easily followed because it demanded from the faithful more than conformity. On that point Bossuet was right. Such elitism, however, was precisely what the church had also always desired. In fact, one of the conditions that the church had always attached to its acceptance of the mystics, whether sensory or negative, was that they be considered as exceptions to the norm and that their particular path to a union with the divine be understood as a gift from God, that is, as an extraordinary intervention in ordinary human beings, often choosing the less than worthy. Aware of the threat that unchecked mysticism posed to its authority, the church thus disallowed mysticism as a model for the common believer and denied that the mystic path was for everyone to pursue. One can imagine how this demand on the part of the church went along with the deepest desires of female mystics, who were granted a prestige and an authority not granted to ordinary women. Bossuet went further than the church in denying the exceptions it had made and conditions it had set for mystics.

Further, in the case of Guyon, Bossuet was wrong to reproach her with elitism, for in this regard she differed from female mystics of the tradition. Guyon understood mystical union as composed of two concomitant steps: the practice of a method that would empty the mind of all volitional or nonvolitional obstacles, and the reaching of a state of void, inhabited by the divine. In this sense, she did not differ from other practitioners of negative mysticism. Unlike them, however, she openly contradicted the church, insisting that everyone was capable of learning how to clear her or his interior path and so unite with the divine, for surely God would act in a soul emptied of its obstacles.[82] Hence, despite the contradiction, Bossuet reproached her both for elitism, and for democratizing mysticism. This echoed the reproach that the church had addressed to Eckhart. Indeed, Guyon wanted to give everyone what the church for centuries had tolerated only for a few. Quoting from her *Moyen Court*, Bossuet reproached her for having written: "As we are all called to salvation, so are we also all called to meditation of silence."[83] He was outraged both for the fact that she, like other mystics, insisted there was another path in spiritual matters than the common one he advocated and for her strong suggestion that passive orison should be taught to children along with catechism.[84] For her, it was a scandal that priests would hide, or be themselves ignorant of, a spiritual path for which so many hungered. For Bossuet, the ecclesiastic par excellence, Guyon's teaching was condemnable not only because it put into abeyance the hierarchy of the church, but also because theologians like himself could no longer fathom the interior voyage of the mystics.

Madame Guyon's democratization of mystical practices was equally viewed with suspicion by those men within the hierarchy of the church, who, unlike Bossuet, understood the mystics of the tradition. For them, the influence of a new epistemology was no ground to dismiss mysticism as superstition; nevertheless, they perceived a danger in allowing the democratization of spiritual practices, a process that might lead the faithful to inner freedom and autonomy and result in the collapse of the hierarchy and authority of the church. One cannot forget that Pseudo-Dionysius, whom the Catholic mystical tradition claimed as its legitimating founder, had constructed a mystical schema that fitted the hierarchy of the church, its powers, and its demand for subordination. According to de Certeau, as a consequence of the breaking up of the unitary theological system, the Dionysian hierarchy that had lent itself to a confusion between stages of spiritual perfection and the hierarchy of the church was abandoned in the sixteenth and seventeenth centuries.[85] It is certain that Guyon was bothered by this hierarchy. It remains to be proven, however, that her resistance to Dionysian hierarchy was a sign of her time, as de Certeau believes was true generally of mystics during this period. Perhaps it is possible to see her form of resistance to Dionysian hierarchy as in keeping with the female mystical tradition, which since the thirteenth century had resisted confusing a hierarchy of spiritual perfection with church hierarchy, as was certainly the case with Marguerite Porète. This subject is too vast to cover in the scope of this study. What is certain is that Guyon, like Porète, was troubled by the confusion of a hierarchy of spiritual perfection with that of the church. What is closer to the beliefs of Guyon is that she clearly disapproved of a hierarchical schema that suggested power and subordination. In a letter to Fénelon, Guyon wrote: "I wish I could explain this admirable hierarchy, and this total dependence [opposing no obstacle] on divine will. . . . But, although there is union [among individuals], there is no subordination."[86]

She interpreted Dionysian hierarchy as a system of communicating vessels: from God there poured forth grace, plenitude, and knowledge, which flowed into the angels, the blessed, and the saints. Because they were in the same degree of perfection (even though some of the saints might be still of this world), they could communicate among themselves and to others. For if everyone could receive divine inspiration, not everyone could communicate it.[87] At the top of this hierarchy reigned the Virgin Mary, who stood above the Apostles, the blessed, the saints (dead or living), and the inferior hierarchies: "The angel saluted the Holy Virgin and filled her with such perfect plenitude that she overflowed and will continue to do so eternally in all the saints. She is their hierarchical queen. It is in this sense that all the graces that God gives to men pass through Mary."[88] It is no wonder that neither the antimystic Bossuet nor the institutional promystics, who in a Dionysian manner confused a hierarchy of spiritual perfection with the structural hierarchy of the church, could agree with Guyon's system in which there is no coincidence between the two hierarchies.

So, whether they were promystic or antimystic, her accusers' alarm was justified. Like accepted mystics, she taught and practiced a path to interior freedom, but unlike them—which is why she was considered as a threat to the church—she made this path accessible to all. This was indeed a most dangerous message for authorities. More than anything else, this explains why everywhere she went the same pattern occurred. At first, those clerics and prelates she met who were already sympathetic to the mystical tradition were interested, fascinated, and persuaded by her teaching. Soon, however, they turned viciously against her. The Chartreux Le Masson, who later made false allegations concerning her misconduct in Savoy, expressed very clearly the danger represented by Guyon's teaching: "I say I know what she is capable of, for her influence might have caused me great troubles, as her book on the Canticle found its way to and multiplied among our women convents in the area."[89]

What worried these clerics was her influence on unschooled minds, and particularly on women. Indeed, her teachings may have taught women how to find freedom and joy despite the many oppressions that constrained their lives. This, in turn, could also have led to an independence of mind, which would have been unacceptable to their male superiors. Guyon was dangerous because her writings could not be proven heretical, and, therefore, her voice, which taught the road to inner freedom or the way to find God outside the church, was all the more capable of reaching not only women in religious orders but lay people as well. According to Marie-Louise Gondal, Le Masson, Bossuet, and Nicole, her three most vociferous opponents, saw her as a rival. This situation had always been the problem of female mystics, and it supports Bynum's argument that female mysticism was a creative response invented by women as an alternative to the priesthood, which men reserved for themselves. To top it all, Guyon designated a woman, Mary, as the archetypal priest: "Did she not sacrifice Him on the cross, in front of which she stood, as a priest who was helping in the accomplishment of the sacrifice that Jesus, as a high priest . . . was making of Himself?"[90] Also, she related in her autobiography how she had successfuly performed exorcism, and that the Devil was afraid of her. Thus she appropriated yet another role priests had reserved for themselves, while they had left women with the dubious privilege of being possessed.[91]

What frightened them was that Guyon's success could not be curbed. She preached everywhere she went; she was listened to, her influence could not be controlled, her writings were not edited, her experience and teachings were not reshaped by conformity or a fear of hierarchy. It was, indeed, absolutely necessary for those in authority to destroy, through calumny and slander if need be, "a venom which goes to the heart by surprise."[92] Le Masson, Nicole, and Bossuet argued on moral, spiritual, and doctrinal grounds that if the voice of Guyon were heard, chaos and apocalypse would ensue; that is, their authority and legitimacy would be destroyed. They were not far from the truth.

Guyon's desire to bring to many a method that would alleviate their inner sufferings, sharing with others the means by which she herself had been cured, led her to a critique of the clergy's prerogative vis-à-vis the laity. She criticized the clerics, their paralyzing knowledge and their abuse of power. She reproached them for predicating in order to receive favors or fame; she blamed them for a spirituality that did not feed the soul, because, precisely, they did not understand its workings. She contended that the faithful ought to be able to read the gospels and prayers in French.[93] She strongly opposed the institution of the church and its demand for lifeless piety and mindless conformity. She reproached the priests for confusing their ecclesiastical function with an apostolic calling:

> Almost all priests believe that because they are priests they necessarily are called to the apostolic path. . . . They cannot suffer that those among lay people who have received the apostolic mission from God answer the call; for, they say, they are not priests. They do not see that these souls are priests according to the order of Melchisédec: they are priests in Jesus Christ. This does not mean that those among the clergy who have an interior life are not called to the apostolate; they have then two functions.[94]

It is obvious that Guyon's demand for spiritual equality, as well as her reproaches to church hierarchy and to the clergy, have a gender dimension as well as a lay dimension. She clearly stated that God did not differentiate between men and women when he bestowed his grace for apostolic mission.[95] First she used the same argument employed by other female mystics to justify their desire to teach:

> God's spirit is communicated to those who belong to Him without reservation. God does not always pay attention to sexual difference because all is equal in His hand. The more the subjects are weak, the better they are to His great designs, because being weak, they are less likely to deflect God's glory onto themselves.[96]

She further warned not to confuse ecclesiastical power with divine empowerment. She stated that God could call to the apostolic mission people who did not yield any power in the hierarchy of the church:

> We should not be surprised that God uses ordinary women to teach the greatest mysteries to learned men. . . . Not only does He permit that great men are instructed by women, but that those among the great men who are later called to the apostolate are sometimes introduced to it by women, and they learn from their mouths the most profound truth.[97]

Her final argument skirts impudence. As a response to Bossuet's insistance that a woman was unable as well as forbidden to teach anything, she responded: "If God is capable of making a she-donkey talk, why not a woman?"[98]

Yet, for all her egalitarian and antiauthoritarian impulses, Madame Guyon did not conceive that society could or should be changed through revolutionary means, or even through vindications of the rights of women. Viewed from the standpoint of the feminists' debate in her own time, such as Marie de Gournay on women's education, Madeleine de Scudéry on marriage, or Poullain de la Barre on biological equality between the sexes, Guyon's position appears especially reactionary. This nonchallenge to the status quo is manifest in the great disparity between the independence Guyon acquired through her spiritual practice and the conformity she imposed upon her daughter through the decisions she made for her. Indeed, in the short moral treatise that she wrote especially for her, Madame Guyon's demanding and heroic mystical principles are transformed into conformist and traditional precepts, whereby she admonishes her daughter to be humble, modest, and self-effacing.[99] Guyon remitted her treatise to Fénelon for his approval. He agreed with her advice to young ladies, especially with respect to the avoidance at all times of worldly display of beauty and wealth.[100] When her daughter turned thirteen, Madame Guyon decided to marry her off. Her haste seems to have been a reaction to the blackmail of Harley de Champvallon, the Archbishop of Paris. It was he who acquiesced to release her from her first incarceration, on the condition that she accept the marriage of her daughter to his nephew, an offer Madame Guyon refused. The haste with which she took it upon herself to act can be understood as a wish to secure for her daughter a husband of whom she, as a mother, approved. Her daughter, however, begged her mother not to marry her at such a tender age.[101] Seeming to forget what she had gone through during her own imposed marriage, and notwithstanding the fact that in her autobiography she had confided that sexuality under such conditions was a kind of hell, Madame Guyon proceeded with the matter.[102] What, no doubt, constituted a drama for the daughter, received but three short entries in Guyon's autobiography. Her daughter's marriage was not an event for her; it was a date, a chronological benchmark in her memory of her own experiences.[103] In her correspondence with Fénelon, the mentions of her daughter's marriage show that the mother perceived it as a business transaction and moral decision.[104] Once she was married, as Guyon confided in Fénelon, she did not think of her daughter anymore: "All I can tell you is that as long as my daughter was my own, I said and did what I thought was my duty. As soon as through her marriage she belonged to another, I felt I let go of everything that concerned her in worldly life, without even being able to have any part in it."[105] On the eve of her daughter's marriage, she described her role as a mother as follows: "My daughter was all the more dear to me, as she had cost me dearly to raise, and in that I had tried, with divine help to uproot her moral defects, and to put her in the disposition of having no will, which is the best disposition for a girl of that age. She was not quite twelve years old."[106] Once a widow herself, the daughter disavowed her mother's intentions for her. She remarried a man who loved and chose her as his wife despite the fact that she could not have children. She was beautiful and enjoyed it, lived a brilliant and worldly life, and tried to prevent the publication of her mother's autobiography, probably because it would embarrass her and compromise the life she had chosen for herself.[107]

Like protofeminists of her time, Madame Guyon attempted to come to terms with the feelings of injustice, revolt, and bitterness.[108] Indeed, there is much evidence that female mystics used silent meditation in order to deal with unbearable suffering, a suffering, which, in the case of women, can be attributed to social oppression. Guyon wrote that in order to bear the suffering of life, nothing less powerful than orison would do.[109] But she and the mystics to whom she can be compared did not project their desire for change upon the world and its status quo; instead they directed it toward themselves. It is as if they were so profoundly convinced that society could not change that they set out to change themselves in order to achieve freedom and fulfillment through means other than challenging the status quo. Their position was that in a world pregnant with suffering and alienation (and that appeared immovable), opposition and revolt could only bring about new suffering. The only solution was for them to employ a powerful mind practice in order to extricate themselves from the contingencies of their world. This is what Madame Guyon suggested:

[A] bone, for instance, which is displaced from the locus in which the economy of divine wisdom had put it, does not cease to hurt until it returns to its natural order. Where do so many troubles, so many reversals come from? It is because the soul did not want to remain in its place, nor be satisfied with what it had and with what happens in time.[110]

Chapter Seven

The Quarrel of Quietism and the Construction of Modern Femininity

istorians agree that the Quietist Affair explicitly put on trial the precepts of Western mysticism. I argue in this chapter that it implicitly also put on trial female mystics and their charismatic claims that, precisely because they were a weaker vessel, they were thus more likely to channel the will and the words of God. Through close reading of Bossuet's theological work, *Instruction sur les états d'oraison*, and his satirical text against Guyon, *Relation sur le quiétisme*, I show that a new conception of femininity was being elaborated at the same time as mysticism was being evacuated from Western epistemology. I follow this construction of a new femininity through the historical texts written over a period of two centuries after the Quietist Affair. These texts, ignoring available archival or published material that would have vindicated Madame Guyon, conferred instead the status of historical truth upon Bossuet's biased narrative of the Quietist Affair. My argument points to the fact that Madame

Guyon was not a mere medium or an alibi in a homosocial struggle between Bossuet and his former disciple, Fénelon. In the Quietist Affair, the female body, once more, became the sight of strategies of control, but this time the antagonists were no longer God and the Devil, nor orthodoxy versus heresy, but rather rationality against superstition, sanity against madness, and masculinity against femininity.

Bossuet, Antimysticism, and the Invalidation of the Female Mystic

Antimysticism in the seventeenth century in general, and particularly Bossuet's antimystic response to Madame Guyon and Fénelon in the Quietist Affair, can be understood as the result of the vast epistemological change that affected Western civilization during the Renaissance. De Certeau has studied the effect of the epistemological transformation on the religious sciences between the sixteenth and seventeenth centuries.[1] Before the Renaissance, religious sciences were divided into three branches: symbolic theology, which ruled the knowledge of sensible things; scholastic theology, which ruled the knowledge of intelligible things; and mystical theology, which described the ascension of the soul to pure divine light.[2] Within the context of an analogical epistemology, these three theologies were understood as part of a unitary system, that is, as branches of a unique knowledge.

According to de Certeau, the unitary system underpinning religious sciences dissolved in the Renaissance; the three theologies remained, but subsequently appeared as competing bodies of religious knowledge, hostile to one another. Most notably, scholastic theology and mystical theology competed against each other, each claiming to possess the truth as well as the only method to reach it. Mystical theology, which referred to the experiences of mystics as the source of divine knowledge, denied scholastic theologians any competence. Cutting ties with the latter, they refined their theology outside the university. They acknowledged the writings of Pseudo-Dionysius as founding the authority to which they subscribed. In return, scholastic theology questioned the validity of the mystics' experience from which mystical theology was drawn, and thus it put into question the validity of the religious knowledge the mystics claimed to have gained from their holy experiences.

At the end of the seventeenth century, fueled by the strengthening of a new epistemology, the clash between the two theologies came to a climax. In the eyes of the antimystics of the time, mysticism, quietism, and pure love became synonymous, thereby taking on a pejorative connotation. Antimystics came to conceive of mysticism as a new invention unauthorized by tradition. Within the church itself, the development of historiography and critical history, ushered in by the work of Richard Simon, was influenced by Cartesianism and reinforced antimystic feelings. According to Jacques Le Brun:

> The theologians close to the Jansenists, such as Nicole, du Vaucel, M. de Ponchâteau, as well as Bossuet, found in the condemnation of Molinos, and in the so-called scandals denounced on this occasion, not only a confirmation of their intellectualism and active piety, but also a legitimation of their hostility to what they called "mystiqueries" (as Ponchartrain wrote in 1687), or "mystagogies" (as Richard Simon wrote in 1690).[3]

We must not forget that Bossuet had Jansenist sympathies, and that some Jansenists such as Nicole, and members of the male coterie residing at Port Royal were much taken by Cartesian philosophy.[4] Bossuet, at one time, even believed he had found in Descartes's thought a reinforcement for the church apologia, even though he later became wary of the repercussions of Cartesian philosopy on traditional faith, because the freethinkers now also invoked their own reason for judging the tradition.[5] Bossuet then pushed Fénelon to undertake a refutation of Malebranche.[6]

Although Bossuet's stand on mysticism is contradictory, it nevertheless is paradigmatic of most antimystic Catholics of the seventeenth century. His objection to mysticism addressed three main topics: authority, anti-intellectualism, and the question of extraordinary graces, manifested as miracles or bodily phenomena.

For Bossuet, there was no doubt that authority was assigned, in a decreasing order, to Scripture, tradition, liturgy, examples, and individuals. As for the latter two categories, they had to be approved by the church and conform to tradition. So it is not surprising that one of his main complaints against Guyon, and mystics in general, should have been centered on their refusal to accept the claim that the institution of the church and its theologians alone retained authority in matters of spirituality. Although the mystics had always had to contend with the church's desire for control and approval, it remained that they understood their relationship to God as direct and unmediated. For Bossuet, on the contrary, the faithful had no business finding their own methods; following common morality and the precepts of the church should suffice. He refused to make an exception for the mystics where the church had made one before. It was unavoidable that Bossuet and Guyon clashed on the ground of authority alone; but a profound epistemological difference ran even deeper.

Bossuet also believed that Christian life was based on an intellectual rapport with the divine and was filtered through the Scriptures, the tradition, the Fathers, and, above all else, the authority of the church.[7] If he harped on the necessity for a faith based on tangible truths, it was because it seemed to him impossible and unintelligible that there could exist contemplation without images, memory, traces in the mind, ideas, or intellectual considerations.[8] It is certain that until the outset of the Quietist Affair in 1692, Bossuet was not aware of any other way of apprehending the divine within his own tradition, not having read the great mystics who flourished from the thirteenth century on. If Bossuet was at first ignorant of the mystical tradition of the church, once he was confronted with it, he revealed that he was unable to accept its doctrine. In fact, he was unaware that the "newness" with which he reproached the mystics was ironically of his own invention. Once faced with the mystical mode of apprehension of the divine (partly through his reading of Madame Guyon's *Justifications*), he could not understand their anti-intellectualism and detachment from even the desire for salvation. He was incensed by their individualism, and, on the whole, antagonistic to the implications of their doctrine. Already in 1691, he opposed the notion of passivity or nonvolition, as well as the idea that one might reach a permanent state of bliss in this life.[9] In 1692, he opposed the idea of detachment and indifference to one's own salvation and to rewards.

Yet, all these mystical notions had previously been accepted by the church for a few chosen.

Finally, Bossuet objected equally strongly to the mystics' notion of extraordinary graces, manifested as miracles or bodily signs. It is in this objection that one can fully appreciate the extent to which Gallican antimystics were, unknowingly perhaps, influenced by a new epistemology. Although Bossuet granted that God could speak directly through a human and that He intervened in the realm of human nature (which was, after all, the essential notion of revelation), this occurred, according to Bossuet, in only very rare instances. In ancient times, all had been revealed once and for all, and therefore there was no need to have it repeated. So Bossuet denied that the mystical experiences (bodily or otherwise) of numerous mystics since the thirteenth century could be of the same miraculous nature as that of Biblical characters, the Apostles, or the Fathers of the church at the time of revelation. Reversing the medieval belief that women were more prone to channel divine will, Bossuet insisted that the Virgin Mary was undoubtedly the only woman who had ever received this extraordinary grace. Such graces granted to the ancient Fathers or the Virgin Mary were, according to Bossuet, bestowed gratuitously by God; in other words, they were not the result of efforts on the part of the faithful and no method could prepare or induce this result, as the mystics claimed. For him, the experiences related by the mystics, from the thirteenth century on, ought to be attributed either to their poetic imagination or to their use of extravagant language. In this way, he satisfied both the tradition that allowed for extraordinary graces and miracles and the new modern epistemology that looked at contemporary miracles and bodily manifestations of piety with suspicion and derision. Last, although he reluctantly admitted that mystical experience was valid only if it matched theological dogma, he was particularly hostile to any mention of bodily experience, as witnessed in his violent reaction to these phenomena in Guyon's autobiography.

Yet, Bossuet could not throw all the mystics into one bag and easily dispose of them, because the church had canonized some and recognized others. He had to take into account François de Sales, Teresa of Avila, John of the Cross, Balthazar Alvarez, Catherine of

Genoa, Ruysbroeck, Tauler, and a few others. He overcame this paradox by reducing those recognized mystics to a banal status and by refusing to admit that their doctrine was similar to that propounded by contemporaries he called the "new mystics." On the contrary, he insisted that what the official mystics related in their spiritual autobiographies was but ordinary, Christian morality and ordinary experience of God's grace.

Sure that his position was a traditional one, in 1697, Bossuet wrote the *Instruction sur les états d'oraison* in which he attempted again to prove that the new mystics, among whom Madame Guyon figured prominently, were heretical and insubordinate. Remaining mainly on theological ground, this work could still give the illusion that the Quietist Affair was strictly a doctrinal debate. Close reading of this text, however, reveals several slippages which point at once to a new epistemology, a dismissal of mysticism, and a novel conception of femininity.

In order to bolster his position and to prove that his was the position the church had always held, Bossuet leaned on Jean Gerson, Grand Chancellor of the University of Paris in the fifteenth century, who had himself wrestled with the intensification of mysticism in his time. Indeed, both Gerson and Bossuet worried that mysticism was taking to the streets and thus was by-passing official hierarchy. Bossuet was concerned that lay men and ignorant women would meddle in theology and in the interpretation of Scripture. Invoking Gerson, Bossuet posed the problem as follows, in the opening of his *Instruction*: "[The new mystics] would have it that experience be the [sole] source of truth; and in order to give free rein to their imagination they disparage knowledge and scholars."[10] Bossuet pursued: "[To trust experience alone] is a devious means to avoid judgements of sound theology, and in general to avoid the authority of ecclesiastical judgements."[11] The true mystics, he added, would be recognized by their total acceptance of the authority of official theologians. He purposely skewed his interpretation of the life of Teresa of Avila when he represented her as an obedient woman who scrupulously mediated her experience through the church and the clerical hierarchy: "In her directors, Saint Teresa wanted to find both knowledge and experience. But if one of these elements came to fail, she preferred a scholar to a priest who would have had only mystical experience."[12] Similarly, he commended Catherine of Genoa for what he claimed to be her exemplary obedience and constant reference to her confessor: "In conformity with [obedience to church hierarchy], [Catherine of Genoa], unlike the mystics of our days, continuously asked her confessor for explanations. Without this constant recourse [to ecclesiatic and scholarly knowledge], she experienced inexplicable torments."[13]

Invoking the sixty-fourth proposition of Molinos, which was condemned in the *Pastor Coelis*, Bossuet attributed it solely to those he called the "new mystics," notwithstanding the fact that several recognized mystics had uttered similar statements:

Theologians [according to the new mystics] are less disposed to contemplation than are the ignorant, because theologians have less faith, less humility, and less concern for their own salvation; moreover, their heads are full of ghosts, images, opinions, and speculations, all of which block the entrance of true light. From such an argument the new mystics conclude that the theologians are not fit for judging such matters, and that contemplation admits no other judges than contemplatives themselves.[14]

The struggle between hierarchical authority and mystical claims is indeed traditional, one also expressed by Gerson in the beginning of his career. Similarly on the doctrinal level, the debate in *Instruction* can appear on the whole traditional, Bossuet charging the new mystics and Guyon with the same accusations that were leveled against Marguerite Porète, the Beghards, and Beguines in the fourteenth century, or Molinos in the seventeenth century: "Before proceeding to the examination [of the new mystics], one must be attentive to the decisions taken by the ecumenical Council of Vienna, in the presence of Pope Clement V, against the Beghards and Beguines, because these decisions have a direct bearing upon the matter [of the new mystics]."[15]

The positions of Bossuet and Gerson are, however, not parallel, as Bossuet was far more categorical than Gerson in his conviction that experience "is subordinated totally to theological science, which is informed by tradition, the only source of true principles."[16] Indeed, Gerson had been writing within the epistemological framework that conceived of the three branches of theology (symbolic, scholastic, and mystic) as contributing equally to one, unique knowledge. Gerson's problem in his *De probatione spirituum* had been to set guidelines to try to discern "true" mystics from "false" ones; that is, he had tried to put scholastic theology in the service of mystical theology.[17] Also, in his *De mystica Theologia* he had attempted to establish the a priori conditions that would allow for a study of the phenomenon of mystical experience. Gerson did not put into question mysticism as a mode of apprehending the divine, as Bossuet did; on the contrary, his own spirituality belonged to what is known as *devotio moderna*, or the devotion of negative mysticism.[18] It is true that Gerson had early reservations concerning the German-Flemish mystical doctrine. In particular, he had objected to the notions that an immovable state of spiritual perfection could be achieved before death, and that human individuality could be dissolved into the divine.[19] Bossuet, of course, amplified Gerson's reservations and elaborated on them, notwithstanding the fact that Gerson later abandoned his objections and espoused the doctrine of the German-Flemish mystics, a reversal that led to his being attacked by official theologians.[20] In her *Justifications*, Guyon also quoted Gerson to support her arguments, and in this she showed that she understood better than Bossuet where Gerson stood vis-à-vis mysticism. Bossuet's endeavor, as opposed to Gerson's, took place within an epistemology in which scholastic and mystical theology had come to be conceived of as two hostile and mutually exclusive ways of understanding the divine. Bossuet's enterprise, unlike Gerson's, was to indict mysticism altogether.

Probably genuinely unaware of the difference between his own framework and Gerson's, Bossuet, leaning on Gerson, operated a first rhetorical manipulation to prove that the mystic movement that sprung up in the thirteenth century was a recent trend, alien to the true, ancient tradition of the church: "A few centuries ago, several people who are called mystics or contemplatives, introduced in the Church a new language which has not pleased all."[21] The adjective *new*, to which Bossuet gave a negative value when it concerned piety or dogma, summarily delegitimizes and marginalizes the German and Flemish school of mysticism of the fourteenth century, despite later corrections to this first assertion. The adjective also allows a juxtaposition and an equation of the mystical

tradition of the church with the new mystics of his century, whom
Bossuet accused of heresy.

A second rhetorical manipulation is effected by Bossuet, one
which concerns Guyon and women in general. Despite his blanket
indictment of all mystics (men and women) and despite the fact
that Guyon was the only woman among the new mystics Bossuet
accused,[22] she was nevertheless the centerpiece of his trial both as
a mystic and as a woman.[23] According to him, Falconi opened the
path, Molinos (a Jesuit) proposed abominable principles, Malaval
(a layman without theology) followed suit, and Madame Guyon, the
worst of the group, explained and systematized these abomina-
tions.[24]

Finally, Bossuet quoted Gerson, who had referred to the heretical Beguines. In order to do a disservice to Guyon, Bossuet implied
that Gerson was speaking of all women who had mystical claims:

> Gerson adds, there are women among [those who measure
> truth solely according to their experience] who are unbelieva-
> bly subtle, whose writings sometimes contain very good things,
> but their pride and the vehemence of their passion persuade
> them that they have received these gifts from God; they de-
> scribe their so-called blessed visions in terms only appropriate
> for eternal bliss.[25]

Through this series of rhetorical blurrings, Bossuet established a
parallel between the fourteenth-century mystics, the new mystics
of his day, and the heretical Beghards and Beguines of the fourteenth century. More particularly, Bossuet established a parallel
between the heretical Beguines and Madame Guyon as "women
who dogmatize under the veil of sanctity."[26] The blurring of distinctions and differences allowed Bossuet to lump together "true" and
"false" mystics, heretical Beguines, and Madame Guyon. This slip-
page, which occurs frequently in Bossuet's writing, allowed him not
only to assimilate all mysticism to heresy, but also to imply that
women, mysticism, and heresy were all but synonymous. For, Bossuet implied, a woman who thinks that God speaks to her and who
believes that she has an apostolic mission *is* a heretic.

Ostensibly Bossuet's endeavor in *Instruction* concerned doctrine alone. But linked to the doctrinal question of mysticism are

the questions of extraordinary graces, miracles, and the role of the body in piety, all of which, in turn, were themselves intrinsically linked to a certain notion of femininity. Again, it is not by chance that it was a woman who served as a catalyst for the elimination of the mystical tradition from Western episteme. Indeed, the status of extraordinary graces and miracles, together with the role of the body in piety, was central to the debate between promystics and antimystics in the seventeenth century. As we might expect, Bossuet's and Guyon's stands on the matter differed.

Guyon's stance vis-à-vis bodily manifestations and extraordinary grace, although contradictory, is traditional, both with regard to sensory and to negative mysticism. On the experiential level, her autobiography does not differ from autobiographies or biographies of many female saints, or from sensory mystics of earlier centuries. It relates that throughout her life she experienced not only dreams (which she interpreted as prophetic) and silent communications with her disciples (during which she claimed she channeled the Holy Spirit), but also various bodily manifestations or illnesses (which she interpreted as holy signs).

On the doctrinal level, however, in keeping with negative mysticism, she stated that extraordinary graces were not the goal of spiritual life but rather intermediary stages or even obstacles.[27] She propounded that "the interior path knows no light, no strength, no power, no ecstasies, no ravishings, no miracles, all of which give credibility and reputation to those who experience them."[28] All these manifestations, she argued, are inferior graces precisely because they use the senses and the mental faculties, and also because they might be illusions or the subterfuge of the Devil.[29] The worst of these phenomena were the ecstasies and the visions,[30] and a good spiritual teacher, she believed, should not let disciples arrest their development at these manifestations.[31] She claimed that the spiritual level she had reached was far superior to all sensory manifestations. She nevertheless considered her perfect state as the most splendid of God's gifts to one of His chosen creatures, and thus as a miracle.[32] We recognize in Guyon's doctrinal stance, if not in the narrative of her life, echoes of Marguerite Porète's disdain for bodily manifestations as well as echoes of John of the Cross's dark path of the *Ascent of Mount Carmel*.

On the doctrinal level, with regard to visions, ectasies, and other extraordinary graces, Madame Guyon expressed the same ideas as Marie de l'Incarnation. In keeping with the teaching of negative mysticism, they both conceived of the spiritual path as stripped of all sensory or parapsychological phenomena. But Marie de l'Incarnation differs from Madame Guyon in that she claimed she stopped experiencing these phenomena. Madame Guyon, according to her autobiography, experienced them throughout her life, and even seemed to waver in her appraisal of the extraordinary. For example, referring to her prophetic dreams, she attempted to apologize for seeming to attach importance to them: "The reader might be surprised that I narrate these dreams while at the same time I pay little attention to the extraordinary." In the same breath, however, she gives three legitimizing reasons for her recounting these experiences: "First, I have promised to omit nothing of what comes through my mind; second, I narrate my dreams because it is the channel God uses to communicate His will to the pure souls, in order that they might know their future. . . . These mysterious dreams may be found everywhere in the Scriptures."[33] In fact, Guyon practiced this double stand constantly: on the one hand, she strongly denied any importance, or even divine origin, to bodily manifestations and to the extraordinary; while on the other hand, her autobiography is permeated with such experiences and she seems, at times, to narrate them in order to legitimize her claim to election. We may recognize in this hesitation the relativization of bodily phenomena de Certeau claims in mystics of the Renaissance and seventeenth century, under the growing suspicion of such phenomena by the theologians. But we must not forget that negative mysticism held bodily manifestations as unreliable or even negative phenomena. Bossuet, not blind to Guyon's ambiguity, later used it against her.

It has been mentioned that in order not to disallow the church's past approval of certain mystics, Bossuet reduced them to a banal status by insisting that what they related in their spiritual autobiographies was but ordinary, Christian morality and ordinary experience of God's grace. It is noteworthy that when Bossuet praised Teresa of Avila, Catherine of Genoa, or other female mystics, he did so by referring to their obedience and to their alleged dismissal of bodily manifestations, as if claiming to have such manifestations, on the part of female mystics, was tantamount to disobedience. The

way he and other antimystics interpreted and used Marie de l'Incarnation is very revealing of the link they were bent on establishing between female obedience, relinquishment of bodily phenomena, and the alleged desire of these female mystics to conform to a
model of ordinariness. Indeed, Marie de l'Incarnation's relinquishment of austerities and extraordinary experiences did not go unnoticed by Bossuet and other antimystics. From 1677, when her
autobiographical accounts were first published with much trepidation by her son, all through the Quietist Affair which started
around 1693, Marie de l'Incarnation remained free of the suspicion
and ridicule suffered by other mystics. Furthermore, during the
Quietist Affair itself, as bitter debates raged between the proponents and adversaries of mysticism, Marie de l'Incarnation as a
mystic found favor in antimystics' eyes. The Jansenist Nicole,
whose antimystical stand is notorious, had but praise for her,[34] and
Bossuet held her as a model for all religious women. To one of his
dirigées who had inquired about how she should feel about the
spirituality of Marie de l'Incarnation, Bossuet wrote in 1695 that
everything in her book was admirable, even though he had just
completed his *Ordonnance sur les états d'oraisons* in which he condemned the books of Molinos, Malaval, Madame Guyon, Dom La
Combe, and mysticism in general. Two years later, in his *Instruction*, he praised "the Mother Marie de l'Incarnation, Ursuline, who
is known as the Teresa of our days and of the New World,"[35] all the
while showing no understanding of, nor tolerance for, mysticism.
One can be certain that his praise was not inspired by Marie de
l'Incarnation's negative theology, for he persistently ignored or at-
tenuated the negative theology of those mystics the church had recognized and whom, therefore, he could not dismiss. I suggest that
what made Marie de l'Incarnation acceptable and even laudable as
a mystic to antimystics of the end of the seventeenth century was
her explicit abandonment of bodily manifestations.[36] It is certain
that the categorical way she expressed these noticeable changes in
her attitude was agreeable to the antimystics who headed the Gallican Church at the dawn of the modern world. In fact they used
her especially as an example by which they could beat the mystics
on their own ground and by which they could propose obedience
and ordinariness as a new model for female religious.

Similarly, in order to justify his choice of Teresa as an authority on questions of orison, despite the numerous and notorious bodily manifestations she experienced, Bossuet said that Teresa looked down upon these manifestations, and that far from considering them as signs of God, she thought of them as weaknesses.[37]

What had disappeared between Gerson and Bossuet is nothing less than the very possibility for women to receive charismatic calling. Assuredly, the church, never lacking in misogynist contempt, had always been suspicious of women who proclaimed that they had been inspired by God, and who, in order to prove it, exhibited paranormal bodily manifestations. Above and beyond a change in epistemology, it is certain that what perturbed Gerson and Bossuet alike was the female body in the midst of piety, and that their common agenda was to curb female enthusiasm and to control women's claim to a charismatic apostolate. However, Gerson and Bossuet differed greatly. True, Gerson had stated:

> The female sex is forbidden on apostolic authority to teach in public, that is either by word of mouth or writing. . . . All women's teaching is to be held suspect unless it has been examined diligently and much more fully than men's. The reason is clear, common law—and not any kind of common law, but that which comes from on high—forbids them. And why? Because they are easily seduced and are themselves determined seducers, and because it is not proved that they are witnesses to divine grace.[38]

But it is also true that something inherent to a premodern epistemology made it possible even for the most misogynist cleric to admit that women could be the channel of God's voice and that their mystical experiences could be an intervention of the divine in human life. It is well established that women were allowed to be prominent in the Western mystical movement and that it was the only movement in Western civilization in which they not only partook but also in which they led. Caroline Walker Bynum has amply documented the prominence of women in sensory mysticism, and she has described fully their role in influencing piety in the late Middle Ages. The same is true for negative mysticism. Certain themes of the spirituality of the two Hadewijchs influenced the whole of German-Flemish spirituality in the fourteenth century, as well as the rest of Europe until well into the sixteenth century: total detachment, loss of self, nudity, vacancy of the mind, simple ground of being, spark of the soul, perpetual mirror within oneself, love without cause, union with the divine without intermediaries. All these themes are immediately recognizable to the readers of Ruysbroeck and Eckhart.[39] The latter owned a copy of Marguerite Porète's book, and others were found in several men's convents in Germany and the Netherlands.

In the seventeenth century, this tradition was renewed with great fervor in Western Europe. In Italy, the mystics renewed a tradition established in the past by Maria Maddalena Pazzi. Madame Acarie, Marie de l'Incarnation, and Madame Guyon were female representatives of the French school of mysticism. Cardinal de Bérulle, founder of this school, was himself inspired by the anonymous *Perle évangélique*, probably written by a Beguine in the sixteenth century, and which is itself inspired by the writings of the Beguine Hadewijch.[40] Other female mystics were also important for the development of mysticism in France during this period. Jeanne Lydie Goré has documented the direct influence of Catherine of Genoa (1447–1510) and also her indirect influence, through John of the Cross, who owned a copy of her *Vita*.[41] Henri Brémond also revealed the impact of the Italian Isabella Bellinzaga, whose *Breve Compendio* was translated, without any mention of her name, by Cardinal de Bérulle.[42]

The fact that Gerson sought to establish guidelines for recognizing "true" mysticism and that he still allowed, although with much suspicion, for the possibility of a "true" female calling, was not reflected in Bossuet's position. It was accepted in premodern times that women were more predisposed than men to channel divine or devilish will, and the problem for theologians had been to discern whether it was God or the Devil who spoke through the mystic (schooled or unschooled, layman or "just woman"). In Bossuet's time things were changing, and it was any claim to mystical experience itself, bodily or otherwise, that was refuted as a basis for truth, together with the conception of the body as a channel traversed with divine will. The repercussion of this new attitude had the potential of placing female religious or female mystics into an extremely difficult position. Since the thirteenth century, bodily experiences had been the only proof they could offer for the recognition of their divine election and their right to name the truth.

Consequently, we may ask: If Bossuet, influenced by new epistemology, held that the body was no longer the locus of divine truth, if female mystics' bodily manifestations were no longer the mark of God, what was then for him the significance of these manifestations?

Either ignoring or denying that at one time the church might have held a different opinion, Bossuet turned to Gerson when he referred to the Beguines' condemnation in the fourteenth century. He attempted to prove that the church had never considered female religious' bodily manifestations as divinely inspired: "They were not listened to at the Council of Vienna; and despite their boasts concerning their [bodily manifestations] which [the Council] looked upon as signs of the Devil's deceptions, *and* in any case as vain transports of an overheated imagination."[43] The copula "and," which I have emphasized, would indicate a series of compatible elements; however the two interpretations Bossuet lends to Gerson and to the Council of Vienna concerning the Beguines' bodily manifestations are incompatible. If these bodily signs are interpreted as an act of the Devil, they cannot be easily dismissed because they are serious. Further, they prove that the body of women can indeed be acted upon by extraordinary forces. But, if they are interpreted as "vain transports of an overheated imagination," that is, as madness, they can be judged as vain and dismissible, or at least of no serious consequence, perhaps even ridiculous. In any case, Bossuet was certainly disconcerted by the question of bodily manifestations. In his *Instruction*, one already witnesses a shift, however faint, within the church itself between an old conception of the body and a new one, an old conception of femininity and a new one.

Toward a Formulation of Modern Femininity

Despite all their attempts to have mysticism condemned by the entire church, Bossuet and the Gallican antimystic faction might not have won if the debate had remained on theological grounds. It should be recalled that the partisans of the Gallican Church, supported by Louis XIV, were angry at Fénelon for having submitted his *Maximes* to the decision of the Pope.[44] On April 30, 1698, the examiners of the Holy Office split the vote: five voted in favor of the orthodoxy of Fénelon's *Maximes*; five voted against it. The split vote in Rome is proof that the antimystic feelings in the seventeenth century were not confined to the Gallican Church but were part of a wider, Western, epistemological change. A victory for Fénelon's orthodoxy meant a victory for Guyon. Encouraged by his nephew, the Abbé Bossuet, who was his supporter in Rome and who assured him that nothing short of character assassination would make the scales tip in the favor of the antimystic faction, Bossuet changed tactics and abandoned doctrinal arguments in favor of personal defamation against both Fénelon and Guyon. Bossuet, prince of the church and eminent theologian, showed that he was indeed capable of resorting to the basest tactics in order to win the debate.

Bossuet singled out the themes of the extraordinary in Guyon's autobiography, focusing on the question of the body's role in piety. By emphasizing her bodily manifestations in order to detract from her negative mystical doctrine, Bossuet drew attention away from the theological debate in which Guyon stood firm. His sole focus on her body made her especially vulnerable to the rationalists' irony. Madame Guyon understood, though unfortunately too late, that her autobiography provided Bossuet with the very weapon that would allow him to emerge victorious.[45] Under his pressure, she started making excuses for these alleged "objectionable" matters; in her first letter to him, just before the Issy examination in 1693, she wrote: "I only beg you, Monseigneur, to consider that I never confused piety with extraordinary manifestations, and that I attribute little importance to them, as I have already told you."[46] At that point, she sensed that the problem of bodily manifestations, which for her was secondary, was being used to obfuscate the primary debate concerning her mystical doctrine and her agreement with the tenets of accepted mystics. Madame Guyon's fears were well founded.

Indeed, Bossuet's hesitations in his *Instruction* regarding the interpretation of female mystics' bodily experiences were resolved in his following work, *Relation sur le quiétisme*, in which they became solely contemptible. Here, Bossuet focused almost exclusively on these experiences, as if by laughing them off or by arousing disgust for them he could automatically dismiss mysticism and disqualify it as an illegitimate experience. His move paid off because the public at large was ripe for such a dismissive attitude.

The *Relation sur le quiétisme* was published in 1698 and presented to the king on June 26 of that year. What doctrinal debate was unable to achieve, satire did. At Versailles, the effect of the book was devastating for Fénelon (Guyon was already in the Bastille), and the examiners and cardinals in Rome who had been up to this point in favor of Fénelon were shaken. Bossuet's uncle, Antoine Bossuet, summed up the effect that Bossuet's satire on Guyon and Fénelon had on public opinion: "All of Marly, from the royal scepter down to the shephard's crook, is reading and rereading the *Relation*; all of Paris is doing likewise."[47] Its publication was instrumental in allowing the pressure applied by Louis XIV and the Gallicans to tip the scales in favor of antimysticism.

By its tone and its literary devices, this work belongs to the genre of polemical and satirical literature, akin to Pascal's *Provinciales* and to Molière's *Les Femmes savantes* and *Les Précieuses ridicules*. Just as Molière's comic representation of the ridiculous "précieuses" succeeded in ridiculing women of learning for centuries to come,[48] Bossuet's *Relation* created its own historical object of derision, the ridiculous mystical Guyon, and, by extension, the ridiculous, lascivious, hysterical female mystic. But what is even more significant is that subsequent historians agreed with Molière and Bossuet and bestowed upon the literary creations of these two men the status of historical and sociological truth.[49]

By its sometimes vulgar and risqué insinuations, *La Relation* is a libelous pamphlet. Citing out of context certain details of *La Vie de Mme* and arranging them according to his own satirical designs, lying, insinuating false accusations, and deforming facts, Bossuet plied his rhetorical wares to denature Guyon's discourse. He was the complete master, all the more so as Guyon was imprisoned by his order and condemned to silence. With a facile and dishonest irony, he subverted Guyon's discourse, strangling her with her own words.[50] Bossuet also proceeded in exactly the same manner with Fénelon, but we know that the effect on Fénelon's life and memory was not as disastrous as for Guyon. Neither Guyon nor Fénelon, whether in their public writings or private letters, delighted in stooping so low and in using a demagogical and satirical tone in order to plead their cause with public opinion. Bossuet's "bourgeois-gentilhomme" mentality could well have been targeted for ridicule by the aristocratic public had either Guyon or Fénelon been inclined to libel or defamation.

Alongside the political intrigues and doctrinal debate, another struggle rages in the *Relation sur le quiétisme*, which is of no lesser importance: the struggle by hierarchical authority to articulate anew its masculine prerogatives around a new epistemology and to rally a concerted defense against the threats represented by a new conception of the female body. The accusation of heresy, which had been in the forefront of the *Instruction* but which had been unable to produce an official condemnation of mysticism or to arouse interest of public opinion, was relegated in the *Relation* to the background, although it did not disappear. While holding on to the notion of heresy, Bossuet's book produced new notions of womanhood that were not always compatible with the old ones, nor with one another. Guyon was portrayed as dangerous, therefore guilty, and deserving the Bastille as well as historical oblivion. At the same time she was depicted as mad, sick, ridiculous, even as a laughing stock, which rendered her innocuous and dismissible. She was portrayed as an ignorant yet sincere woman, who, having acknowledged her mistakes, submitted to the orthodoxy of the church, and thus allowed herself to be controlled; she was also presented as a salacious woman hiding her carnal desires under the cover of piety, like a female Tartuffe; and finally, she was characterized as a woman who claimed authority and demanded a voice and was, therefore, both criminal and ridiculous—both dangerous and dismissible.

According to Bossuet, Guyon's published books threatened the "whole church," the "whole earth," and the "whole universe."[51] Moreover, she was "the true cause of the problems of the church."[52] Forgetting that she was not the only new mystic he condemned, he made her solely responsible for what he considered a heretical movement: "An affair by which indeed the whole church was affected, as what was at stake was nothing less than to prevent the rebirth of quietism, which as we see through the writings of Madame Guyon, was spreading again in this kingdom."[53] He made her responsible for the epistemological and theological debate raging within the church: "It is clear why, in the end, I denounce a woman who is the cause, still today, of the dissentions within the church."[54] He deemed it his duty to reveal to the world the extent of her pernicious doctrine:

> I confess that this was in fact the work of darkness which one ought to keep hidden, and I would have hidden it for ever, as I had done for over three years with an impenetrable silence, if my discretion had not been excessively abused, and if the matter had not reached a point where we must, for the good of the church, make known what is quietly being plotted in its midst.[55]

Not only was the altar threatened with destruction by this one woman, but the throne as well:

> [The king] had learned from a hundred sources that Madame Guyon had found a defender in his court, in his very house, among his princely children; his displeasure was in proportion to his deep piety and his great wisdom . . . for everything was catching fire: all of Europe, and even Rome, where universal astonishment followed the publication of the news.[56]

Bossuet insisted Guyon was dangerous because her doctrine was seductive. She had even seduced a man like Fénelon, a prince of the church, and she was supported by a "party": "The faithful must be forewarned against a seduction which still subsists: a woman who is capable of deceiving souls by such illusions must be exposed, especially since she finds admirers and defenders and a large party on her side, waiting for her novelties."[57] Fénelon was seduced to such a degree that he was beyond recognition, refusing to see the truth about her: "I thought to myself: What? It will be brought to light that if he is breaking with his brethren, it is because he is supporting Madame Guyon? Everyone will therefore see that he is her protector? This suspicion, which dishonored him in the eyes of the public, will become a certitude?"[58] She was so seductive that Bossuet had to brace himself against her power: "I, myself, was full of trepidation, and at each step I feared I might also fall victim to her as such an intelligent man [Fénelon] had done."[59] But above all, Guyon was guilty of separating the "breth-ren" by introducing dissention among them: "You will now see clearer than day what is all too clear already. It is, after all, Ma-dame Guyon who is at the bottom of this affair, and it is solely the desire to support her that separated this prelate from his breth-ren."[60] Bossuet repeated insistently that it was beyond imagination that "a woman who should never have written and who was sen-tenced to eternal silence"[61] could be given so much credit by an intelligent and influential man, and that this man, Fénelon, could thus, for her sake, sever the bond between men and undermine the church, the monarchy, and the social fabric.[62] Her madness could not be simply dismissed, precisely because of Fénelon's support. All of these reasons made her dangerous. Bossuet writes:

> It's already too much to be known publicly as the protector of a [woman] who is a self-appointed prophetess set on seducing the entire universe. If it be said that I speak too harshly against this woman whose frenzy approaches madness, so be it, unless her madness indeed is not fanaticism, unless this woman is not possessed with the will to seduce, unless this Priscilla has not indeed met her Montan to defend her.[63]

For all his talk about the danger that Guyon represented to the altar, the throne, and the brethren, Bossuet was also intent in his *Relation* to ridicule her, knowing very well that ridicule kills. Fe-male mystics' bodily manifestations, which for premodern religious men had been understood as a mark of the divine, became in Guyon's autobiography, under Bossuets' pen, an occasion for laugh-ter and ridicule:

> I had to shed light upon the false mystery of our time. Here is an abbreviated account of it . . . : a new prophetess took it upon herself to resuscitate the *Guide* of Molinos and the ori-son which he taught; her words are stamped with his influ-ence; mysterious woman of the apocalypse,[64] she is pregnant with his teachings. The work of this woman is not finished: she calls our time an age of persecutions, in which martyrs [of her kind] will have to suffer. The time will come, and accord-ing to her the day is already upon us, when the reign of the

Holy Spirit and of her orison, which is the same as Molinos's, will be established, accompanied by a series of miracles that will surprise the universe. Hence her communications of graces; hence her power [to free people of evil]. Her words prove that she has forgotten she has signed before me and my superiors a condemnation of her books and of her doctrine.[65]

She was so ridiculous that Fénelon was reduced to "find[ing] excuses for the enormous boasts of a woman who claimed to be a prophetess and an apostle, with the power to free people from evil, full of overflowing grace and endowed with such an eminent perfection that she could not tolerate the rest of mankind."[66] She was a deluded woman who, in her own opinion, was a "communicator of grace in the unique and prodigious fashion which I have related; furthermore prophetess and accomplishing miracles."[67] It was incomprehensible that a man such as Fénelon could have been taken by her: "I withdrew, astonished to see such a fine mind admiring a woman whose intelligence was so limited, whose qualities so frail, whose illusions so evident, and who played the role of a prophetess!"[68] Fénelon, as an Archbishop, owed it to the church to see through this woman: "As a consequence of her erroneous doctrine and of her unbridled behavior . . . Madame Guyon had become so ridiculous and so odious that prudence and caution should have dictated to Fénelon, from the moment he was named Archbishop of Cambrai, to refuse to commit himself on her behalf."[69]

In order to paint a more effective portrait of Guyon as a person who could be dismissed easily, Bossuet wanted to pass her off as "an ignorant woman who, dazzled by a specious spirituality, fooled by her directors and applauded by a man of [Fénelon's] importance, recanted her error when someone took the trouble to instruct her."[70] He wanted his public to believe that Guyon herself recanted, repented, and admitted she was heretical, which she never did. He wrote that "she accepted the condemnation of her books as containing an erroneous doctrine. She has, moreover, accepted our censorship whereby her published books and all her doctrine were condemned: in the end she has expressedly rejected the major propositions upon which her system rested."[71] She was so submissive, according to him, that all he had to do was to prohibit her "from communicating them, from writing anymore, from teaching, from formulating dogmas, from counselling, condemning her to silence and retreat as she herself requested."[72] She was so insignificant that there was absolutely no reason for Fénelon to make so much of an issue in defending her nor to say that Bossuet had represented her as a monster: "[Your friend was not] 'a monster on earth,' but an ignorant woman who, bedazzled with a specious spirituality, deceived by her directors, applauded by a man of your importance, agreed with the condemnation of her error, when it was pointed out to her."[73] This contradicted, of course, the image of Guyon he also had put forth as a monster of pride. In contrast with the female mystics recognized by the church whose obedience to church hierarchy and whose humility, according to Bossuet, had been their marks of distinction, Guyon and the medieval female heretics were presumptuous.

To win the debate and ensure that laughter would arise on his side, Bossuet did not hesitate to add licentious innuendos to his portrait of Guyon's relationships with her first confessor, La Combe, and also with Fénelon. He compared Fénelon and Guyon to Montanus and Priscilla, Christian sectarians of the early church, who, according to legend, had a sexual relationship. Further, in the Latin version of the *Relation*, which he sent to Rome, Bossuet translated the term *amie*, which Fénelon had used to designate Guyon, with the term *amica* which had the connotation of "mistress." Given this license for a risqué interpretation of Fénelon's own word, Bossuet's nephew, the Abbé Bossuet, alluding to the comparison of Fénelon and Guyon to Montan and Priscilla, added: "There are people prudish enough to prefer using Montanus, instead of Montan [in French, 'mounting'] in order to avoid any [obscene] double entendre."[74]

Bossuet took particular advantage of Guyon's bodily manifestations to ridicule her, although on this score, Guyon was rather sober when compared to Tauler, Teresa of Avila, or Catherine of Genoa, whom he had praised, or Surin, whose book he had authorized.

In the autobiography of this lady, I read that God bestowed upon her such an abundance of grace that she literally was bursting, and that her corset had to be unlaced. She did not forget to mention that a Duchess had once performed this office. In such a state, she often was placed upon her bed; one would just remain seated near her in order to receive her overflowing grace, and this was the only means for giving her relief.[75]

The silent communications between Guyon and her disciples, which, according to him, were sought for their physical effects, were especially revolting to Bossuet: "My heart which would rise up in disgust against her doctrine was even more upset with her silent communications."[76] His first response was to forbid them,[77] for to him they were a proof of her pride and sensuality, the source of her dogmatic error. Presented with such a portrait, the court did not recoil in fear of the dangers supposedly represented by Guyon; it simply laughed and was surprised that she was put in the Bastille rather than in a madhouse.[78]

Perfectly lucid and serene, Madame Guyon challenged Bossuet's contradictory portrait: "Either I am an irresponsible, ignorant and stupid woman, and in that case I am clear of all charges, or else I am fully responsible and lucid and deserve to be judged with attention and good faith."[79] She also pointed out that although Bossuet claimed she was ignorant, he nevertheless treated her with as much severity as he would have a learned theologian who, in full conscience, preached heretical teachings.[80]

With Bossuet's satire of mysticism in his *Relation sur le quiétisme*, mystical experience was firmly reduced to the absurd, to the insignificance of glossolalia, to unreason, to madness. I do not intend to argue, however, that Bossuet, as he was articulating a new notion of femininity, was a misogynist, while Fénelon and the old epistemology were not.

A reading of Fénelon's *De l'éducation des filles* is further evidence that Fénelon was no champion of women's freedom. Both Bossuet and Fénelon were in favor of women's submission, but according to a different episteme.[81] According to Fénelon's older model, although women were inferior, they could nevertheless enjoy charismatic authority, and this is particularly evident in his correspondence with Guyon.[82] But, according to Bossuet's newer model, while women were not only inferior and ignorant, they were also prone to strange, comical, repulsive bodily movements, which referred to nothing but their own uncanniness. As Brémond stated, Madame Guyon and Isabela Bellinzaga[83] (c. 1552–1624) were persecuted largely because they exerted great influence on prominent men (Bellinzaga, on the Jesuit Gagliardi, 1537–1607 and on several other Jesuits besides him) and because they had many followers (Guyon, among members of the *Dévot* Party and St. Cyr).[84] The controversy concerning Guyon and Bellinzaga arose also from the fact that it had become unacceptable for a woman to exercize the role of spiritual director to men.[85] Already in *Instruction*, Bossuet accused Guyon of wanting "to dictate the law to priests and apostolic men,"[86] and he found it scandalous that a man thought he could learn anything from a woman: "[Fénelon] often frightened us, telling us that he had learned more from her than from all learned men together."[87] The time had passed when men thought they could learn God's will through women. Femininity, combined with mysticism, was projected as the "other" of modernity, reason, and masculinity. In the religious arena, the reworking of femininity led to the delegitimization of female claims to charismatic power, with or without psychosomatic manifestations.

Madame Guyon clashed in every way with the demands of the modern church as represented by Bossuet and his antimystic allies. She opposed the rule that women remain silent, obscure, and obedient. She refused the notion that piety must follow unquestioningly the mediation of the clerics. She refuted the claim that the supernatural or the extraordinary be dispelled by reason and common sense, or be reserved to ancient and very selective cases, such as that of the mother of Christ. Finally, she did not believe that the dogma of the Catholic Church should be upheld by the faithful as the only truth or that the body no longer be the locus of God's truth. It is in keeping with what he believed and represented that Bossuet sought a victory over Guyon on authorial and doctrinal grounds. But, the questionable means he employed to achieve his goal reveal also a new era in which Scriptures and alleged divine authority were no longer effective means to disempower women; other discourses had to be invented in order to disqualify them.

Positivist Historiography: The Historian as Hysteric

Bossuet's fabrication of a new femininity, characterized by the mad mystic woman, was perpetuated during the two centuries that fol-

lowed. In the eighteenth and the nineteenth centuries, events related to the Quietist Affair were transposed onto an increasingly
secularized world in which doctrinal debates no longer held the
theoretical weight they had once assumed. The universities were
reformed, a national literary canon was fabricated, and Bossuet
and Fénelon both were enshrined as "classics" of French literature.
Bossuet was dubbed the "Eagle of Meaux"; he represented the *sum-
mum* of French "classical" eloquence. He was represented as a man
whose imposing stature and authority were equal to the reign of
the Sun King, in whose grandeur an increasingly secularized and
democratized France still basked. Fénelon served instead as a second type of national image, one just as important as that of the
imposing authority and "juste mesure" of the reign of Louis XIV.
He was known as the "Swan of Cambrai," a precursor of the French
Revolution and of the Romantic movement.[88]

For two centuries following the Quietist Affair, historians of
seventeenth-century France were divided into two hostile and separate camps: the Bossuetists and the Fenelonians. For Bossuetists,
Fénelon's image remained mainly that given by Bossuet in his *Relation sur le quiétisme*. According to this perspective, Fénelon was
mendacious and infatuated with a madwoman. Fenelonians, in
turn, accused Bossuet of bad faith, and they minimized the impact
that Guyon exerted on Fénelon's spirituality. Although Bossuetists
and Fenelonians were antagonistic to each other, both camps were
invested in making certain that Guyon disappear from history. Her
existence was detrimental both to the memory of Bossuet as a hero
of "classicism" and "juste mesure," and to the memory of Fénelon
as an elegant and sober precursor of the Enlightenment. At the
expense of Guyon, Bossuet's reputation was saved from accusations
that his actions in the Quietist Affair had been reprehensible and
that he had been dominated by less than admirable considerations.
Fénelon, in turn, was saved from having been the disciple of
Guyon, from admitting to childish behavior while following her
spiritual advice, from acknowledging he learned much from a
woman, and from being blamed for having missed the chance of a
great career at court because he defended her. Bossuet states
(words which the Fenelonians internalized): "It was not worthy
of him, of his character, of his public image, of his reputation, of
his mind, to defend the books and the dogma of a woman of that

kind."[89] Unable to make her disappear completely, both camps chose to perpetuate Bossuet's image of Guyon and to minimize her role in the affair. They represented her as psychologically unbalanced, sickly, bizarre, impudent, ridiculous, even monstrous, while minimizing the danger she might have represented to church and throne. Her writing was never included in anthologies of French literature or in literary history until the publication of Jean Rousset's anthology of Baroque poetry in 1961.[90] When Bossuet's views on the Quietist Affair were revised, owing to Fénelon's documents on the affair, historians then chose to present the quarrel as the history of a political and personal confrontation between two great prelates. From Bossuet's contradictory portrait of Guyon as dangerous, mad, and ridiculous, posterity inherited only the view that Guyon was mad and ridiculous.

One historian—Voltaire—perpetuated the idea that the affair was a confrontation between two powerful individuals. In his *Siècle de Louis XIV*[91] Voltaire deprecated both religion and mysticism, and he also dismissed the entire Quietist Affair as much ado about nothing. Yet what is also evident in this work is his great admiration for Bossuet and Fénelon, along with his disdain for Madame Guyon. It is evident that Voltaire did not read *La Vie de Mme*, nor any other work by Madame Guyon. He gleaned certain details of *La Vie de Mme* from the *Relation sur le quiétisme*, which Bossuet had exploited in order to ridicule her. For example, Bossuet had written: "In the autobiography of this lady, I read that God bestowed upon her such an abundance of grace that she literally was bursting, and that her corset had to be unlaced."[92] Voltaire copied the anecdote almost verbatim from Bossuet: "It was strange that [Fénelon] was seduced by a woman of revelations, prophecies, and gibberish, who suffocated from interior grace, to the point of having to be unlaced."[93] The historian Michelet repeated the anecdote in the nineteenth century.

Voltaire added a twist to Bossuet's portrait, which is the version that survived a long time. He invented the fact that she was young and pretty and that her success in spiritual matters was owing to this physical trait: "Tender and impressionable imaginations, especially those of women and some young monks, who love above all to hear the word of God from the mouth of a beautiful woman, were easily touched by this eloquence of speech, so fit to bend ready minds."[94] This is gratuitous invention, for at the time of her successes, Madame Guyon was no longer young, not to mention that she had long been disfigured by smallpox. In addition, Voltaire radically minimized Guyon's role in the affair by insisting on the fact that she was of no importance. He added condescension to ridicule: "[She was] imprisoned at Vincennes, as though she had been a person dangerous to the state. She could not have been, and her pious reveries did not deserve the attention of the sovereign."[95] This was, of course, not the opinion of Bossuet, who wanted to pass her off, or who thought of her, as dangerous, having her arrested by thirty armed men and put in the political prison of the Bastille.

Had Voltaire read her work, he would have recognized in Guyon the tolerance he himself preached but had not always practiced. But could Voltaire have been fair to a woman when it meant that he had to go against the reputation of a "great man" of the past? Probably not. The man who won Voltaire's respect was Bossuet, the champion of the principle of authority and of the spirit of orthodoxy, highly intolerant, and at times dishonest. In Voltaire's dictionary of the major writers of the seventeenth century, in which Guyon is not included, he even found excuses for Bossuet: "Moreover, it was claimed that this great man had philosophical sentiments different from his theology, rather like a wise magistrate who, judging according to the letter of the law, sometimes secretly raises himself above it by the strength of his genius."[96]

In the nineteenth century, the Sorbonne and intellectuals were adamant supporters of Bossuet. Rare were those individuals who attempted a different version or who searched for yet uncovered archives. In 1881, in a dissertation at the Sorbonne, M. Guerrier was more sympathetic to Guyon than his masters, and he dared to present a version of Bossuet as a man who was subject to human frailties. Brunetière, the famous literary historian of the century, rebuked him. According to Brémond, the Sorbonne's phobia for Guyon reached an apogee with Croulé's fanatical denunciation of Guyon's La Vie de Mme on the ground that it was a masterpiece of fabricated accusations against Bossuet. Twentieth-century research has, on the contrary, proven that Guyon's testimony on the affair is credible, while Bossuet's is libel.

The fate of the six-year correspondence between Fénelon and Guyon tells much about the positions historians defended. Only thirteen or fourteen months survive of this correspondence. In 1767 and 1768, Jean-Philippe Dutoit, a pietist disciple of Madame

Guyon, published a new edition of her *Lettres chrétiennes et spiri-tuelles*, to which he added the private letters between Fénelon and Guyon. These letters reveal many aspects of Fénelon's personality and spirituality that ought to have interested historians and editors of his works. The Bossuetists could have pounced on the occasion to vilify Fénelon even more but nothing of the sort occurred and the edition went unnoticed.

Further, from 1820 to 1830, Gosselin, Fénelon's friend, published the latter's entire opus in thirty-four volumes, but omitted Fénelon's letters to Guyon on the pretext that they were apocryphal. No one protested, not even the Bossuetists who could have fueled their cause by pointing to this omission. In 1892 when E. Ritter republished the thirty-eight remaining letters from Fénelon to Guyon, he succeeded in presenting them as unknown, as if they had never been published. This publication, however, did not give rise to the kind of critical discussion that Ritter wished, and only the Bossuetist, Brunetière, mentioned the letters in the bibliographical notes to his article, "Fénelon et la Grande Encyclopédie." The task of authenticating these letters fell to Maurice Masson in 1907, and they changed forever the image of Fénelon that posterity had fabricated. Indeed the silence that surrounded Madame Guyon by Bossuetists and Fenelonians alike underscores the degree to which the historians of the eighteenth and nineteenth centuries needed to adhere to the dominant view not only of Guyon but of femininity.

It was inevitable that the nineteenth century would represent Guyon as simply hysterical. Having been sent to the Bastille, however, gave her an importance belied by this radically simplified portrait. In 1880, Brunetière, who never questioned the facts given by Bossuet concerning the Quietist Affair, attempted to explain why Bossuet would have put Guyon in the Bastille rather than in a madhouse. His reasoning was that while in the seventeenth century hysteria had not yet been discovered, during his own era people knew better; such a woman would have been shut up in the Salpêtrière, the infamous nineteenth-century psychiatric hospital for hysterics, directed by Doctor Charcot.[97]

Brunetière's resolute avoidance of consulting newly found archives, the anti-Guyon fanaticism of Crouslé, and other historians' rage against her all seem to indicate that, even though they could not admit to it, historians perceived her as posing a danger. The portrait they fabricated of Guyon as a dismissible hysteric was to ward off some unspoken fear.

As several critics have shown, Freud's texts on femininity are enlightening about masculine fears and about what men construe as the feminine.[98] They give us a clue as to the danger Guyon represented for these secular, often anticlerical men who could no longer translate their fear in terms of danger to the altar, or to the throne, as Bossuet had done. Sarah Kofman, in her interpretation of Freud, shows how, although rich in his insights, Freud was prisoner of the most traditional ideology concerning the sexes. He hesitated between two accounts of femininity: woman as hysterical, that is, repressed but not knowing the truth about her repression and woman as radical other, narcissistic, and criminal because she knows the truth about women's repression yet dissimulates her knowledge.[99] Whereas the criminal knows men's secret but hides it, the hysteric has a secret of which she is ignorant and which she hides from herself, except that her "symptom" reveals her secret to the public. Kofman adds that even though Freud polarized the hysteric and the criminal woman, he nevertheless thought that the hysteric is always somewhat criminal, because she, too, although unconsciously, dissimulates. So, woman is also always guilty and dangerous, even if she is hysterical and therefore dismissible—a victim of repression or of an oppression of which she is unconscious. Kofman writes:

> It is as if Freud (and men in general) "knew," dream-like fashion, that women were "great criminals," but nevertheless strove, by bringing about such a reversal as occurs in dreams, to pass them off as hysterics, for it is very much in men's interest that women should share their own convictions, should make themselves accomplices to men's crimes, in exchange for a pseudo-cure, a poison-remedy, a "solution" that cannot help being pernicious since it restores speech to women in order to model it on men's, only in order to condemn their "demands to silence."[100]

If we follow this line of thought, the eighteenth- and nineteenth-century historians of the Quietist Affair who wrote about Guyon are the hysterics: they had forgotten something or pretended that Guyon's message constituted no danger to their world. In order to prevent their secret from being discovered, they bandied the image of Guyon as a hysteric, unable to discern the radical implication of her teaching and her practice. Faced with the unprecedented accomplishment of personal freedom on the part of a woman who refused to dissimulate, posterity could only laugh nervously.

Despite trying to pass her off at times as ridiculous and mad, Bossuet had known better. He reproached Guyon for the final state she said she had attained: a naked, desireless state, without intermediary, which placed her beyond the rites and sacraments and which made prayer to the saints, to the Virgin, to Christ or God Himself, useless or impossible. In this state, Guyon could escape Bossuet, and he knew it. For Guyon, the elimination of the logos and of representation culminated in a perfect detachment, in which fear and its corollary, belief, dissolved. She became indifferent to her possible damnation and "even to her salvation and the joys of paradise."[101] The disappearance of logos and of representation preserved her from any possibility of ideological influence. As for detachment and lack of desire, they are not a matter of speculation for her, but rather constitute a rare, lived state. They result in the dissolution, at the ontological level itself, of the master-slave dialectic and of their relationship in a mediated desire. Bossuet threatened Guyon with the stake and with excommunication; he had her thrown in prison for seven years, formally forbade her to write, speak, preach, or meditate. In his own words, he "impose[d] upon her an eternal silence."[102] Not only did he fail to obtain her submission, but what is more, he and everything he represented were negated by her nondesire. Through her nondesire, Guyon made of Bossuet and of the social and ecclesiastical hierarchy with which he so proudly identified an empty theater, void of players and spectators. According to her, the essential happened elsewhere, and all of Bossuet's anger amounted to nought. By the double maneuver of her complete, outward acceptance of orthodoxy and her firm refusal to be cowed by authority, Guyon exposed the superfluous aspect of dogma. She offered an external and conventional obedience to authority, an obedience that in no way encroached on her internal freedom. This significance of Guyon's teaching and resistance was lost on eighteenth- and nineteenth-century positivist historians who, basing themselves on Bossuet's account, retained only the dismissible female mystic.

Chapter Eight

Guyon's Autobiography at the Crossroads of History

For Augustine as well as for female religious autobiographers within the mystic tradition, the individual life and the self were given meaning and coherence solely in reference to God. The new epistemology of the Renaissance and seventeenth century displaced God as the origin of the coherence of the personality, and the cohesion of the self was no longer perceived as originating from divine designs, but rather from human factors. This shift resulted in a change in self-representation.

Most studies concerning autobiography as a genre date the manifestations of a new representation of the self as early as the Renaissance, but agree that it fully bloomed only in the eighteenth century.[1] According to some critics, this new representation of the self is characterized by the ideology of individualism, which is defined as a set of beliefs that fosters a conception of "man" as a metaphysical, universal entity: as a self, existing independently of any particular discourse or style of self-expression, and logically prior to all literary genres and even to language itself. These studies acknowledge Rousseau's *Confessions* as the prototype of this new genre and accept Montaigne's *Essais* as a precursor. They assert, in addition, that Rousseau's *Confessions* differ from earlier representations of the self in that he establishes the origin of personality in the experience of childhood and in social conditions, and that he is the first author to elaborate a causal childhood narrative. Finally, modern autobiography is characterized by the author's reveling in intimate disclosure.[2] Historically, critics link these characteristics of modern autobiography to the development of bourgeois sensibility and social demands. The link made between modern autobiography, the ideology of individualism, and the emergence of democratic demands is supported by Paul Delany in the case of English autobiography.[3] More recently, William C. Spengemann situates autobiography at the center of modernist concerns, and he suggests that the very idea of literary modernism is synonymous with that of autobiography à la Rousseau.[4] In agreement with this point of view, Philippe Lejeune's early studies on autobiography in France strictly reserve the generic label, autobiography, for the literature of the self that appears in the eighteenth century. Some critics support this argument by referring to the fact that the neologism, *autobiographie*, appears in the French language shortly after Rousseau's *Confessions*, precisely to name this new genre as characteristic of the Enlightenment.

While agreeing on the whole with this definition of modern autobiography, Yves Coirault contests the restriction of the term *autobiography* to modern manifestations alone. He feels that certain seventeenth-century memoirs, particularly those of the Cardinal de Retz (written between 1671 and 1675) and those of the Duke of Saint Simon (written in 1699) are indeed autobiographies. According to Coirault, although these two works do not contain childhood narratives, they nevertheless constitute the history of a personality and of a self, as it can represent itself in a certain class and at a certain time. In agreement with Georges Gusdorf, Coirault declares that the opposition between memoirs and autobiography is futile, since memoirs, like the more modern autobiography, derive from an apologetic intent and express a "theodicity of the personal being."[5]

This revision, however awkward it may be in its search for sources and generic ancestors, has the merit of emphasizing the false problematics that preside over the dispute concerning the definition of autobiography as a genre. The point is not to define a genre and then to test which work fits the category, but rather to analyze the evolution of the representation of the self throughout the centuries. As Coirault points out, in fact, there is nothing in Cardinal de Retz's or Saint Simon's memoirs that disqualifies them as autobiographies. As they are memoirs written by aristocrats, they reveal a conception of the self specific to this social group, at a certain time, that is, a theatrical and social self that cannot be conceived in the margins of history. From the same point of view, *The Confessions* would characterize a certain bourgeois sensitivity that favors the individual and his personal history, at the expense of the political and historical circumstances that support the aristocratic self. Seen according to this perspective, autobiography in the mode of Rousseau appears less as a new, "truer" kind of self-representation than as a specific historical mode of representation of the self.

Although Philippe Lejeune's study narrows down the notion of autobiography, it has the merit of emphasizing the importance of the birth of the childhood narrative in the modern conception of the self. This new place of origin of the self was endorsed later, as we know, by psychoanalysis, the "science" that both conveys a bourgeois ideology and analyzes a bourgeois unconscious.

Another kind of historical account of autobiography places the emergence of individualism in the late Middle Ages and in the Renaissance. In her chapter "Did the Twelfth Century Discover the Individual?" Carolyne Walker Bynum (1982) speaks of the "revolt of the medievalists" who, in the last fifteen years, have claimed for the twelfth century many of the characteristics once given to the fifteenth century by Michelet and Burckhardt: humanism, renaissance, and the discovery of nature and man.[6] To this they have added the discovery of the individual, and, consequently, the birth of autobiography.

Bynum refutes the entire argument, but I do not wish to enter into the dispute as it does not directly bear on the issues that I address in this chapter. I only wish to point out a possibly useful distinction, advanced by Karl Joachim Weintraub, in which he posits a separation between the ideology of individualism and individuality as a self-conception.[7] Weintraub defines individualism as a social theory that encourages the least possible social control over the individual so that he be free to define himself. This social theory can be considered as constitutive of the modern mind. By contrast, individuality, as self-conception, occurs at different periods in history and refers to the perception of oneself as a unique personality, one who feels unique rather than conforms to a model. Seen according to this perspective, the debate of the medievalists who claim individualism for the medieval period might indeed be moot. In any case, what is important for my purpose is the fact that whether historians of autobiography place its beginning in the twelfth or in the eighteenth century, women autobiographers are surprisingly absent from their studies, despite the existence of a rich tradition of female spiritual autobiographies from the thirteenth to the seventeenth century and beyond.

Indeed, these views on autobiography have been challenged by the introduction of the category of gender into the study of the literature of self-representation.[8] Feminist scholars have done archeological work on women's autobiography in the last fifteen years and have produced a body of important studies on the subject. As Domna Stanton, Sidonie Smith, and Nancy K. Miller pointedly remark, literary history written by traditional (androcentric) critics is paradoxical because it judges most female literary production as dismissible on the ground that it is mainly autobiographical, while it excludes women from serious studies that address the problematic of autobiography. This exclusion is explained by arguing that women's autobiographies do not fit the established criteria of what self-representation ought to be, namely, male self-representation. Hence, there is a complete lack of interest in the rich tradition of female spiritual autobiographies from the thirteenth until at least the seventeenth century. Madame Guyon's autobiography is no exception to the rule, and in the flurry of criticism on autobiography written in the past three decades, in France, England, and in the United States, Guyon's *La Vie de Mme* is seldom mentioned. When it is the object of a more serious study, as is the case in Weintraub's or Gusdorf's works, the gender of the author and narrator is not taken into account in the analysis of the negotiations of self-representation.[9]

I wish to emphasize that *La Vie de Mme. J. M. B. de la Mothe Guion écrite par elle-même* holds a unique place in the history of autobiography and in the history of the representation of the self, a fact which has hitherto not been acknowledged. Both a spiritual narrative in the tradition of the female mystics and a memoir in the aristocratic tradition of the sixteenth and seventeenth centuries, Guyon's *La Vie de Mme* also adheres to the definition Philippe Lejeune gives for modern autobiography in the style of Rousseau. The difference is that the social condition to which Guyon attributes her destiny is not class, but rather gender. As the creation by a woman, by an aristocrat, and by a mystic, Guyon's *La Vie de Mme* is essential for understanding the discontinuities that exist in literary history between female, medieval, mystical autobiographies, and sixteenth- and seventeenth-century aristocratic memoirs on the one hand, and Rousseau's *Confessions* in the eighteenth century on the other. In its multiple models of self-representation, *La Vie de Mme* exemplifies the passage in the collective consciousness from a representation of the self as inscribed in the eternal (as is the case for female mystical autobiography), or as written within the history of its century (characteristic of aristocratic memoirs), to a representation of the self as originating in the individual's childhood, or in keeping with her/his social conditions. In the case of Guyon, this passage is recorded not as a conception of "man" as universal, but in a gendered conception of self.

Madame Guyon and the Traditional Representations of the Self

Guyon's *La Vie de Mme*—begun in 1682 in Thonon, then continued in 1686 during her first incarceration, and finished in 1709 in Blois, eight years before her death—covers the period from 1648 to 1709. The very circumstances of its publication exemplify once more the vagaries that texts written by women incurred, starting with the very conditions that allow them to be written and extending through their publication and ultimate preservation. When she finished putting the last corrections to her manuscript of *La Vie de Mme*, which she then entrusted to Pierre Poiret, her disciple and publisher, Guyon stipulated that it should not be published before her death. The manuscript she gave to Pierre Poiret after 1709 was first published posthumously in Amsterdam in 1720, and then republished in Lausanne in 1791 by Jean-Philippe Dutoit.

From the correspondence exchanged among her Scottish disciples, one learns that even though they were very eager to publish her autobiography, there was some opposition in France that tried to prevent Poiret from publishing it. In fact, the delay in its publication was due to her daughter (whom one of the Scottish disciples called an "artful political Lady"), who apparently put pressure on the Marquis de Fénelon (nephew of Fénelon) and on Michael Ramsey (Guyon's secretary and disciple in Blois) to prevent the publication of her mother's autobiography.[10] The Scottish disciples won, and, in another letter, Dr. James Keith wrote: "The *Life* I hope will be speedily put to press, without consulting the French friends any further about it."[11] If Guyon had not had such devoted disciples outside France, her autobiography would surely not have been published.

Shortly after its publication in 1720, it was translated into several languages and widely read outside of France and the Catholic world. The work was also widely read in sectarian Protestant circles in the eighteenth century and even in the nineteenth. It is, according to Gusdorf, the most important text in Quietist literature.[12] In France, however, literary and social historians alike have ignored it, and to this day, the first three volumes have not been reissued in a critical edition. Owing to the scholarly efforts of Marie-Louise Gondal, it is now also known that Madame Guyon did not give her publisher the entire manuscript.[13] Instead, she truncated the text and retained the part of the manuscript that dealt with her last seven years of captivity, first at Vincennes, then in the convent of Saint Thomas de Villeneuve, and, finally, at the Bastille. The manuscript of this last part was found and published in 1992 by Gondal, in a perspicacious critical edition under the title *Récits de captivité*.[14] Why did Madame Guyon, who wanted to be vindicated by posterity, renounce the publication of this part of her life? Most probably because it indicted many members of the high clergy, and she wanted to shield her family and friends from their vindictive power.

At the crossroads of history, literary genres, and epistemologies, Guyon's autobiography juxtaposes several kinds of representations of the self belonging to different social registers and originating in different epochs, from the thirteenth century to the eve of modernity. By its very title, *La Vie de Mme J. M. B. de la Mothe Guion écrite par elle-même*, this text imposes itself at the same time as a hagiography, a spiritual narrative, and a book of memoirs. In a Catholic context, the title *La Vie de Mme* evokes the life of saints or of religious persons. The name Mme. J. M. B. de la Mothe Guyon, however, devoid of any religious title but bearing the nobiliary particle, reminds the reader of aristocratic memoirs. Then the end of the title, "written by herself," dissociates the writer from the narrator and refers the reader to the hagiographic tradition, in which a privileged witness who has shared the life of the model—one who can combine intimacy with serenity and objectivity—tells the life of the model. The last part of the title thus serves to remind us what autobiography owes to the biographical genre. The title of Guyon's autobiography could, at a cursory glance, simply be seen as a convention; analysis reveals instead that the claim to objectivity suggested in the hagiographic convention is used here strategically for purposes of edification and self-representation.

This strategy allows the author to establish three sources of enunciation, with three levels of narrative. Mme. J. M. B. de la Mothe Guyon is the object of her own narrative, in which she relates experiences that she had without knowing their meaning. The reference in the title to "herself" represents the narrator, who was later given the chance to understand and interpret these experiences for the edification of others and for the glory of God. The third source of enunciation and instance of narrative is suggested, but not named, by the religious title. It is God Himself who ordered the writing of this autobiography, and who wrote it in Guyon's hand. The interplay of these three voices produces a hagiography of the self that partly aims at anticipating and disarming criticism. When Bossuet reproached Guyon for reveling in extraordinary silent communications with her followers, or for claiming that God's grace had filled her to the point of ripping her clothing, "herself" was able to explain that this behavior conformed to mystical models. As the object of divine intervention, she narrated the extraordinary occurrences she experienced; as subject, speculating on her experiences, she reminded the skeptical reader that nothing was too extraordinary for God, that even more extraordinary behavior could be witnessed in the life of those mystics who had been accepted by the church, and that, in any case, although these occurrences had happened to her, she did not give any importance to them. Similarly, when the narrator-interpreter "herself" was blamed for having taken liberties with dogma and orthodoxy, she could reply that it was not she, a poor ignorant woman, who had written this, but God through her hand, and that it was neither her own nor God's fault if men's dogma was not in agreement with divine law.

La Vie de Mme is, for the most part, a spiritual account, reporting the progress of a soul in its journey toward perfection and recording the moments of intense emotional contact between God and the soul. But it is also the account of the difficult and dangerous voyage of a woman seeking official recognition of her mystical calling, while refusing to betray her personal experience in order to make it fit the hierarchy's notion of "true experience" or accepted, female behavior. As the author of a mystical narrative, Guyon scrupulously follows the conventions of the genre. She is unworthy but chosen. She does not reveal her self of her own will, but she is ordered to do so by her confessor. Her personal experience sticks scrupulously to the experience of the mystics. Her suffering, her madness, her confusion, she says, were due to the fact that she could not assign meaning to her experiences, for she was unfamiliar with the mystical writings that would have enabled her to see them in the proper context. Once the meaning of her experience was made apparent to her, everything fell into place. Like all authors of spiritual autobiographies, whether Catholic or Reformed, she weighed, classified, and compared all the events in her life so that they conformed to a preconceived plan. There is no originality in all this, whether in the Catholic or in the Reformed tradition.

In both the hagiographical and the spiritual levels of her narrative, Guyon totally adopted the subservient and humble position of women, although she subverted it, as do all mystics, by invoking God's call to her in particular, because she is such a lowly vessel and a woman. Guyon also claimed for herself the charismatic and ahistorical power claimed by numerous female mystics from the thirteenth century on. She tread what I have elsewhere called the tightrope of all mystics who were recognized by the church. Like them, she negotiates the humble, unworthy, passive role demanded of women by family, church, and society (which relegated her to the enclosed spheres of home or convent), with the opposite, personal claim to singular charismatic election and a claim to be entrusted with a mission in the public sphere of society.

Guyon's *La Vie de Mme* incorporates yet another genre practiced by the mystics, which expresses a concern for the ecclesiastical court. It has to do with the justifications by which the author wanted to prove her orthodoxy when she aligned her experiences and doctrine with the experiences and writings of the mystics of the past who were accepted by the church. The justifications aim at situating the self in the history of mysticism in the Roman Catholic tradition. Transgressing the ignorance imposed on her sex, she displayed her knowledge of the Scriptures, as well as of both past and contemporary mystical tradition. In this transgression she deliberately abandoned claims to female ignorance and humility, which would have protected her from the accusation of willfull heresy, and donned the masculine privilege of intellectual debate, reason, and knowledge about divine truth, which allowed her to defend her doctrine.

Guyon's autobiography can also be seen within the perspective of the mass of memoirs that the French nobility produced during the seventeenth century.[15] Indeed, *La Vie de Mme* also presents itself as a memoir: the depository of truth regarding the Quietist Affair, and as such, a rectification of Bossuet's *La Relation sur le quiétisme*. She expounded her belief that her books would be read by posterity.[16] She justified herself before posterity by reproducing documents and letters which she had sent or received.[17] In its claim as a book of memoirs, her autobiography thus served both as a dossier, prepared for the tribunal of posterity, and as a testimony of an event that the author had experienced, in which her memory and honor were at stake. In this vein, Guyon was conscious of her rank in society as an aristocrat and of belonging to a class for whom reputation and honor were more important than wealth. She was also conscious of belonging to a group of high-ranking aristocrats whose mystical tendencies produced many enemies. The side of *La Vie de Mme* that echoes the memoir tradition indicates its author's will to place herself in history and in the temporal register, a desire to save the reputation of her family and that of her influential friends of the court. Here, Guyon situated herself not as a female aristocrat, proud of her caste, but nevertheless bound to a self-effacing role while extolling the glory of the men of her caste;

on the contrary, she played the male persona on whose pen depended the memory and the honor of her caste, her family, and herself.

At the same time she invoked the authority of Augustine, Guyon evoked the vanity and the ridicule of all worldly and political life dominated by the absurd and by death. Under the cover of antimemoirs, which allowed her to belittle concerns for posterity and the temporal (in which she had just placed herself with the memoirs), she did not hesitate to analyze the temporal institutions of the church, the lowly acts that could be committed by the clergy and even by the higher pontifs for the sake of ambition, money, or glory. This allowed her to transpose herself to the order of the eternal, and she thereby established a difference between those who, taking advantage of their temporal power, allowed themselves to judge her, and herself, whom God alone could judge. The order of the eternal also allowed her to transcend gender and be neither male nor female, but a soul in front of God.

Having borrowed thus from a number of cultural conventions, each of these constituting a brush stroke defining the self-portraitist, Guyon's *La Vie de Mme* is surely a self-portrait, as Michel Beaujour defines it in *Poetics of Literary Self-Portrait*—that is, a grab bag of cultural clichés. Striking a fatal blow to the myth of the literature of the self as a naïve genre and as a revelation of a unique and original self, Beaujour demonstrates that it is precisely when one wants to represent oneself as unique that one borrows the collective discourses of one's culture.[18] Indeed, *La Vie de Mme* was an ingenious demonstration of the monumental fabrication of the self, a coherent elaboration that linked and weaved together literary genres, events, metaphysics, dogma, prophetic dreams, and proofs from the Holy Scripture. Not satisfied, however, with juxtaposing them, she organized, modified, and subordinated these elements according to the ontological imperatives of her personal life. If there was little originality in the cultural elements that *La Vie de Mme* borrowed, there was, nevertheless, a great dexterity in their assemblage. The work demonstrated Guyon's superb craftsmanship and keen knowledge of the rhetorical intention of each literary genre that she used. Her work illustrates that autobiography is not so much the locus wherein the uniqueness of the individual is revealed as it is a panoply of social codes and socially determined selves that restrict individual freedom and expression. One could interpret this plethora of self-representations as a desire to organize the autobiographical narrative for an eschatological and totalizing purpose—a desire which, according to Gusdorf, invariably animates the autobiographical project.

A New Representation of the Self

Jonathan Dewald has analyzed a shift in self-representation in the aristocratic memoirs of the seventeenth century, a shift that responds to the preoccupation of a modern world, revealing a modern sensibility: "Seventeenth-century nobles became preoccupied with the nature of selfhood, ideas that poorly fitted with the aristocratic ideological schema."[19] Accordingly, the ingenious organization of conventions and recourse to the polysemy of traditional genres, by which the identity tries to define itself, make of Guyon's *La Vie de Mme* a successful prototype of modern autobiography. The originality of Guyon's *La Vie de Mme* as an autobiography, however, lies not in its borrowing of multiple representations but in its momentary hesitation in its teleological intent. It is in this hesitation that the reader can discern an attempted emergence of a modern autobiography, as characterized by childhood narrative, individualism, and intimate revelations. Guyon's, indeed, is one of the few autobiographical texts in the seventeenth century to present in a coherent manner a modern childhood narrative and a sketch of a social discourse on the origin of personal fate and social injustice. As if seeking to escape the available modes of self-representation, Guyon, in *La Vie de Mme*, sought to invent new ones and thus stumbled upon the modern autobiography. Her text irrefutably corroborates de Certeau's assertion that at the beginning of the modern world, mystical discourse, by deconstructing its own premises, produced, from within, the elements that made it divert toward other genres and other discourses.[20] It is as if, all of a sudden, abandoning its alleged ahistoricity, mystical discourse started to look for a different origin and to give a name other than that of God to the locus of its production; in other words, it is as if mystical discourse suddenly felt the need to compensate for the displacement of God by focusing on the social production of the individual.

It is important to specify that certain childhood narratives have always been a part of the conventions of spiritual autobiography. During the seventeenth century, in France as well as in England, authors of spiritual autobiographies continued to find it appropriate to deplore the depravation of their youth, and even their infancy. They described the most trivial events of childhood, in which they read the unique designs of God upon them. This type of childhood narrative is very much present in Guyon's autobiography. It functions as it does traditionally in mystical or religious autobiographies, showing the depravity of the child and her coming to God, or rather her being chosen by God despite her depravity, and how the present divine election can already be deciphered in the events of childhood.

In addition, however, and intermixed with the religious childhood narrative, there is another kind of childhood narrative. Childhood is perceived as the time when individual destiny is shaped, situating the birthplace of personal fate within the family.[21] On the one hand, in keeping with the logic of traditional childhood narrative, Guyon allegorized the struggle between life and death as a struggle between good and evil. This struggle, she said, foreshadowed the struggle that occupied her life and made her oscillate between spiritual death (sin—the Devil) and life (God the Father). She wrote:

> There was a struggle between death and life: death believed it would conquer and dominate life; but life remained victorious. Oh, if I were allowed to have this confidence and if I could believe at last that life will always be victorious over death. This would no doubt be if You alone lived in me. Oh, my God who now seem to be my only life and my only love.[22]

However her allegory is not abstract, associating the mother with death or evil and the father with love and God. In Guyon's text, the mother was identified as the origin of Guyon's fate to suffer, even before she was born: "I was not born at term: for my mother was so horribly frightened that she gave birth to me in the eighth month during which it is said that it is almost impossible to survive. . . . No sooner was I given life than I thought I was losing it."[23] While she believed that the mother inflicted suffering and death, the father, on the other hand, was designated as he who gave love and life. He would have been afflicted if she had lost her life, and he worried about her physical and spiritual health: "I was taken to a nurse; no sooner was I with her than my father was informed that I was dead. He was very afflicted by it. . . . Immediately, my father brought a priest to me."[24]

Immediately after her birth, Guyon fell extremely ill, and on several occasions it was expected that she would die. On the one hand, as in traditional, religious, childhood narratives, she attributed her survival to God's will: "Such a surprising illness at such a tender age would normally have deprived me of life; but oh, my God! since You wanted to make of me a subject of Your greatest mercy, You did not allow it."[25] On the other hand, a few lines later, the origin of her fate of sufferings and illnesses that led her to follow the mystical path pointed again to the family, and, in particular, to the mother, who regarded son and daughter unequally: "My mother, who did not like daughters very much, neglected me somehow and abandoned me too much to the care of women who also neglected me."[26]

Her uncertainty about whether her fate was owing to the designs of God to which her father's love for her was associated, or instead, to the mother's hatred of her, led Guyon to two different discourses. From divine and fatherly love derived the mystical discourse that enabled the author to see a posteriori the events and accidents in her life as signs sent to her by God: "Oh, my God! it seems to me that You have allowed such a strange behavior towards me [her mother's hatred], only to make me understand the greatness of Your kindness to me, and how You wanted that I be indebted to You alone for my salvation, and not to the doing of any other creature."[27]

As in the works of other mystics, the subject was singled out as a chosen, unique, and privileged being, engaged in a dialogue initiated by God and assigned a mission to accomplish. Mystical discourse also enabled her to put order into her meaningless life, arrange its events in line with spiritual betterment, and present it as a progressive journey toward a predetermined goal: "These alternatives of life and death at the beginning of my life were fatal omens of what was to happen to me one day, at times dying from sin, at times living through grace."[28]

At the same time, however, her attributing the origins of her troubles to maternal hatred gave rise to what I will call a proto-political discourse that contradicted mystical discourse. The reported memories of her premature birth and difficult beginnings, which were associated with the mother, were followed by memories of maternal neglect: "As soon as I was sent back to my father's home, my mother left me as before in the charge of servants, because there was a maid whom she trusted."[29] This neglect, she implied, was at the source of her difficulties: "Assuredly, it was a crime to bring me up badly: for I was naturally disposed to virtue and I loved good actions."[30] She attributed her mother's neglect to the latter's preference for sons: "As my mother only showed love for my brother and as she did not show any sign of tenderness towards me, I readily distanced myself from her."[31]

From her personal history she moved to comment more universally on mothers who, because they did not love their daughters and preferred their sons to them, were a source of social injustice:

I cannot here refrain from pointing out the fault committed by mothers, who under the pretext of devotion or occupation, neglect to keep their daughters near them. . . . I cannot refrain from condemning these unjust preferences made between one child and another which cause the division and loss of families, whereas equality binds the hearts and fosters charity.[32]

She did not feel that she was a unique case, but rather part of a class or a category of individuals who were unjustly treated. She perceived mothers' hatred for their daughters and preference for their sons as a social problem shaping women's lives. This perception of injustice and its origin in the family organization contradicted mystical discourse, according to which no injustice could exist, since everything was ordained by God for reasons that could sometimes be understood but most often remained mysterious.

This is followed by some other remarks concerning the fate of women: "This negligence causes the loss of most young ladies. How many of them would be angels, whom freedom [i.e., neglect] and idleness turn into devils?"[33] In this passage she perceived her mystic fate as a deviance from the norm due to a lack of love. She identified neglect as well as lack of autonomy as the origin of women's suffering, for mothers who neglected their daughters also sinned out of selfishness by treating their daughters as prisoners: "What still contributes to this is that these devout mothers hold them so tightly that they do not give them any freedom, holding them like those birds that are kept in a cage, and which, as soon as they find any opening, fly away and do not come back."[34] Accordingly, she would have flown far away from the mother and become a mystic to escape the stifling, loveless atmosphere in which her mother was keeping her. She then reprimands such selfish mothers who force their daughters to seek elsewhere (in mysticism perhaps?) what they were unable to give them: "May they devote themselves to never pushing their daughters away from them: may they treat them as sisters and not as slaves . . . and finding much tenderness near them, they [the daughters] will not seek it elsewhere."[35] She seems to imply that if her mother had loved and directed her, her life would have been different.

Her admonishment to mothers leads to a utopian vision of order and peaceful relations. If the present conditions were changed, that is, if mothers loved their daughters as they love their sons, the face of the earth would change:

> If one acted in this fashion, the course leading to disorders would soon be stopped! There would no longer be bad daughters or bad mothers, for, with these daughters becoming mothers, they would raise their children like they would have been raised themselves. . . . This would foster union, whereas from the unjust preferences made for some children spring jealousy and a secret hatred, which increase with time and remain until death. How many children do we see as idols in their homes, who act as sovereigns and treat their siblings like slaves following the example of the fathers and mothers; you would think that the ones are the servants of the others.[36]

This inequality in the treatment of children by the parents is the cause of social and religious disorder:

> If we loved them equally, we would no longer force some children to enter a convent, and we would no longer sacrifice some in order to raise others. It would follow that there would

be no more disorder in the cloisters, because there would only be sincere vocations. . . . Those parents who force their children into a convent are the cause of their despair and of their damnation through the irreconcilable hatred that they conceive against their brothers or sisters.[37]

Not only does Guyon attribute the origin of her fate to the family, but her discourse also constitutes a protofeminist discourse concerning demands for social reform, in which the individual woman identifies social injustice done to women as a group, and proposes a way to change that injustice. She claims for all daughters the right, equal to that of sons, to be loved by their parents. This scenario of personal fate, based in the family and rooted in social realities, anchors the individual destiny in the social and family structure and expels divine eschatology inherent in mystical discourse.

This embryo of sociopolitical discourse is supported by flashes of insight into oppression, which lead to flashes of intimate revelation. Indeed, it seems that Guyon, before Rousseau, is the first French autobiographer to have believed that the minutiae of childhood and the details of private life were significant enough to be included in an account of one's life. These revelations, rare in the seventeenth century, constitute a personal testimony of the experience of a woman.

After having spent a neglected childhood in different convents and having endured the ill treatments of her mother, she was married off at age sixteen, not to the cousin she liked but to a gentleman from her area who had considerable wealth. She writes: "This was done without my being informed of anything, the day before Saint François de Sales's day, on January 28, 1664; and I even had to sign the articles of the marriage without being told what they were."[38] Since this marriage was arranged by her father, to whom she would not dare reproach anything whatsoever, the revelation of her tribulations is made in the tone of a simple observation. The images, however, are so strong that this confession constitutes a poignant testimony to the social destiny of a woman:

I did not see my betrothed until two or three days before my wedding. . . . I was extremely happy to be married, for I imagined that I would thereby have complete freedom and that I would be freed from the bad treatments of my mother. . . . [But on the day of the ceremony] the joy surrounding this wedding was universal in our town and in the midst of this rejoicing I was the only one to be sad. I could neither laugh like the others nor even eat, so heavy was my heart. I did not know the cause of my sadness.[39]

Soon after the wedding, the convent seemed to her to be a fate infinitely more pleasing than married life.

I was hardly married when I was overcome by the memory of the desire that I had to be a nun. . . . All those who came to compliment me the day following my wedding could not help mock me because I was crying bitterly; and I told them, "Alas! I had wanted so much to be a nun, why am I presently married, and by what fatality did this happen to me?"[40]

When she became a widow, she was free to choose her destiny; she firmly resisted the injunctions of the priests and prelates who pressed her to become a nun in order to restrict, within the walls of a convent, her zeal for preaching and her will for freedom, and to silence her exuberant pen.

As for her sadness in her married life, which she had to hide in order to look happy so as not to dishonor her husband, she described it as follows: "I was on this occasion [of some festivities] like those animals bound for the butcher, which on certain days, are adorned with flowers and greenery and which are led this way around town before being slaughtered."[41]

Yet, the radical potential of the protopolitical discourse to be found in Guyon's autobiography is narrowly circumscribed. She did not delve into the reasons mothers hate daughters, just as women hate themselves when forced to endure a patriarchal social arrangement. Guyon's hints of a political analysis of women's conditions in her society are blurred by her not identifying patriarchal authority behind women's depreciation of individuals of their own sex. Her protopolitical discourse is short circuited and short lived, and it gravitates toward, on the one hand, the fantasy of the F(f)ather's love for his daughter and, on the other hand, toward mysticism, which teaches her to work around the status quo rather than to challenge it.

Her dual failure (at political analysis and in not confronting the role of patriarchy) might explain why Madame Guyon repeated with her daughter the same fate she had herself bemoaned earlier. Despite her abundant use of childbirth and motherhood as metaphors for spiritual creativity, she exposed her daughter to undue hardship while searching for her mission, and she was aware of it.[42] There are many other signs of obvious neglect of the child, which Guyon justified by saying that God wanted it that way or that she trusted God would take care of her daughter. On an occasion of the latter's illness, aggravated by the instability of life with her mother and the lack of good food and doctors in Savoy, Guyon, comparing herself to Abraham, implied that this situation was ordered by God: "I offered You her illness, O my God, as a sacrifice, and it seemed to me that, like a new Abraham, I was holding the knife that would slaughter her."[43]

Of course the topos of the abandonment of children for the love of God figures in Madame Guyon's spiritual narrative, conforming to the genre. As a widow, she spent some time in Paris where, one day, she entered a dark and unfamiliar church. She went to confession, and according to her narrative, the priest, struck by something she had said, was moved to respond that surely she must have been given a mission by God, adding that "nothing must prevent [her] from accomplishing God's will" and that "she ought to abandon her children in order to accomplish her mission."[44]

What conclusions can be drawn at this point from this analysis of Madame Guyon's embryo of a modern autobiography, an analysis that raises questions concerning a certain number of generally accepted ideas on autobiography? As I have already mentioned, it seems clear, first of all, that modern autobiography was not born spontaneously when Rousseau's *Confessions* were published. The sensibility that characterizes modern autobiography was already at work by the end of the seventeenth century, as Dewald has shown in the case of aristocratic memoirs and is present in Guyon's *La Vie de Mme.*

Second, Rousseau's *Confessions* might have a debt to female mystical accounts, one that has never been acknowledged. Georges Gusdorf has shown that the history of modern literature of the self in France cannot be understood if it is restricted to the national limits of the French territory and if the history of religious consciousness, which has asserted itself since the beginning of the seventeenth century in the European Pietist and Quietist currents, is not taken into account. At the end of the seventeenth and during the eighteenth century, these movements contained the liveliest elements in Christianity outside confessional barriers, forming an international, religious force that led to the *Sturm und Drang* in Germany, a highly intimist movement, and which still had echoes in the nineteenth century in the works of Novalis, Schleimacher and Kierkegaard.[45] As already shown, Madame Guyon was close to Pietist circles when she lived in Blois after her release from the Bastille, and it is thanks to her Pietist disciples that her work was published after her death. According to Gusdorf, Rousseau, who remains outside the Germanic tradition, is nevertheless connected to European Pietism through the Vaudois circles and to Quietism through the influence of Madame de Warens.[46] The Germanic domain, thus brought to light by Gusdorf, enables us to see the connection between Guyon and Rousseau, a connection that does not appear in literary history as practiced in France, since Quietism and Guyon have been virtually erased from it. It is also very important to recall that Rousseau was an avid reader of Bérulle, the founder of the "French school" of mysticism in the seventeenth century, whose method of meditation was developed even further by Guyon. This connection helps one to understand that the religious tones found in the most famous of modern and secular autobiographies, Rousseau's *Confessions*, do not come solely from a reference to Augustine's *Confessions*. Rousseau naturally invoked Augustine, but an Augustine read and practiced by all the authors of Pietist, Quietist, or reformed spiritual autobiographies of the seventeenth century.

Gusdorf's thesis is useful for two reasons: first, he asserts the fact that literary history of any European nation remains blind if it does not take into account the literary history of Europe as a whole during the same period; second, he claims that religious literature before the eighteenth century cannot be separated and excluded from analyses of secular literature without risking historical distortions. In fact, with the exception of the writings of Pascal and François de Sales, few religious works have been taken into consideration in French literary history. To these theories, I add a third point. Works of women, be they religious or secular (or the absence of such works) must be considered together with works written by men of the same period, if we want to avoid facile generalizations.

Finally, it is necessary to nuance the thesis that too closely and exclusively links modern autobiography with bourgeois ideology of individualism, the claims of the bourgeois class, and the idea of the rights of man. Guyon was not bourgeois but aristocratic—was wealthy, and belonged to the most restricted circles that had access to the throne. Thus, reasons for her vocation to democratize mystical practices, which were reserved up to then to a small elite closely watched by the ecclesiastical authorities, and her determination to write an autobiography, which invents a modern way of conceiving personal fate, must rely on other sociopolitical criteria.

In *Holy Feast and Holy Fast*, Carolyn Walker Bynum implies that female mysticism arose from the erosion of sacerdotal and temporal powers that women endured with the Gregorian Reform of the twelfth century. In *The Mystic Fable*, Michel de Certeau further suggests a link between mysticism and a general loss of power; he points out that during the sixteenth and seventeenth centuries, both women and men mystics tended to belong to regions and categories affected by a socioeconomic recession, unprivileged by change, marginalized by progress, or ruined by wars. Therefore, in these early modern centuries, mysticism especially attracted those who were lacking or losing power. In addition, it is known that a particular female genre of spiritual autobiography arose from the medieval, female mystical movement. Finally, Paul Delany says, with respect to autobiography, that during the seventeenth century in England, all social classes participated in the proliferation of secular and religious autobiographies except the small elite of the Anglican establishment who, being highly learned and aristocratic, had the leisure of expressing themselves through genres that were more respected than autobiography. He adds that religious autobiography in England during this time seems to be linked to social demands, feelings of injustice and persecution. Thus one can conclude that with Rousseau and other modern biographers at the dawn of the modern world, individuality and the autobiographical impulse, which had always been the characteris-

tic of female mystics, merged with bourgeois sensibility, the ideology of bourgeois individualism, and a demand for social recognition
and justice.

Identity Destroyed and the Ruin
of the Autobiographical Project

Guyon's autobiography offers yet a further avenue of speculation.
There exists in her text a tension between, on the one hand, the
humanist-modernist project of inscribing the self in history, together with the desire for social reform, and on the other, the anti-
humanist desire of pointing out the illusory nature of the self by
the emptying of the subject. One can, indeed, only be surprised
that Guyon wrote an autobiography at all, and, moreover, one that
used so great a variety of the choices in self-representations that
were available to her. It is all the more surprising for her spiritual
doctrine pushed the unraveling of the ego and the quieting of the
logos to the limits of orthodoxy, both of which were beyond the
tolerance of an age increasingly enamoured by reason. What should
be made of the cultural clichés that multiply in her autobiography,
in light of her spiritual practice, which aims at clearing away all
images, language, and emotions in order to attain a state devoid of
discursive patterns?

It is precisely Guyon's diversity of self-representations that un-
dermines the autobiographical project itself and with it the very
notion of self-representation. In Guyon's *La Vie de Mme*, negative
mysticism works at emptying the self that the autobiographical
project had constructed, and thereby a variety of possible selves is
produced. The plethora of self-representations that she deploys
points to the multiplicity and instability of identity and the revelation that when all is said, nothing remains. With the coherence of
the self dismantled, Guyon's autobiography closes with a meditation on the nothingness of self-representation.

The last part of her autobiography, *Récits de captivité*, (which
she had not wished to be published even after her death and which
has only recently been found and published by Marie-Louise Gondal) abandoned all the genres used in the first three volumes. This
section stands as her testimony to the friends and disciples who

requested it and to posterity. The tone is different; it is a straightforward narrative of events and is as stripped of teleological or mystical interpretation as it is of anecdotes. Written around 1709 or 1710, six and a half years after her liberation from the Bastille, it contains events that were unknown to her while she was in prison but which she learned of later. In the first pages she was faithful to the rhetoric of the *via negativa*. She described her current mental state: "There, there is no clamor, no pain, no sorrow, no pleasure, no uncertainty. . . . I go without leaving, with no goal in mind, without knowing where I go. I have neither trust nor distrust, in a word nothing, nothing, nothing"[47] At this point the significance of her life and of her autobiographical project seemed to have dissolved: "If *La Vie de Mme* had not been written, it would run a great risk of never being written."[48] But, she also adds this: "And yet I would rewrite it at the slightest pretext without knowing what I want to say."[49] Does this mean that in an existence deprived of intelligibility, repetition becomes not the mark of meaning but of the absurd? As for God's designs on her, they are paradoxical and she can no longer discern them. She remains sure that He gave her a mission, but she does not know whether or not she has accomplished it, no more than she knows the meaning of her life:

What I have said or written is past; I do not remember it. It is as if someone else experienced it. I am unable to desire justification or esteem. If God wants either one, He will do what He wants, I do not care. Whether He is glorified through my destruction or through the clearing of my reputation, the one is equal to the other in the scale.[50]

The autobiography, which established a place for her in the eternal, in the temporal, and in the future, exits into nothingness. The personal problematic that was posed in terms of the divine, of church doctrine, and within a precise political and sexual configuration, is resolved in "a chaos without confusion."[51] God is no longer, as with Augustine, the guarantor of identity, but, as with the Dionysian mystics, the occasion of its dissolution. In this regard, Guyon is not a modern. She is either a premodern or a postmodern, in so far as postmodern French thinkers such as Lacan,

Derrida, or Foucault have extolled the necessity to question the subject and its identities.

Notwithstanding its lack of adherence to normative notions of autobiography, Guyon's work, which juxtaposes all the modes of representations of the self while at the same time undermining their validity, ought to have interested postmodern critics who tend to debunk the unity and authenticity of the autobiographical self by uncovering its multiplicity, its conventions of representation, and its teleological myth. Indeed, Guyon's attempt at self-representation is a demonstration of how different conventions of the representation of the self, although penned by the same author, can produce totally different and incompatible selves, and ultimately invalidate the very project of autobiography. Guyon reveals autobiography not as a place of authenticity, singularity, and unity of the subject, but as a place both of uncovering and covering, a place to negotiate conventions, a place where one tries to give to oneself and to the reader an acceptable image of oneself. It is also a place where, when everything has been said, nothing is left of the self. Further, this text can teach us that gender, far from being an essential category that disallows the inclusion of female autobiographers within the history of autobiography, is but one identity among others, which the female autobiographer plays with, accepts, challenges, or negotiates. This choice either to highlight gender identity or not according to the need of the autobiographer suggests that postmodern male critics' neglect, not only of female autobiographers but also of gender, might be due to the fact that they have not gone far enough in the deconstruction of the self. They still hold masculinity as a fixed, stable, and essential identity, one they will not relinquish despite the wreckage of identity they themselves have instigated.

Conclusion

tarting with the writings of two female mystics of the seventeenth-century Catholic world, heirs of Medieval mysticism, this study has led us to the New World and to eighteenth-century European religious and political sensibilities, through diverse literary genres, self-refashionings, and a different way of apprehending the world. Its focus has been the impact of a shift in epistemology in the Renaissance and the seventeenth century upon the mystical discourse of two well-known female mystics. As such, this study supports Michel de Certeau's assertion, according to which mystical discourse in the seventeenth century produced from within its own realm the elements that made it migrate toward other genres and discourses.

This study also supports Caroline Walker Bynum's view that female mysticism in the Western tradition has to do with issues of authority and female, creative resistance.

However, in other regards, this study challenges both de Certeau's and Bynum's assertions on many issues. On the one hand, the category of gender, brought to bear on the mystical movement in the seventeenth century, revises some of de Certeau's generalizations; on the other, not losing sight of the ways misogyny has

221

shaped theology allows us to nuance Bynum's glorification of female mystics' agency. The three-way dialogue between de Certeau, Bynum, and my reading of these two mystics allows for a revised answer to the questions posed by the predominant role of women in Western mysticism. Specifically, was female mysticism a successful means for women of the past to subvert patriarchal power? And, more generally, what can be learned from the encounter between female mystical tradition and the modern world?

I have responded to these questions amply enough as concerns sensory mysticism not to warrant further elaboration. I agree with those who argue that sensory mysticism allowed female mystics a charismatic power and an access to transcendence otherwise denied them. However, sensory mysticism does not, in my opinion, constitute a space of disruption within the patriarchal order, because it is precisely through their bodies, which misogyny identified and marked as wicked flesh, that female mystics were allowed power and transcendence. Therefore, it can be concluded that female mystics who identified with sensory mysticism paid for the extraordinary privileges they enjoyed by acting out (albeit quite creatively) the self-denial dictated to them by a misogynous society.

What, then, about negative mysticism? The potential of negative mysticism as a means of leaving the patriarchal order behind has been neglected in studies on the subject of female mysticism. Indeed, because both female mystics and sensory mysticism with which they had been associated were devalued by historians and theologians, recent revaluations of female mysticism have focused on a rehabilitation of sensory mysticism. Has one not, however, missed the point by searching for resistance, dissent, and freedom in the bodies and discourses of female mystics rather than in examining their practice of negative mysticism? Weren't female mystics' creative attempts to disturb patriarchal order more successful through their practice of silence than through a theology that involved the female body shaped by medieval theology? Indeed, the practice of silence could lead them to a psychic space beyond a logos, imagination, representation, and identity marked by patriarchy, while their bodies were irremediably marked by their being identified with the wicked flesh.

There is no doubt that female mystic practitioners of negative mysticism often took the lead in the mystical movement. The sociopolitical, theological, and literary domains were not the only ones on which they left their mark. Their accomplishments on the psycho-spiritual level, although more difficult to define and also more individual, are no less striking. During the latter half of their lives, some female mystics appear to have attained, along with what they called "permanent union," a great psychological independence, an inner force that freed them from guilt and was accompanied by a profound compassion and inner peace. One can sense in the writings of some of the female mystics that, after a long journey full of torments, they attained a spiritual level that allowed them to transcend the psychological fragmentation and internalized self-loathing that was the lot of women destined to live in a highly misogynous culture and religion.

Paradoxically, however, they achieved freedom and peace of mind while they accepted and played with the negative images of women and of the feminine imposed on them by their culture. They went so far as to claim for themselves this negativity, in order to better reverse the values that produced it. De Certeau has shown that the theme of the idiot, the fool, the insane, or the ignorant person who is wiser than all the doctors and the prelates, although not new in the late Middle Ages, for it can be found in the ancient Christian tradition, remained constant in the mystical movement of the thirteenth through the seventeenth centuries.[1] It is of special importance that female mystics made an extensive use of this theme throughout this period, for it is hardly surprising that women identified with the traditional "poor in spirit," given the intellectual, political, social, and symbolic privations they repeatedly withstood. De Certeau shows how the alleged spiritual superiority of the first female "lunatic" of this tradition (recorded in the fourth century) was used by male teachers in order to humble religious men.[2] This objective attained, she disappeared from the records. In contrast, the female mystics discussed here utilized this identification with the "poor in spirit" in order to operate a reversal of power within the institution and to inscribe themselves in history.

Female mystics like Marie de l'Incarnation, Madame Guyon, and many others claimed that they achieved peace of mind through their practice of silence. It even seems that they perceived this peace of mind as one of their most important spiritual achievements. Indeed, this was no small feat considering the frustrating and psychically destructive constraints and deprivations these particularly capable women endured. Also, I have suggested that the practice of negative mysticism might have been responsible for Marie de l'Incarnation's creative vision of a femininity impossible to conceive of within the confines of Western, gendered epistemology. Further, as seen, Madame Guyon also claimed that her practice of silence lifted all inhibitions weighing on her mental faculties, thus allowing her to be free from disabling fears. More clearly than other spiritual writers, Guyon was able to describe how the practice she used and refined induced an inspired state that allowed her to overcome internal and external obstacles, in order to tap a dynamic source of energy.

Yet, notwithstanding their many accomplishments and sometimes overt resistance, Marie de l'Incarnation's and Madame Guyon's respective attitudes vis-à-vis the gendered status quo are in some respects meek. Although surpassing her contemporaries in her bold vision of a different option for femininity and even though leaving a testimony of women's work in the establishment of a French colony in America, Marie de l'Incarnation was timid in her questioning the status quo for women in religious orders—a status quo that her contemporaries in Canada, Louise Bourgeoys and Jeanne Mance, successfully opposed.

As for Madame Guyon, there is indeed a fundamental tension between her mystical search, from which, in the end, she profited greatly by achieving inner freedom, and her acceptance of the status quo, which imprisoned women and which, in part, she helped to perpetuate.

The modern world, with its new epistemological and geographic horizons, did bring these two mystics new possibilities; but it also seems that for both Marie de l'Incarnation and Madame Guyon, these opportunities translated only into bold new visions of inner freedom, rather than into an attempt to shape society so as to make it better suited to their desire for freedom. Consequently, I arrive at the same conclusion that de Certeau stated for ordinary, daily practices of opposition. However bolder were the negative mystical practices than practices of everyday life and however stronger their effects manifested themselves, they did not fundamentally perturb the status quo. The meaning produced by female mystical practices may have deeply disturbed the intent of the dominant power and produced in the individual's mind a space of freedom, without subverting that power altogether nor preventing deep, unsurmountable contradictions for the individual. Hence, perhaps, the many persistent somatizations female mystics endured. Given the total lack of vision for changes in the world, it is no wonder that psychosomatization did not disappear from the lives of most female practitioners of negative mysticism, even though they devalued these experiences and notwithstanding their otherwise outstanding achievements.

Yet one should not draw from this the conclusion that the powerful mental practice of silence, from which the female mystics of the past drew so much strength, is of no use for social activism. Women of the twentieth century, steeped in a democratic tradition, have learned from experience that new visions, as well as political and social demands, can effect changes in the social fabric. I suggest that an alloy fabricated from political and social activism and intellectual pursuit, on the one hand, and a practice of mental liberation from representations, on the other, can, indeed, constitute the most effective tool that will allow a coming to terms with the history of female oppression and thus will permit women to take the lead again, but this time in a movement that would give to the word *democracy* its full meaning.

Notes

Introduction

1. Michel de Certeau, *Heterologies: Discourse on the Other*, trans. Brian Massumi (Minneapolis: University of Minnesota Press, 1986); *The Practice of Everyday Life*, trans. Steven F. Rendell (Berkeley: University of California Press, 1984); *The Writing of History*, trans. Tom Conley (New York: Columbia University Press, 1988); *The Mystic Fable*, trans. Michael Smith (Chicago: University of Chicago Press, 1992); "Mysticism," trans. Marsanne Brammer, in *Diacritics*, 22:2 (1992), 11–25; "On the Oppositional Practices of Everyday Life," *Social Text*, 1:3 (1980), 3–43; "The Gaze: Nicolas de Cusa," trans. Catherine Porter, in *Diacritics*, 17:3 (1987), 2–38; *Political Writing*, trans. Tom Conley (Minneapolis: University of Minnesota Press, 1996).

2. Caroline Walker Bynum, *Jesus as Mother* (Berkeley: University of California Press, 1982); *Holy Feast and Holy Fast* (Berkeley: University of California Press, 1987); *Fragmentation and Redemption* (New York: Zone Books, 1991).

3. De Certeau, *Fable*, 4.

4. Ibid., 4.

5. See de Certeau, "Mysticism," 14. See also Marsanne Brammer, "Thinking Practice: Michel de Certeau and the Theorization of Mysticism," in *Diacritics* (1992), 22:2, 30.

6. Brammer, "Thinking Practice," 28.

7. De Certeau, "Mysticism," 13.

8. Ibid., 16.

9. Ibid., 16.

10. Ibid., 16.

11. Ibid., 14.

12. De Certeau, *Fable*, 16.

13. Ibid., 5. "But already in [John of the Cross's] works, or in those of Teresa of Avila (more 'modern' than he) and after him, the approach took physical forms, more concerned with a symbolic capacity of the body than with an incarnation of the Verb. . . . It spoke less and less. It was written in unreadable messages on the body transformed into an emblem or a memorial engraved with the sufferings of love."

14. In *Gender and the Politics of History* (New York: Columbia University Press, 1988), 42, Joan Wallach Scott defines gender as "a constitutive element of social relationships based upon perceived differences between the sexes, and gender is a primary way of signifying relationships of power."

The second volume of de Certeau's *The Mystic Fable*, still to be published, will reportedly consider the issue of sexual difference in the mystical movement. See Guy Petitdemange, "L'Invention du commencement: *La Fable mystique* de Michel de Certeau," in *Recherche de Science Religieuse*, 71:4 (1983), 519, n.32. The lack of such address in his first volume points to the necessity to delve further into the question of gender as a category of historical inquiry if we are to better understand a movement which, as historians agree, was largely dominated by women. All the more so as de Certeau's work is predicated on the assumption that "spiritual perception does indeed unfold within a mental, linguistic, and social organization that preceded and determined it." De Certeau, "Mysticism," 21.

15. De Certeau, *Fable*, 36–44.

16. Brammer, "Thinking Practice," 27.

17. De Certeau, "Mysticism," 18.

18. Ibid., 29.

19. Ibid., 31.

20. De Certeau, *Writing*, 156.

21. De Certeau, *The Practice*, xix.

22. This exclusive privilege, together with the interdiction for women to touch the Eucharist, had profound repercussions for female mystics for whom Eucharistic devotion and *imitatio Christi* are intrinsically linked. See Bynum, *Jesus*, 15, 297.

23. On the increasing loss of status for women from the late Middle Ages onward, see Joan Kelly, "Early Feminist Theory and the *Querelle des Femmes*, 1400–1789," *Signs* 8 (1982), 4–28. Kelly refers to the development of the nation-state as adversely affecting women's political position. See also Natalie Zemon Davis, "Women on Top," in her collections of essays, *Society and Culture in Early Modern France* (Stanford: Stanford Uni-

versity Press, 1975), 124–28, as well as Sarah Hanley, "Engendering the State: Family Formation and State Building in Early Modern France," *French Historical Studies* 16 (1989), 4–27. On the deterioration of women's economic status in the late Middle Ages owing to growing guild restrictions, increased technological changes, and the advent of capitalism, see Merry E. Weisner, "Spinning Out Capital: Women's Work in the Early Modern Era," in *Becoming Visible: Women in European History*, ed. Renate Bridenthal, Claudia Koonz; and Susan Stuard, 2d ed. (Boston: Houghton, 1987), 221–49 and David Herlihy, *Opera Muliebria: Women and Work in Medieval Europe* (New York: McGraw, 1990).

24. Bynum explains that before the thirteenth century women had a certain clerical authority (they preached, heard confessions from the sisters placed under them, and gave benedictions), as Pope Innocent III learned to his great surprise in 1210. But these activities were increasingly being criticized and repressed. Around 1245, Bernard of Parma declared that whatever the custom had been before, from now on women were no longer allowed to teach, preach, touch the Eucharist or the sacred vessels, give the veil to new nuns, confess and absolve them, nor exercise their own judgment. See Bynum, *Jesus*, 15.

25. In this, Bynum agrees with André Vauchez that female mysticism is not only the manifestation of a loss but also the occasion of an empowerment. For Vauchez, mysticism, with its emphasis on the sensory, provided women with a privileged access to the divine that was otherwise denied to them. See André Vauchez, *Les Laïcs au Moyen Age: pratiques et expériences religieuses* (Paris: Editions du Cerf, 1987), 202.

26. Bynum, *Holy*, 294.

27. Ibid., 294.

28. Ibid., 295.

29. Ibid., 295.

30. Simone de Beauvoir, *The Second Sex*, trans. H. M. Parshley (New York: Bantam, 1970), 630–38.

31. Bynum, *Holy*, 29. See also her note 73.

32. Ibid., xvi.

33. Cited in Laurie Finke, *Feminist Theory, Women's Writing.* (Ithaca, N.Y.: Cornell University Press, 1992), 23.

34. Bynum, *Fragmentation*, 65. See also 324 note 46.

35. De Certeau, "Mysticism," 16.

36. Bynum, *Fragmentation*, 55.

37. Bynum, *Holy*, 277–96.

38. Finke states: "Bakhtin's notion of the dialogized word is useful to feminist critics precisely because it refuses to see the oppressed or marginalized as passive victims of their oppression; it returns them to a cultur-

ally specific agency and the power to participate in defining their struggles, in turning the oppressor's words against him" (14). For such a view
see also S. R. Bordo, "Anorexia Nervosa: Psychopathology as the Crystallization of Culture," in *Feminism and Foucault: Reflections on Resistance*,
ed. I. Diamond and L. Quinby (Boston: Northeastern University Press,
1988), 87–118; idem., "The Body and the Reproduction of Femininity: A
Feminist Appropriation of Foucault," in *Gender/Body/Knowledge: Feminist Reconstructions of Being*, ed. A. M. Jaggar and S. R. Bordo (New
Brunswick, N.J.: Rutgers University Press, 1989), 13–33.

    39. Beckwith, "A Very Material Mysticism," 36.

Chapter 1. Female Mysticism

    1. For an evolution of the words *mystic* and *mysticism* see de Certeau,
"Mystique au XVIIe siècle," in *L'Homme devant Dieu; Mélanges offerts au
Père Henri de Lubac* (Paris: Aubier, 1964), vol. 2. Before the seventeenth
century such a person would have been called "contemplative" or "spiritual."

    2. See Bynum, *Jesus*; idem., *Holy Feast and Holy Fast*; idem., *Frag-
mentation and Redemption*; Rudolph Bell, *Holy Anorexia* (Chicago: University of Chicago Press, 1985); Donald Weinstein and Rudolph Bell, *Saints
and Society: The Two Worlds of Western Christendom* (Chicago: University
of Chicago Press, 1982); Richard Kieckhefer, *Unquiet Souls: Fourteenth-
Century Saints and Their Religious Milieu* (Chicago: University of Chicago
Press, 1984). See also, de Certeau, *Fable*, 21–22, for the sixteenth and
seventeenth centuries.

    3. About the female mystical movement, Bynum says: "For the first
time in Christian history we can document that a particular kind of religious experience is more common among women than men. For the first
time in Christian history certain major devotional and theological em-
phases emanate from women and influence the basic development of spirituality." See Bynum, *Jesus*, 172.

    4. Bynum, *Jesus*, 172. See also Weinstein and Bell, *Saints and Society*
and Kieckhefer, *Unquiet Souls*.

    5. For this historical framework see Bynum, *Jesus*.

    6. Pseudo-Dionysius is the name given by modern historians to an
anonymous Greek writer of the fifth or sixth century, whose works had
been wrongly attributed to Denys the Areopagite who lived in the first
century.

    7. See de Certeau, *Fable*, 90.

8. On the preference traditionally given to negative theology see Sarah Beckwith, "A Very Material Mysticism: The Medieval Mysticism of Margery Kempe," in *Medieval Literature: Criticism, Ideology and History*, ed. David Aers (Brighton: Harvester, 1986), 38–39. Theologians' favoring of negative mysticism is one of the themes in Karma Lochrie, *Margery Kempe and Translations of the Flesh* (Philadelphia: University of Pennsylvania Press, 1991).

9. The themes of negative mysticism in the vernacular started with the Beguines in the thirteenth century. See *Dictionnaire de spiritualité ascétique et mystique* (Paris: Beauchesne, 1937), "Béguines," 1:1350. This work will be hereafter referred to as *DSAM*. Translations from this work are mine. Among other famous female mystics who developed or prolonged this trend, one finds the two Hadewijchs and Marguerite Porète in the thirteenth century, Catherine of Sienna in the fourteenth century, Catherine of Genoa in the fifteenth century, Teresa of Avila (to a certain extent) and Isabella Bellinzaga in the sixteenth century, and Madame Acarie, Marie de l'Incarnation and Madame Guyon in the seventeenth century. For the influence of the Beguines on Meister Eckhart see Bernard McGinn, *Meister Eckhart and the Beguine Mystics* (New York: Continuum, 1994).

10. For a further contrast between female and male mystics at the symbolic level, see Lochrie, *Margery Kempe*, 50, 227, and Bynum, *Holy*, 100–20. As Bynum explains, when men of the Middle Ages (and this is also true for later male mystics) described other men or themselves as women, they did so in order to symbolize what they must give up in order to attain God. Namely, they had to give up temporal power, fortune, authority, knowledge, and reason. In other words, they had to deprive themselves of all that constituted male privilege, except that of ruling over women.

11. The Beguines, although now more closely controlled by the institution of the church, were given permission to expand in the middle of the century. See Bynum, *Holy*, 22.

12. According to Bynum, the epoch produced a new image of God as father/mother/lover/friend, as well as an image of the priest as necessary intermediary between the soul and God. In proportion as the priest became more distant and more holy, God became more accessible and more human. Bynum, *Jesus*, 19.

13. Clare of Montefalco's sanctification in the beginning of the thirteenth century is one of the first to be based on paraphysical phenomena. See Lochrie, *Margery Kempe and Translations of the Flesh*, 14.

14. Elizabeth Rapley, *The Dévotes: Women and Church in Seventeenth-Century France*. (Montreal: McGill-Queen's University Press, 1990), 21.

15. Ibid., 41.

16. Ibid., 27.

17. Ibid., 6.

18. Ibid., 6.

19. Ibid., 8.

20. Works devoted to the history of science and philosophy, such as *Science, Culture and Popular Belief in Renaissance Europe*, ed. Stephen Pumfrey, Paolo L. Rossi, Maurice Slawinski (Manchester: Manchester University Press, 1991), and in this volume particularly, Luce Giard's, "Remapping Knowledge, Reshaping Institutions," 19–47, define rationality by its characteristic classification of knowledge, whether it be in relation to the philosophy of nature, analysis of religious phenomena, or the conception of the human body.

21. See, for example, Thomas S. Kuhn's classic, *The Structure of Scientific Revolutions* (Chicago: University of Chicago Press, reprint 1970). Kuhn argues that there are discontinuities between the types of theories before and after the scientific revolution.

22. See the exhaustive and excellent study on women, culture, and mysticism in seventeenth-century France by Linda Timmermans, *L'Accès des femmes à la culture (1598–1715)* (Paris: Champion, 1993).

23. According to Georges Gusdorf, *Dieu, la nature, l'homme au siècle des Lumières* (Paris: Payot, 1972), this religious liberalism is echoed in the thought of Rousseau, Kant, and Kierkegaard; it was also influential in the formation of the German *Sturm und Drang* and, more generally, of European Romanticism.

24. See for example, Dorothy Backer, *Precious Women* (New York: Basic, 1974); Carolyn C. Lougee, *Le Paradis des Femmes: Women, Salons and Social Stratification in Seventeenth-Century France* (Princeton, N.J.: Princeton University Press, 1976); Ian Maclean, *Woman Triumphant (1610–1652)* (Oxford: Oxford University Press, 1977); Timmermans, *L'Accès des femmes à la culture.*

25. What is known as the collective convulsions of Saint-Médard occurred in 1727, around the Jansenist cult of François de Pâris, deacon of the Church of Saint-Médard. The Jansenists attributed the bodily manifestations of the Jansenist women to the intervention of God, as a proof that they held the truth. The official church, however, looked upon the phenomenon as a demonic possession and a proof of the heresy of the Jansenists. The king ordered the army to close the church and the cemetery where the convulsionaries were meeting. His ordinance was based on two points that evaded the dialectic of the church (possession by God or the Devil). The first point was that the medical doctors had pronounced that the fantastic bodily manifestations of the Jansenist convulsionaries were neither supernatural nor natural, but simply a fraud. The second point

was that the phenomenon had sexual overtones. See Gérard Wajeman, *Le Maître et l'hystérique* (Paris: Navarin/Seuil, 1982), 105.

26. The last phenomenon of collective possesssion in Europe occurred in 1878, in the commune of Verzegnis, in the Italian Frioul. See Wajeman, *Le Maître et l'hystérique*, 77.

27. For the description of the collective possession of Morzine and its interpretation whithin a psychoanalytical framework, see Wajeman, *Le Maître et l'hystérique*, 35–77.

28. J. M. Charcot and P. Richer, *Les Démoniaques dans l'art, suivi de la foi qui guérit*, ed. P. Fedida and J. Didi-Huberman (Paris: Macula, 1984).

29. The idea propounded by Descartes of the body as a pure mechanism found its utmost expression at the end of the nineteenth century in Charcot, who went so far as to deny any correlation between symptoms and psychic life in the women he called "hysterics" and on whom he experimented at the Salpêtrière hospital. Faced with this severe and destructive consequence of positivistic thought, one can gauge the importance of Freud's contribution, which brought back the unity of body and mind, although that unity was no longer the same as that of premodern times, for he emphasized a body and mind that refer to themselves and not to God. I must add that despite Freud's breakthrough in understanding that it was the symptom itself of the suffering woman that ought to be decoded, his own conservatism stood in the way of a political analysis of women's suffering in patriarchy. For it is not by questioning the suffering woman that an answer can be given to the enigma of female suffering, as the unconscious of both the woman and the psychoanalyst repress the keys to the enigma. An understanding can take place only by directing the questioning to the civilization that produced enigmatic female suffering.

30. *Histoire de la vie privée.* Under the direction of Philippe Ariès and Georges Duby, vol. 4. (Paris: Seuil, 1987).

31. Ibid., 579.

32. Bynum, *Holy*, 8.

Part 1. Marie de l'Incarnation

1. I have drawn this information mainly from Dom Guy Oury, *Marie Guyart (1599–1672)*, trans. Miriam Thompson (Cincinnati, Oh.: Specialty Lithographing Company, 1979) and also from Françoise Deroy-Pineau, *Marie de l'Incarnation. Marie Guyart femme d'affaires, mystique, mère de la Nouvelle France* (Paris: Laffont, 1989). Natalie Zemon Davis's excellent study on Marie de l'Incarnation in *Women on the Margins: Three Seven-*

teenth-Century Lives (Cambridge: Harvard University Press, 1995) came out after I had sent my manuscript to the publisher.

Chapter 2. The Female Mystical Body in Transition

1. Weinstein and Bell, *Saints and Society*, 2.
2. Marc Bloch, in *The Royal Touch* (London: Routledge, 1973), argued well before Foucault for a shift in the perception of the body in the eighteenth century when he stated that the belief that touching the king would bring cure of illnesses suddenly disappeared in France and England at that time. Bloch's suggestions for a different understanding of the body remained without echo until Foucault. Since Foucault, American as well as European historians of the body have argued that, indeed, such a shift occurred in the eighteenth century and even before.

For example, in *Body Guards*, ed. Julia Epstein and Kristina Straub (New York: Routledge, 1991), there are two articles that address more specifically how the body, sexuality, and gender come to be understood in different ways in the Renaissance, eighteenth and nineteenth centuries. Randolph Trumback's "London's Sapphists: From Three Sexes to Four Genders in the Making of Modern Culture" (112–41), together with Ann Rosalind Jones's and Peter Stallybrass's "Fetishizing Gender: Constructing the Hermaphrodite in Renaissance Europe" (80–111), argues for a shift in the understanding of sex and gender from fluid positions to fixed characteristics.

Michel de Certeau's *La Possession de Loudun* (Paris: Gallimard, 1980) (to be published in English translation by the University of Chicago Press) also indicates, apropos of the bodily manifestations of the possessed women of Loudun, the emergence of a new way to conceptualize such manifestations in the seventeenth century.

Ruth Richardson's *Death, Dissection and the Destitute* (London: Routledge, 1988) examines the way corpses became available to medical schools in the eighteenth and nineteenth centuries. Until the early nineteenth century, corpses available for medical use were bodies of criminals, supposedly desacralized by their sins. In the early nineteenth century, however, demands for corpses by the medical schools became greater than the supply, and grave robbing by thieves, who then sold corpses to these schools, began to thrive. In an attempt to reintroduce some civic order, English law decreed that bodies of the destitute coming from poorhouses would also be used for medical purposes. Richardson argues that the decree points to the shift, which had already taken place, from an understanding of the body as inhabited by a soul (which required intactness for resurrection) to a secularized view of the body.

3. In *The Order of Things* (New York: Vintage, 1973), Michel Foucault termed this phenomena "episteme." Foucault suggested that there are moments in history when texts produced by different disciplines express a coherence in which one can discern patterns of structures and meaning that are different from what preceded. It is this coherence and rupture at given historical moments that he called "episteme." With this notion of episteme in mind, Foucault argued that such a textual phenomenon is evident starting in the Renaissance and then especially in the eighteenth century. This discontinuity between ways of understanding and assigning meaning to the world eventually affects social structures.

4. Weinstein and Bell, *Saints and Society*, 4.

5. Marie de l'Incarnation, *La Vie*, 48. Dom Claude Martin, the son of Marie de l'Incarnation, published her autobiographical writings in 1677 under the title: *La Vie de la Vénérable Mère Marie de l'Incarnation*. As Dom J. Lonsagne warns us in his introduction to the reproduction of 1981, this is a complex work, for when Dom Martin published his mother's autobiographical texts he interspersed them with biographical commentaries of his own. Besides, he admits to having corrected her style, which, he said, would have appeared archaic to readers in the latter part of the century. When quoting from Marie de l'Incarnation's texts I cite her name in the notes; when quoting from the commentaries by Martin, I cite his name. Dom Claude Martin also published his mother's *Correspondence* in 1681, and a new and more complete edition of this work was published by Dom Guy Oury at Solesme in 1971. Translations from both of these works are mine.

6. Marie de l'Incarnation, *La Vie*, 49.

7. This is underscored by many, including Weinstein and Bell, *Saints and Society*; Rudolph Bell, *Holy Anorexia*; Caroline Walker Bynum, *Holy*; idem., *Fragmentation*.

8. On the circumstances of Marie de l'Incarnation's choice of an order and the way she interprets it, see Dom Guy Oury, *Marie Guyart*, 120–28.

9. For a history of the Ursuline order in Italy, France, and Quebec, see Rapley, *The Dévotes. Women and Church in Seventeenth-Century France*; Jegou, Marie-Andrée, *Les Ursulines du Faubourg Saint Jacques à Paris 1607–1662* (Paris: Presses Universitaires de France, 1981); Lemoine, George Louis, *Les Ursulines de Québec depuis leur établissement jusqu'à nos jours* (Québec: C. Darveau, 1866–78), 4 vols.; Oury, *Marie Guyart*, 134–45.

10. Oury, *Marie Guyart*, 141–42; Rapley, *The Dévotes*, 142–47.

11. Marie de l'Incarnation, *La Vie*, 180–81.

12. Quoted by Rapley, *The Dévotes*, 142, from *Les Chroniques de l'Ordre*

des Ursulines recueillies pour l'usage des Religieuses du mesme Ordre, par M(ère) D(e) P(ommereu) U(rsuline) (Paris, 1673), part 1:8–9.

13. The Ursulines in Tours and the nursing nuns in Dieppe were the first in the French Church to have undertaken such an enterprise. The Spanish Church had, however, earlier founded a monastery of regular canonesses of Saint Augustine (the Incarnation) in Lima, Peru, in 1572; before 1585, that of the order of Saint Clare (the Conception); in 1584 a monastery of Cistercian nuns was created (the Trinity). See Oury, *Marie Guyart*, 233, n.57. The only other precedent for women missionaries occurred in the eighth century when Boniface chose an English nun, Leoba, to accompany him on his mission to Christianize Germany.

14. Marie de l'Incarnation, *Correspondance*, 814.

15. Ibid., 764.

16. Ibid., 342.

17. Cornelius Jaenen, *Friend and Foe: Aspects of French-Amerindian Cultural Contact in the Sixteenth and Seventeenth Centuries* (Toronto: McClelland and Steward, 1976), 69.

18. Ibid., 70.

19. Martin, *La Vie*, 403–404.

20. Not only was Marie de l'Incarnation consulted by many officials of the colony, she was also sought after for her spiritual advice and teaching by the population, as well as by the Jesuits. According to the *DSAM*, "Marie de l'Incarnation" (1980), 10:498, several Jesuit missionaries came to her for spiritual direction and for advice, particularly A. J. Poncet, P. -M. Chaumonot, and Ch. Garnier.

21. Marie de l'Incarnation, *Correspondance*, 229.

22. Ibid., 314.

23. Ibid., 390.

24. Ibid., 550.

25. Ibid., 589.

26. Ibid., 800.

27. Ibid., 826.

28. Ibid., 939. More mentions of her good health are to be found in *Correspondance* in her letters of the following dates: 1654, 1656, 1659, 1660, 1663.

29. Ibid., 477.

30. Ibid., 482.

31. Ibid., 499.

32. Ibid., 477.

33. Ibid., 396.

34. Ibid., 790. She speaks at length about her illness for the first time in 1665.

35. Ibid., 791.

36. Ibid., 795.

37. On her confrontation with her superiors see Oury, *Marie Guyart*, 288–89, 335–44.

38. Bynum, *Holy*, 8.

39. Ibid., 298.

40. Bynum, *Fragmentation*, 23.

41. Oury, *Marie Guyart*, 125.

42. She could also have chosen to join one of the new congregations that had neither *clausura* nor solemn vows. In this case, she would have had even more freedom than the Ursulines offered, while still serving the church as a religious woman. These congregations, however, lacked the prestige of regular orders, and her family (or she herself) might have considered this position beneath their social status.

43. Bynum, *Holy*, 6.

44. Beckwith, "A Very Material Mysticism," 54. As a parallel we can invoke feet-binding of young girls by their mothers in not-so-ancient China or sexual mutilation of young girls in Africa performed by the adult women themselves. These mutilations of the female body are given cultural and religious meaning by the women who have been subjected to it and who, in turn, perform it on the young girls. In their fight against what their culture perceives as Westernization, the women performing excision have even been persuaded by the men of their culture to defend it as a right in which their national, religious, and sexual identity lies. But can we really stretch cultural relativism to the absurd and affirm that because the women of these particular cultures give these mutilations cultural and religious meaning, these practices therefore become dignified? And can we affirm that because they give a cultural or religious meaning to the sexual mutilation of little girls these women are not acting out of internalized self-hatred?

45. For an incisive analysis of the problem of consent, see Nicole-Claude Mathieu, "When Yielding Is Not Consenting," *Feminist Issues*, 9:1 (1989), 3–49 and 10:1 (1990), 51–90.

46. Bynum, *Fragmentation*, 18.

47. Bynum, *Holy*, 22.

48. Ibid., 21–22.

49. Ibid., 22.

Chapter 3. From France to Canada/From Motherhood to Subjecthood

1. See Oury, *Marie Guyart*, 131, n.98. See also Oury's introduction to the *Correspondance*, xv and xvii.

238 NOTES (CHAPTER 3)

2. See letter of August 9, 1654, *Correspondance*, 525, which Claude Martin reproduces in its entirety in his preface to the publication of his mother's work, as if to prove that indeed she had unveiled her most intimate secrets out of motherly love.

3. Sigmund Freud, "Femininity," *The Standard Edition of the Complete Psychological Works of Sigmund Freud*, ed. James Strachey (London: Hogarth, 1953–74), 22:133.

4. Cited by Jean-Noël Vuarnet, *Extases féminines* (Paris: Arthaud, 1980), 79. My translation.

5. Claude Martin alludes to this scandal in *La Vie*, 171.

6. Marie de l'Incarnation speaks of this abandonment in numerous letters: *Correspondance*, 130, 316, 384, 527, 658, 725, 836–837, 898.

7. Ibid., 115.

8. Ibid., 130–31.

9. Ibid., 130–31.

10. Ibid., 316.

11. Ibid., 837.

12. Ibid., 837.

13. Ibid., 837.

14. Oury, *Marie Guyart*, 64–5.

15. Marie de l'Incarnation, *Correspondance*, 399.

16. Ibid., 525.

17. Ibid., 526–27.

18. Ibid., 527.

19. Ibid., 186.

20. Ibid., 525.

21. Ibid., 527.

22. Ibid., 224.

23. Ibid., 572.

24. Ibid., 898.

25. Martin, *La Vie*, 171.

26. Marie de l'Incarnation, *Correspondance*, 318.

27. Ibid., 661.

28. Ibid., 318.

29. Ibid., 515.

30. Ibid., 532.

31. See introduction to Elisabeth A. Petroff, *Medieval Women's Visionary Literature* (Oxford: Oxford University Press, 1986), and Peter Dronke, *Women Writers of the Middle Ages* (Cambridge: Cambridge University Press, 1984).

32. Marguerite Porète, *Le Miroir des âmes simples et anéanties* (Paris: Albin Michel, 1984). Marguerite Porète is the most outstanding exception

to the pattern of tightrope walking that is so characteristic of female mystics, because she made no compromise. It is interesting to observe that Marguerite Porète's mystical treatise was not autobiographical but merely speculative, in contrast to the texts of the bulk of mystics for whom charismatic authority and the recognition of the church were based on personal, extraordinary, and physical experiences. Also, Porète was opposed to visions, which were another source of authorization for mystics in general. Finally, unlike those mystics considered to be orthodox, Marguerite Porète made no excuse for being a woman writing on theology.

33. Martin, *La Vie*, ii.
34. Ibid., iv.
35. Ibid., v.
36. Marie de l'Incarnation, *La Vie*, 1.
37. Marie de l'Incarnation, *Correspondance*, 317.
38. Ibid., 184.
39. Ibid., 343.
40. Ibid., 317. My emphasis.
41. Ibid., 343.
42. Ibid., 425.
43. Ibid., 526. My emphasis.
44. Marie de l'Incarnation had compelling reasons for not wanting her experience to be divulged in her lifetime. It must be borne in mind that while the female mystic was still revered in the midseventeenth century, she was also open to suspicion, and Marie de l'Incarnation alludes in her letters to being aware of the religious quarrels raging in France. Had she been accused of quietism, her undertaking in New France would have been endangered.
45. Marie de l'Incarnation, *Correspondance*, 426.
46. Ibid., 515.
47. Ibid., 517. See also Oury, *Marie Guyart*, 201–202.
48. Marie de l'Incarnation, *Correspondance*, 837.
49. Ibid., 184.

Chapter 4. The Double Bind

1. For an alternative definition of history that allows an evaluation of women's historical undertaking, see Natalie Zemon Davis, "Gender and Genre: Women as Historical Writers, 1400–1820" in *Beyond Their Sex. Learned Women of the European Past*, ed. Patricia A. Labalme (New York: New York University Press, 1980), 153–82; Joan Kelly, *Women, History and Theory* (Chicago: University of Chicago Press, 1984); Scott, *Gender*

and the Politics of History; Faith E. Beasley, *Revising Memory: Women's Fiction and Memoirs in Seventeenth-Century France* (New Brunswick, N.J.: Rutgers University Press, 1990). Natalie Zemon Davis's *Women on the Margins* considers specifically Marie de l'Incarnation as a writer of history.

2. Beasley, *Revising Memory*, 7.

3. Her historiographical writings can be found in her *Correspondance*, ed. Dom Guy Oury (Solesme, 1971), and in Dom Claude Martin, *La Vie de la Vénérable Mère Marie de l'Incarnation* reproduction of the original 1677 edition, (Solesme, 1981).

4. *The Jesuit Relations and Allied Documents*, ed. Reuben Gold Thwaites (Cleveland, Oh.: Burrows 1890–1901). Hereafter refered to as Thwaites.

5. François Du Creux, *Historiae Canadensis* (Paris, 1664).

6. Scott, *Gender and the Politics of History*.

7. I refer to the hagiography of Mother Marie de Saint Joseph, in the *Correspondance*, 436, and which is included in *The Jesuit Relation* (Thwaites, 38: 70). Certain pages are also included in the *Chroniques de l'ordre de Sainte-Ursule* of Mother de Pommereu, published in 1673. Marie de l'Incarnation also wrote a short hagiography of Anne Bataille de Saint Laurent, which Mother de Pommereu used in her *Chroniques* 2: 458–62. See *Correspondence*, 848, n.1.

8. In fact, the Indians of the Northeast were very tolerant in matters of religion, and no Jesuit was ever martyred because his beliefs differed from theirs. Jesuits were sometimes killed when they were perceived as exercising bad magic against the Indians. See Joseph LeCaron, *Au Roy sur la Nouvelle-France* (Paris: 1626), cited by Cornelius J. Jaenen, "L'Autre en Nouvelle France/The *Other* in Early Canada," *The Canadian Historical Association, Historical Papers*, 1989, 11.

9. Mme de la Peltrie, the lay founder of the Ursulines in Quebec, although not bound by *clausura* and thus theoretically able to go on a mission among the tribes, was very strongly discouraged by the Jesuits. Consequently she did not venture forth.

10. See the introduction to the English translation of François Du Creux, *History of Canada*, trans. Percy J. Robinson, ed. James B. Conacher, (Toronto: Champlain Society, 1951).

11. There was a special parlor shared by the Mother Superior and the treasurer, or sometimes there were two individual parlors, depending on the amount of business to be conducted. The grill in the parlor had shutters and curtains, not opened for everyone. With the exception of the missionaries and Indians, all visitors were met by covered faces. It is true that the *clausura* of the Ursulines in Quebec was less rigorous than in France,

and that when Marie de l'Incarnation was about to die, those who wanted to see her were allowed to come in and do so. Nevertheless, the nuns were not permitted to go out of their convent. See Oury, *Marie Guyart*, 411.

12. Ibid., 411.

13. Ibid., 521.

14. Marie de l'Incarnation, *Correspondance*, 132.

15. On the use of the diminutive to designate women's work, see Timmermans, 536–37.

16. Thwaites, 38: 70.

17. Marie de l'Incarnation, *Correspondance*, 853.

18. Ibid., 521.

19. Ibid., 642.

20. Ibid., 146.

21. Ibid., 146.

22. Ibid., 146.

23. Ibid., 818.

24. This is what she wrote to Mother Marie-Alexis Boschet, Superior of the Ursulines of Le Mans in 1663: "I begged the reverent Father du Crux (Creux) to visit you and to make known to you what I wrote on the subject of the great earthquakes that occurred in this country" (*Correspondance*, 719).

25. Ibid., 768.

26. Ibid., 791.

27. Ibid., 802.

28. Thwaites, 52:98.

29. Marie de l'Incarnation, *Correspondance*, 485.

30. Ibid., 131.

31. Ibid., 801.

32. Ibid., 801.

33. Ibid., 801.

34. Ibid., 476.

35. Ibid., 634.

36. Ibid., 140.

37. Ibid., 156.

38. Ibid., 868.

39. Ibid., 549.

40. Women of all classes displayed an interest in the New World for many different reasons. For example, in the sixteenth century, Louise de Savoy, mother of Francis the First, possessed the journal of Pigafetta, which made known the Spanish circumnavigation of the world. Certain women of the aristocracy, free to dispose of their fortune, took part in the adventure of the New World by financing certain colonial enterprises. In

the seventeenth century, Madame de Guercheville provided large sums of money for commercial expeditions and explorations. Madame de Combalet, later Duchess d'Aiguillon, founded the Quebec Hospital. Madame Bullion set up the *Hospitalières* of Montreal. Charlotte de Montmorency provided the funds for a mission to aid and convert the Indians of the Petun nation. Madeleine de la Peltrie, who would spend thirty years in New France, devoted herself to various religious works and provided funds for the foundation of the Ursulines in Quebec. Among bourgeois women, Jeanne Mance founded the *Hotel Dieu de Montréal* in 1643. See Marcel Trudel, *Initiation à la Nouvelle-France* (Montréal: Holt, 1968). Marguerite Bourgeoys founded the *Congrégation des Filles Séculières de Notre Dame in Ville-Marie* in 1669 for the education of children, and she instituted avant-garde teaching methods therein. She openly stood against the cloister and solemn vows, refusing to take an oath of obedience to the clergy. This officially sanctioned congregation was among the first in the seventeenth century to bring together women who lived a religious life outside the cloister and who worked to provide for their own subsistence. See Elizabeth Rapley, *The Dévotes*.

41. Marie de l'Incarnation, *Correspondance*, 398.

42. Ibid., 873.

43. The study of civil proceedings shows women in nearly all social occupations: commerce, production of textiles and clothing, fur trade, spirits, utensils, and management of inns, cabarets, and brothels. Collectif Clio, *L'Histoire des femmes au Québec depuis quatre siècles* (Montréal: Quinze, 1982), 24.

44. Davis, "Gender and Genre", 174.

45. Marie de l'Incarnation, *Correspondance*, 832.

46. Ibid., 873.

47. Ibid., 844.

48. Ibid., 845.

49. Ibid., 833.

50. Ibid., 832–33.

51. Ibid., 126.

52. Ibid., 451–52.

53. Ibid., 181.

54. I disagree with Timmermans who states that Marie de l'Incarnation conceived of female apostleship in terms strictly considered proper for women, that is as small works rather than as teaching and preaching actively outside the convent. See 535–36.

55. The Jesuits' story is included in Thwaites, 22: 142–44.

56. Marie de l'Incarnation, *Correspondance,* 64.

57. The missionaries encouraged the segregation of Christianized In-

dians from those who resisted Christianization. They also encouraged the *dogiques*, that is the older men, to assume responsibility for catechism and to police the young in the Christianized community. On the Indian reservations, the *dogiques* imposed a theocratic rule. The whip was used by the missionaries and by the *dogiques* on the converts in order to make them observe French and Christian disciplines. See Jaenen, *Friend and Foe*, 70–71.

58. The excessive zeal of certain converts embarrassed even the ecclesiastic authorities. At Tadoussac, in 1645, the Jesuits had to interveve in order to stop public penitence and bloody sessions of self-flagellation. See Jaenen, *Friend and Foe*, 70–71.

59. Marie de l'Incarnation, *Correspondance*, 164.

60. Thwaites, 50: 126.

61. Marie de l'Incarnation, *Correspondance*, 774.

Chapter 5. The Confrontation between "Civilized" and "Savage" Femininity in the New World

1. I do not always distinguish between groups of American Indian women, not because the groups with which the French came in contact were indistinguishable, but because the distinction does not bear on the subject of Marie de l'Incarnation's perception of them. These Indians included Huron, Algonquin, Montagnais, and later, Iroquois. Although cultural differences existed between them, as occasionally acknowledged by seventeenth-century writers, the missionaries generally made only one sharp distinction, setting the Iroquois apart from the others. There are three reasons for this. First, the Iroquois were not their allies; second, they were more sedentary and seemed to have had a more tightly knit social structure; third, the French came in contact with their villages and civilization later than with the other Indians mentioned above. Furthermore, according to Conrad Heidenreich, *Huronia: A History and Geography of the Huron Indians 1600–1650* (Ontario: McClelland, 1971), "most of the generalities made about Hurons' technology and resources are also applicable to other tribal societies of shifting cultivators [in the American Northeast], as are Huron social values and political concepts" (296). This also seems to be the opinion of Elizabeth Tooker, "Women in Iroquois Society," in *Extending the Rafter*, ed. Michael Foster and Deborah Welch, (New York: New York State University Press, 1984).

2. In the sixteenth and seventeenth centuries, the French constructed their images of the American Indians from their contact with Brazilian and Northeast Indians. See Cartier, Léry, Thevet, Roberval, Saintonge,

Villegagnon, Ribaut, Lescarbot, Sagard, Dollier de Casson, and *The Jesuit Relations*. According to Cornelius J. Jaenen, "Amerindian Views of French Culture in the Seventeenth Century," *The Canadian Historical Review*, 55:3 (1974): "In the seventeenth century Europeans invariably assumed that Europe was the center of the world and of civilization, that its cultures were the oldest, that America was a new continent and that its peoples were necessarily recent immigrants. . . . The conceptual frameworks of Europeans—whether Spaniards, French, or English, or whether Catholics or Protestants—were remarkably indistinguishable whenever the circumstances of contact were similar" (264).

3. *New World Encounters*, ed. Stephen Greenblatt (Berkeley: University of California Press, 1993), vii–viii.

4. See Jaenen, *Friend and Foe*; Norman Clermont, "La Place de la femme dans les sociétés iroquiennes de la période du contact," *Recherches Amérindiennes au Québec* 13:4 (1983); Dominique Deslandres, "Marie de l'Incarnation et la femme amérindienne," *Recherches Amérindiennes au Québec* 13:4 (1983).

5. Jaenen, "Perceptions françaises de la Nouvelle France et de ses peuples indigènes aux XVIIe et XVIIIe siècles," *Recherches Amérindiennes au Québec* 13:2 (1983), 111. Sharing this vision, Marie de l'Incarnation called the missionary church "a first-century church" or sometimes "the new church."

6. Greenblatt identifies a third position: it is an ironic critique of the "vision of the victors" that views European colonization not as an epiphany but as a material, cultural, and religious piracy as illustrated by Swift's *Gulliver's Travels*. This position is neither represented in Marie de l'Incarnation's writing nor in that of the Jesuits, except maybe when they criticize the French who provide alcohol to the Indians in order to get something in exchange.

7. Ibid., viii.

8. For European myths about American Indians see Jaenen, "Perception." The existence of the New World came initially as something of a surprise, since Scriptures made no mention of it. The surprise was overcome by turning to various mythical traditions in the European heritage and by trying at all costs to integrate the unknown into the known, European scheme of things. It was suggested that America was indeed a new world, created after that of Adam and Eve and that the American Indians were new human beings, more recent additions to the history of the human race, as was borne out by their small numbers, their ignorance, and the meager progress made in the arts by the more civilized among them. Others suggested that this was the lost paradise: the natural beauty of the

country and its animals, the trust and innocence of the naked Indians who lived in accordance with the "natural" laws, all attested to this. Others, following the scheme of Hesiod as adopted by Fontenelle and Turgot, believed that the history of humanity could be divided like that of an individual into stages or periods, and they viewed Indian society as the infantile state of the Golden Age. It was suggested in opposition to this thesis that the barbarian or savage state belonged to a degenerative phase of the human race. There were even those who claimed that Indians represented an intermediary species between the human and the animal. Finally, certain people wondered whether America was not the monstrous, damned, satanic world in which terror reigned, located by philosophical tradition in the "forest" or at the "end of the earth," and whether the Iroquois were not the living image of the devil, who could only be eliminated by holy war. These contradictory notions of the "savage" can all be found within the same period and often in the works of the same author.

9. Jaenen, "Perception," 10.

10. See Alan C. Kors, *Atheism in France: 1650–1729.* (Princeton, N.J.: Princeton University Press, 1990).

11. Thwaites, 5: 180.

12. Clermont, "La Place," 287.

13. De Certeau, "Writing vs. Time: History and Anthropology in the Work of Lafiteau, *Yale French Studies,* 59 (Summer, 1980), 37–64.

14. My translation from Joseph F. Lafiteau, *Moeurs des sauvages américains comparées aux moeurs des premiers temps,* 2 vols (Paris: Saugrain, 1724), 71–72.

15. Continuing the patriarchal policy of the Jesuits, the federal law of Canada in 1869 stripped American Indian women of all their ancient rights and prerogatives and forced them to submit totally to white and American Indian men. In the 1970s, inspired by the feminist movement, American Indian women attempted to reclaim their ancient rights. On the federal level, they have as yet had little success; on the national level, they have come up against the American Indian males who do not want to cede their new-found prerogatives, despite the fact that these were granted to them by their conquerors. For a history of Indian women of the Northeast see Collectif Clio, *Histoire des femmes au Québec depuis quatre siècles.*

16. Thwaites, 5: 180.

17. The role of women and the relationship between the sexes in Iroquoian society has attracted, and continues to attract, the attention of equally large numbers of historians and ethnographers. For a revaluation of the place of Iroquoian, Algonquian, and Huron women in their society, see Tooker, "Women in Iroquois Society"; Clermont, "La Place"; Deborah

Welch, "American Indian Women: Reaching Beyond the Myth," in *New Directions in American Indian History*, ed. Collin Calloway (Norman and London: University of Oklahoma Press, 1988).

18. See Heidenreich, *Huronia*.

19. Marie de l'Incarnation, *Correspondance*, 546.

20. Ibid., 671.

21. Ibid., 123.

22. Thwaites, 6: 254.

23. Marie de l'Incarnation, *Correspondance*, 483.

24. Jaenen, "*L'Autre*," 3.

25. Thwaites, 30: 254.

26. Ibid., 30: 254.

27. Marie de l'Incarnation, *Correspondance*, 329.

28. Thwaites, 30: 254.

29. Marie de l'Incarnation, *Correspondance*, 331.

30. Thwaites, 30: 288.

31. Ibid., 30: 294.

32. Louis Montrose, "The Work of Gender in the Discourse of Discovery," in *New World Encounters*, 201.

33. Marie de l'Incarnation, *Correspondance*, 563.

34. Ibid., 604.

35. Thwaites, 44: 100.

36. This is a question Inga Clendinnen asks regarding Cortés's narrative in "'Fierce and Unnatural Cruelty': Cortés and the Conquest of Mexico," in *New World Encounters*, 14.

37. On the transformative violence of the encounter with the Other, see Luce Giard, "Epilogue: Michel de Certeau's Heterology and the New World," in *New World Encounters*, 317.

38. See Clermont, "La Place," 286–90; Rayna Green, *Native American Women: A Contextual Bibliography* (Bloomington: Indiana University Press, 1983), 248–67; Tooker, "Women in Iroquois Society."

39. Rapley's *Dévotes* gives a good account of the history of *clausura* in Europe, particularly in the seventeenth century when it comes to be questioned by religious women who wanted to devote their lives to charitable work in the world. For how *clausura* functioned in New France, see Oury, *Marie Guyart*, 411.

40. Marie de l'Incarnation, *Correspondance*, 108.

41. Ibid., 802.

42. Ibid., 828.

43. Ibid., 718.

44. While missionaries were immunized, the Indians were not, and they

died in great numbers as soon as the missionaries arrived in their territories and brought diseases with them. Surprised by these epidemics, the missionaries explained them by invoking God's will. The Indians, however, intuited a link between the diseases and the missionaries and thought that the latter had bewitched them. Later, decimated by disease and harassed by the Iroquois, the Huron neophytes closed ranks or mingled with other tribes in southern Quebec, leaving the French to face a void where the other had been. In 1650, when the French population was multiplying, only three hundred Hurons remained in Quebec, out of the twelve thousand present in 1639 and of the thirty thousand in 1634. See Oury, *Marie de l'Incarnation*, 431.

45. Marie de l'Incarnation, *Correspondance*, 734.

46. Ibid., 507.

47. Ibid., 936.

48. Cited by Jaenen, "*L'Autre*," 12.

49. Ibid., 12.

50. Jaenen, *Friend and Foe*, 69.

51. See Deslandres, "Marie de l'Incarnation," 281; Jaenen, *Friend and Foe*, 76.

52. Deslandres, "Marie de l'Incarnation," 283; Collectif Clio, 27; Jaenen, "*L'Autre*," 11.

53. Heidenreich, *Huronia*, 370; Tooker, "Women in Iroquois Society," 718.

54. Jaenen, "*L'Autre*," 11.

55. Collectif Clio, 20.

56. Marcel Trudel, "The Meeting of Cultures," in *Beginnings of New-France*. (Toronto: McClelland, 1973), 150–62.

57. Marie de l'Incarnation, *Correspondance*, 809.

58. Ibid., 829.

Part 2. Madame Guyon

1. For bibliographical information on Madame Guyon, I relied on Henri Brémond, *Apologie pour Fénelon* (Paris: Perrin et Cie., 1910), Louis Cognet, *Crépuscule des mystiques* (Paris: Desclée, 1958), and Marie-Louise Gondal, *Madame Guyon 1648–1717: Un Nouveau visage* (Paris: Beauchesne, 1989). For a complete bibliography of Madame Guyon's published and unpublished writings, as well as for a chronology of the publication of Madame Guyon's work, see Gondal, *Nouveau visage*, 286–90. Translations from these works are mine.

2. See Jonathan Dewald, *Aristocratic Experience and the Origins of Modern Culture: France 1570–1715* (Berkeley: University of California Press, 1993), 81.

3. Gondal, *Nouveau visage*, 211.

4. Ibid., 118, n. 5.

5. Ibid., 120.

6. Pierre Nicole, *Réfutation des principales erreurs des quiétistes contenues dans les livres censurés par l'ordonnance de Mgr l'arch. de Paris du 16 oct. 1694, précédée de l'ordonnance de l'arch. de Paris* (Paris, 1695), 1: 29.

7. I. Le Masson, *Eclaircissements sur la vie de Jean d'Arenthon* (1699).

8. Brémond, *Apologie*, 149.

9. Gondal, *Nouveau visage*, 149.

10. The Brief *Cum Alias* only condemned the *Maximes des saints*, not the defenses of Fénelon. A first vote had produced a tie of five against five. See Brémond, *Apologie*, 187.

Chapter 6. A Figure of Transition

1. In my doctoral dissertation on Madame Guyon I analyzed Guyon's persecutions as part of a paranoid discourse. Although I believe a historical perspective does not invalidate my previous analysis, my thesis is now more complex. See *Mysticisme et Psychose: l'autobiographie de Jeanne Guyon*, unpub. diss., University of California, Berkeley, 1980. *Dissertation Abstracts International*, Ann Arbor, XLII (81), 237 A–238 A.

2. Brémond, *Apologie*, 127. My translation.

3. Brémond, *Apologie*; idem., *Histoire littéraire du sentiment religieux en France depuis la fin des guerres de religion jusqu'à nos jours* (Paris: Bloud et Gay, 1921–1933), vol. 11. Brémond benefited from a series of previously published studies on Guyon. Masson recognized the importance of the corrrespondence between Guyon and Fénelon, which Jean-Philippe Dutoit had published two centuries earlier but which most historians had preferred to ignore: Maurice Masson, *Fénelon et Mme Guyon* (Paris: Hachette, 1907). In addition, several archival documents had already been published: Charles Urbain and Eugène Lévesque, *Correspondance de Bossuet* (Paris: Hachette, 1909–1925), 15 vols.; Eugène Griselle, "Interrogatoires de Mme Guyon, à Vincennes, le 26-12-1695," in *Documents d'Histoire*, 1 (Feb. 1910), 98–120 and 457–68. Emile Faguet also published very important archival documents in *Documents d'Histoire*, particularly the interrogation of Mme Guyon at Vincennes, while Albert Chérel resumed the

entire documentation in "Mme Guyon directrice de conscience," *Revue Fénelon*, (1910).

4. Cognet, *Le Crépuscule des mystiques*; idem., "Guyon," in *DSAM* (1967) 6: 1306–36; idem., "La spiritualité de Mme Guyon," *XVIIe Siècle* (1951–52), 269–75.

5. Jean Orcibal, "Une Controverse sur l'Eglise, d'après une correspondance inédite entre Fénelon et P. Poiret (1710–1711)," *XVIIe Siècle*, 25–26 (1955), 396–422; idem., "Le Cardinal Le Camus, témoin au procès de Mme Guyon," in *Le Cardinal des Montagnes, E. Le Camus, évêque de Grenoble (1671–1701)*, ed. Jean Godel (Grenoble: Presses Universitaires de Grenoble, 1974), 123–40; idem., "Mme Guyon devant ses juges," in *Mélanges de littérature française offerts à Mr. Pintard*, ed. Noémie Hepp, Robert Mauzi, and Claude Pichois (Strasbourg: Centre de Philologie et de Littératures Romanes de l'Université de Strasbourg, 1975) 409–23; François de Salignac de la Mothe Fénelon, *Correspondance*, ed. Jean Orcibal, 13 vols. (Paris: Klincksieck, 1972).

6. Gusdorf, *Dieu*.

7. Marie-Louise Gondal, *Nouveau visage*; *Madame Guyon: La Passion de croire*, ed. Marie-Louise Gondal (Paris: Nouvelle Cité, 1990); Madame Guyon, *Récits de captivité: inédit*, ed. Marie-Louise Gondal (Grenoble: Jérôme Millon, 1992). Translations from these works are mine.

8. Madame Guyon, *Lettres Chrétiennes et spirituelles sur divers sujets qui regardent la vie intérieure, ou l'esprit du vrai christianisme*, ed. Jean-Philippe Dutoit (1767–68), 4:519. Translations from this work are mine.

9. Madame Guyon, *La Vie de Mme J. M. B. de la Mothe Guion écrite par elle-même*, ed. Jean-Philippe Dutoit (1790), 1: 103. Translations from this work are mine.

10. Guyon, *Lettres Chrétiennes*, 4:519.

11. Madame Guyon, *Les Torrents spirituels*, in *Opuscules Spirituels*, ed. Pierre Poiret (1720), 253.

12. See Brémond, *Apologie*, 38; Le Brun, introduction to Fénelon, *Oeuvres*, xix; Orcibal, introduction to Fénelon, *Correspondance*, 11.

13. Fénelon, *Réponse à la Relation*, in *Oeuvres*, ed. Le Brun, 1156.

14. See Fénelon, *Correspondance*, ed. Orcibal, 3:241 and also 3:251, n. 5. See also Brémond, *Apologie*, 32–37.

15. See Fénelon, *Correspondance*, ed. Jean Orcibal, 3:193, n.14; 3:171, n.22; 3:199, n.25; 3:209, n.4.

16. Maurice Masson, *Fénelon et Mme Guyon*, 114, n.1; 139, n.3; 177, n.1; 228, n.2; 264, n.3; 306, n.3.

17. For Fénelon's statements affirming that he read everything Guyon sent him and for denials on the part of Orcibal, who was the editor of part of the *Correspondance*, see Fénelon, *Correspondance*, ed. Jean Orcibal. In

the letter of July 26, 1689, Fénelon writes to Guyon that he reads everything she sends him. In the letter of August 11, Fénelon tells Guyon that he reads with pleasure her *Petit abrégé de la voie et de la Réunion de l'âme à Dieu*. In the letter of August 31, he asks her to send him one of her writings for his edification. On June 3 of the same year, Fénelon tells Guyon that he has read her *Instruction chrétienne d'une mère à sa fille*, adding: "I have read it with the pleasure I read everything that comes from you." Orcibal does not provide a note for this letter; however, he repeats (in 3:179, n.2) that Fénelon not only did not like Guyon's writings but that he did not even read them. In the letter of June 12, 1689, however, Fénelon told Guyon: "I have taste for no kind of readings except for your letters when they arrive." Orcibal provides the following note to this statement: "For the first time Fénelon seems seduced by Mme. Guyon. But only by her letters and not by her works."

18. Barbe Jeanne Avrillot, wife of Pierre Acarie. She founded the French Carmelites in 1604 with Cardinal de Bérulle. When she was widowed, she entered the Carmelites herself under the name of Marie de l'Incarnation. She must not be confused with the other Marie de l'Incarnation (Guyart) who was a missionary in Quebec. The procedures for her beatification started in 1622, and she was beatified in 1791.

19. Jeanne-Françoise Frémiot, wife of Christophe de Rabutin, Baron de Chantal. In 1610, widowed, she founded, with François de Sales, the *Visitation Sainte-Marie* in Annecy. This institution became the regular order of the Visitation in 1619, which later multiplied throughout France. Jeanne de Chantal was also the grandmother of Madame de Sévigné. She was canonized in 1767.

20. Madame Guyon, *Les Justifications de Madame J. M. B. de la Mothe Guion, écrites par elle-même, suivant l'ordre de Messieurs les Evêques ses examinateurs, où l'on éclaircit plusieurs difficultés qui regardent la vie intérieure* (1720), 3 vols. The list of mystics she cites is extensive, and I offer it here with Guyon's spelling: Albarado, Albert le Grand, St. Ambroise, Ambroise Florentin de l'ordre des Camaldules, La B. Angèle de Foligni, St. Augustin, Constentin Barbançon, Bede, Benoît Justinien, St. Bernard, Bartelemi of the Martyrs Archbishop of Brague, Blosius, St. Bonaventure, Cardinal Cajenatus (Thomas de Vivo), Benoît de Canfeld, Cassien, Ste. Catherine de Gênes, Cornelius à Lapide, St. Denis, Denis le Chartreux, S. Diadoche, Epiphane Louis (abbé d'Estival), St. François de Sales, Gerson, Gilbert (l'abbé), Michel Gislerius, St. Gregoire le Grand, Harpuis, Hugues de St. Victor, Le P. Jacques de Jesus (Jacques d' Ypres, Evêque de Trarassone), Jean Chysostome, St. Jean Climaque, Le B. Jean de la Croix, Le P. Jean de Jesus-Maria, Le Fr. Jean de s. Samson, St. Jerôme, Le P. Il-

defonse d'Orosco, Kempis, Le P. Louis de Leon, Le P. Louis du Pont, Marie de l'Incarnation Superieure des Ursulines du Canada, Marie Rosette, Le P. Nicolas de Jesus-Maria, St. Nilus, Mr. Olier, Picus de la Mirande, St. Prosper, Richard de St. Victor, Antoine Roias, Rossignolius, Le P. Ruis de Montoya, Rusbroche, Suarez, Le P. Surin, Suso, Taulère, Ste. Thérèse, St. Thomas, Le P. Thomas de Jesus, Le B. Thomas de Villeneuve, Tolete.

21. Jean Baruzi, *Saint Jean de la Croix et le problème de l'expérience mystique* (Paris: Alcan, 1924), 449–54. See also Cognet, "La Spiritualité de Mme Guyon," 274. According to Cognet, Madame Guyon is virtually the only mystic author in the seventeenth century who constructed a coherent theory of passive purification. Her mysticism is essentially one of annihilation of the self (ego). She is an excellent theorist of the theopathic state, a state in which the human and the divine unite.

22. Henri Delacroix, *Les Grands mystiques chrétiens* (Paris: Alcan, 1938), 235.

23. Guyon, *La Vie de Mme*, 2:129, 140–42.

24. Ibid., 2:263.

25. Ibid., 2:132.

26. Cited by Vuarnet, *Extases féminines*, 39.

27. Guyon, *La Vie de Mme*, 2:98–99.

28. Ibid., 2:131.

29. Guyon wrote that La Combe had power over her illnesses (*La Vie de Mme*, 2:27, 103). She also stated that she had the power to heal others miraculously (*La Vie de Mme*, 2:230).

30. On the trial of Marguerite Porète, see Paul Verdeyen, "Le Procès d'inquisition contre Marguerite Porète et Guiard de Cressonessart (1309–1310)," in *Revue d'Histoire Ecclésiastique* (1986) 81:1–2, 47–94. For a comparison between Marguerite Porète and Madame Guyon, see Franz-Joseph Schweitzer, "Von Marguerite Porète (+1310) bis Mme Guyon (+1717): Frauenmystic im Konflikt mit der Kirche," in *Frauenmystik im Mittelalter*, ed. Peter Dinzelbacher and Dieter R. Bauer (Stuttgart: Schwabenverlag, 1985) 256–74. Modern researchers do not concur on the question of Porète's orthodoxy, but it is likely that the church had good reasons to exterminate her, notwithstanding questions of orthodoxy. Her *Miroir* professed absolute, undisguised, and unqualified opposition to the clergy and to the teachers of theology who were considered to be the guardians and interpreters of Scripture. According to Marguerite Porète, the latter could not comprehend or teach the Holy Word because they derived their understanding from Reason, whereas truth could only be revealed by Love. Marguerite Porète attacked ecclesiastical power at precisely the time when the church was endeavoring to establish its authority.

31. Guyon, *La Vie de Mme*, 2:74.

32. On the numerous spiritual biographies written in the seventeenth century, see Le Brun, "Biographies spirituelles françaises du XVIIe siècle. Ecriture féminine? Ecriture mystique?" in *Esperienza religiosa. Escritture femminili tra medioevo ed età moderna*, ed. Marilena Modia Vasta, 20 (Università di Catania: Bonanno Editore, 1992), 135–50.

33. Guyon, *La Vie de Mme*, 2:149.

34. For the history of quietism I have used Brémond, *Histoire littéraire du sentiment religieux en France*, especially vol. 11; I am particularly indebted to Fénelon, *Oeuvres*, ed. Le Brun; Jacques Le Brun, *La Spritualité de Bossuet* (Paris: Gallimard, 1982) and idem., "Quiétisme," in *DSAM* (1985), 12:2806–42.

35. Similar accusations in the fourteenth century led to the burning at the stake of Marguerite Porète (1310) and to the condemnation of the Beghards by the Council of Vienna and of Meister Eckhart in the *In Agro Dominico* Bull in 1329. In the sixteenth century, the first Jesuits, as well as the mystics of the Spanish reformed Carmelites (Teresa of Avila, her confessor Balthazar Alvarez, and John of the Cross), encountered great resistance on the part of the church hierarchy for similar objections.

36. Brémond, *Histoire littéraire du sentiment religieux en France*, 11: 109.

37. Isabelle Christina Bellinzaga (1552–1624) and her disciple, the Jesuit Achille Gagliardi (1537–1607), from whose *Breve compendio intorno alla perfezione cristiana* Bérulle drew his free translation *Bref discours de l'abnégation intérieure* (1597), were also suspected of quietism. See Brémond, *Histoire littéraire du sentiment religieux*, 11:185. The fifty editions and translations into French of Bellinzaga's *Breve compendio*, inspired by Catherine of Genoa, had a considerable influence on French spirituality in the sixteenth century. See *"Breve compendio,"* in *DSAM* (1937), 1:1940–42. For a history of the attribution of this book see Brémond, *Histoire littéraire du sentiment religieux*, 11: 3–22.

38. See Fénelon, *Oeuvres*, commentary by Jacques Le Brun, 1532.

39. This sort of condemnation did not deter many believers from reading these texts. For example, Dom Claude Martin did not pay much attention to the official condemnation of Bernières's *Chrétien intérieur*, and still praised it in 1695. See Le Brun, *La Spiritualité de Bossuet*, 461.

40. Bossuet implicitly assimilated mysticism and extraordinary phenomena. See Le Brun, *La Spiritualité de Bossuet*, 457.

41. It is interesting to note that while Bossuet held a strong rational and authoritarian antimystic position and manifested equally strong bon vivant characteristics, one of his youngest sisters, Marguerite Bossuet, became a Dominican nun in Toul when she was fourteen years of age, and

displayed a pronounced fervor for suffering and humiliations, together with an aptitude for ecstasy. She died in 1658 at the age of twenty-three. See Le Brun, *La Spiritualité de Bossuet*, 22–23.

42. The Synod of Dordrecht (1618–1619) is, in the Calvinist world, the equivalent of the Council of Trent. With the help of a small-scale Inquisition, it instituted repressive measures against nonconformists.

43. Le Brun, *La Spiritualité de Bossuet*, 454–55, n.110.

44. See Orcibal, "L'Originalité théologique de John Wesley et les spiritualités du continent," in *Revue Historique*, (July–September 1959), 222: 51–80. John Wesley owned many works by Madame Guyon, and in 1776 he republished her autobiography, which had been translated into English by a Quaker. See also Gondal, *Nouveau visage*, 51.

45. See Gondal, *Nouveau visage*, 40.

46. Madame Guyon, *Poésies et cantiques spirituels sur divers sujets qui regardent la vie intérieure, ou l'esprit du vrai Christianisme*, 4 vols (1722). Consequently, Cowper published a number of Guyon's poems in English translation: *Poems Translated from the French of M. de la Mothe Guyon*, (1782). In addition, Cowper mentions Madame Guyon's poetry in his *Correspondence of W. Cowper*, 4 vols. (T. Wright, 1904) 2:5, and declares "her verse is the only French verse I ever read that I found agreeable; there is a neatness in it equal to that we applaud with so much reason in the composition of Prior." In another letter he states: "The strain of simple and unaffected piety in the original is sweet beyond expression. She sings like an Angel, and for that very reason has found but few admirers." Quoted in G. D. Henderson, *Mystics of the North-East* (Aberdeen: Spalding Club, 1934) 175, n.8.

47. Gusdorf, *Dieu*, 41.

48. Ibid., 62.

49. Guyon, *La Vie de Mme*, 1: 120.

50. Ibid., 2:23.

51. Brémond, *Histoire littéraire du sentiment religieux*, 11: 19.

52. He was arrested under the pretext that he had not respected the order to remain under forced residence given to him by the official. However, as he was purposefully never given that order, it was a trumped-up charge. His *Apologie*, written while in prison, after he had tried without success to appeal to Rome, contests thirty-six lies accumulated against him. His testimony often corroborates Guyon's. This *Apologie* was published in *Revue Fénelon* (September 1910–11), 67–87 and 139–64.

53. See the perspicacious study by Patrick D. Laude, *Approches du quiétisme* (Paris-Seattle-Tübingen: Biblio 17, 1991), which successfully compares Guyon's spirituality to Oriental, mainly Buddhist, spiritual practices.

54. On the contrary, with Bossuet we see the church seeking a solid theological foundation, its authority fixed in historical precedent, thus protecting it from accusations of innovation and arbitrariness. Moreover, this solid foundation would reduce the element of the supernatural, which was feared, to an ordinary and reassuring condition. See Le Brun, *La Spiritualité de Bossuet*, 13.

55. Guyon, *La vie de Mme*, 1: 58.

56. Ibid., 1: 115.

57. The five ordinances are the pastoral letters of J. D'Arenthon, Bishop of Geneva (November 4, 1687); Harley de Champvallon, Archbishop of Paris (October 16, 1694); Bossuet, Bishop of Meaux (April 16, 1695); L. A. de Noailles, Bishop of Chalons (April 25, 1695); and Godais des Marais, Bishop of Chartres (November 21, 1695). The prohibition of Guyon's *Moyen Court* cannot be considered an excommunication.

58. Cited by Gondal, *Nouveau Visage*, 109.

59. Ibid., 109. My emphasis.

60. Gusdorf, *Dieu*, 61.

61. See also Madame Guyon, *Courte apologie du Moien Court*, in *Les Opuscules spirituels de Madame J. M. B. de la Mothe Guion*, ed. P. Poiret (1720), 127 and *La Vie de Mme*, 3:165.

62. *La Vie de Mme*, 3: 80.

63. See Gusdorf, *Dieu*, 46.

64. For this information on the discourse of tolerance in the sixteenth century, I would like to thank Elisabeth Caron, author of *Les Essais de Montaigne ou les échos satiriques de l'humanisme* (Montréal: CERES, 1993).

65. Gusdorf, *Dieu*, 50

66. Ibid., 48.

67. For Hildegard of Bingen (1098–1179) see "Hildegard de Bingen," in *DSAM* (1969), 7:505–21. For her attitude towards heretics, see 508.

68. See "Marguerite-Marie Alacoque," in *DSAM* (1980), 10:349–55.

69. Cited by Mallet-Joris, *Jeanne Guyon*, 92.

70. Le Brun, introduction to Fénelon, *Oeuvres*, ix.

71. Cited by Albert Chérel, *Fénelon au XVIIIe siècle en France* (Paris: Hachette, 1917), 55. My translation.

72. *Supplément à La Vie*. This manuscript, not written by Madame Guyon but probably by one of her disciples, can be found, together with the manuscript of her autobiography, in the Bodleian Library.

73. Guyon, *La Vie de Mme*, 1: 11.

74. Ibid., 2:54.

75. Several of the Protestant disciples of Guyon and of Fénelon belonged for the most part to Scottish landed gentry, who were Episco-

palians, Jacobites, and leisured, educated men: Dr. Garden, Lord Forbes of
Pitsligo, Dr. George Cheyne, Dr. James Keith William, the fourteenth Lord
Forbes, Andrew Michael Ramsey, Lord Deskford. There was also Pierre
Poiret, a Protestant Frenchman who published Madame Guyon's unpub-
lished work in the Netherlands after her death. In Switzerland we can identify
M. de Wateville, and in Germany, M. Fleisbein. For Guyonian legacy in the
United States see Patricia A. Ward, "Madame Guyon in America: An Anno-
tated Bibliography," in *Bulletin of Bibliography*, 52:2 (June 1995) 107–11.

76. From a letter of June 11, 1717, from Dr. James Keith to Lord Deskford, we learn that Michael Ramsey, George Garden, Lord Forbes and his
brother James Forbes, were present at the deathbed of Madame Guyon.
See G. D Henderson, *Mystics of the North East* 143.

77. See Masson, *Fénelon et Mme Guyon*, 360, n.1.

78. Several letters of the group are cited in Henderson, *Mystics of the
North-East*. Gondal also cites an unpublished letter from Madame Guyon
in *Nouveau visage*, 47.

79. For more information on the subject of Guyon's Scottish and English disciples, see Gondal, *Nouveau visage*, 48, n.4.

80. Gondal, *Nouveau visage*, 70.

81. In her autobiography, Guyon wrote that Bossuet wanted to prove to
her that all Christians with a common faith, and with no "interior" [prac-
tice of silence and detachment], might arrive at deification. *La Vie de Mme*,
3:204.

82. Ibid., 1: 112.

83. Bossuet, *Instruction sur les états d'oraison*, in *Oeuvres complètes de
Bossuet*, ed. Lachat, (Paris: Louis Vivès, 1862–66) 18:535. Translations
from this work are mine.

84. Ibid., 260.

85. De Certeau, "Mystique au XVIIe siècle," 277–78.

86. *Madame Guyon et Fénelon. La Correspondance secrète*, ed. Benjamin Sahler (Paris: Dervy-Livres, 1982), 240.

87. Guyon, *La Vie de Mme*, 2:141, 214.

88. Ibid., 2:213

89. Autograph letter of Le Masson to Mme de Vancy, *Dame de St-Louis*.
of September 3, 1686, (Library of Grenoble, N. 808), cited by Gondal, *Nouveau visage*, 73. Le Masson refers to Madame Guyon, *Le Cantique des Cantiques de Salomon interprété selon le sens mistique et la vraie représenta-
tion des Etats intérieurs* (1688).

90. Guyon, *La Vie de Mme*, 3:122.

91. Ibid., 2:125–26, 200.

92. Le Masson, a letter to Mme de Vancy, cited by Gondal, *Nouveau
Visage*, 74.

93. Madame Guyon, *Moyen Court et très facile de faire oraison*, in *Les Opuscules spirituels*, ed. Pierre Poiret (1720), 16.

94. Madame Guyon, *La Sainte Bible ou le Vieux et Nouveau Testament, avec des explications*, ed. Jean-Philippe Dutoit (1790), 12:601. Cited by Gondal, *Nouveau visage*, 104. My translation.

95. Guyon, *La Vie de Mme*, 3:159.

96. Guyon, *La Passion de croire*, ed. Marie-Louise Gondal (Paris: Nouvelle Cité, 1990), 215.

97. Guyon, *La Passion de Croire*, 215.

98. Guyon, *La Vie de Mme*, 3:156.

99. Guyon, *Instruction chrétienne d'une mère à sa fille*, in *Opuscules spirituels*.

100. *Madame Guyon et Fénelon. La Correspondance secrète*, 152.

101. See the letter Guyon addresses to Fénelon on this subject: *Madame Guyon and Fénelon. La Correspondance secrète*, 163.

102. Guyon, *La Vie de Mme*, 1:110; 3:197.

103. Ibid., 3:120–22.

104. Fénelon, *Correspondance*, ed. Jean Orcibal, 2:131, 3:184, n.3.

105. See Guyon's letter to Fénelon in *Madame Guyon et Fénelon. La Correspondance secrète*, 248.

106. Guyon, *La Vie de Mme*, 3:43.

107. See Fénelon, *Correspondance*, ed. Jean Orcibal, 3:184 n.3; also Albert Chérel, *Michael Ramsey*, and Voltaire, *Le siècle de Louis XIV*.

108. Marie de Gournay, *Egalité des hommes et des femmes* (1622); idem., *Le Grief des Dames* (1595); Madeleine de Scudéry, *Clélie, histoire romaine* (1654–1660); idem., *Mathilde d'Aguilar* (1667); François Poullain de la Barre, *De l'égalité des deux sexes* (1673); idem., *De l'éducation des Dames* (1674); idem., *De l'excellence des Hommes, Contre l'égalité des sexes* (1675).

109. Guyon, *La Vie de Mme*, 2:194–95.

110. Ibid., 2:108.

Chapter 7. The Quarrel of Quietism and the Construction of Modern Femininity

1. De Certeau, "Mystique au XVIIe siècle," in *Mélanges de Lubac*, 2:267–91.

2. For an indepth study of medieval theology and its breakup in the Renaissance, see Mino Bergamo, *La Science des saints. Le Discours mystique au XVIIe siècle en France* (Grenoble: Jérôme Millon, 1992), 76–121.

3. Fénelon, *Oeuvres*, 1532, Le Brun's commentary. My translation.

4. This of course is not true for the whole Jansenist movement, as exemplified by the nuns of Port Royal, as well as by Pascal in his mystic fervor, which was pronouncedly antirationalist and anti-Cartesian.

5. Gusdorf, *Dieu*, 42.

6. Fénelon, *Réfutation du système de Malebranche* (1684).

7. On Bossuet's spirituality, I am indebted to Jacques Le Brun, *La Spiritualité de Bossuet*.

8. Ibid., 621.

9. Ibid., 464.

10. Bossuet, *Instruction*, 18:368.

11. Ibid., 18:374.

12. Ibid., 18:371.

13. Ibid., 18:587.

14. Ibid., 18:368.

15. Ibid., 18:600.

16. Ibid., 18:374.

17. See "Jean Gerson," in *DSAM* (1967) 6:314–31.

18. See "Mystique," in *DSAM* (1980), 10:1907–11.

19. See "Gerson," in *DSAM* (1967), 6:322.

20. Ibid., 6:322, 329.

21. Bossuet, *Instruction*, 18:383.

22. The other mystics condemned by Bossuet are Falconi, Malaval, Molinos, and La Combe.

23. Guyon's works, which Bossuet attacked in his *Instruction*, are *Moyen Court, Interpretation du cantique des cantiques, Les Torrents, La Vie de Mme*, and *Règles des associés à l'enfant Jésus*.

24. Bossuet, *Instruction*, 18:403.

25. Ibid., 18:370.

26. Ibid., 18:391.

27. Guyon, *La Vie de Mme*, 2:39.

28. Guyon, *Explication*, 7:235, cited by Gondal, *Nouveau visage*, 104.

29. Guyon, *La Vie de Mme*, 1:82.

30. Ibid., 1:83.

31. Ibid., 1:82.

32. Ibid., 1:87.

33. Ibid., 1:279.

34. See introduction to *La Vie*, reproduction of 1981, 18.

35. "Marie de l'Incarnation," in *DSAM* (1980), 10:506.

36. It is true that other female mystics have shown the same pattern, but the pressure of the Inquisition or of the clergy can often be detected behind their belated scorn of bodily manifestations. It is also true that the theologians of negative mysticism considered bodily manifestations, vi-

sions, ecstasies, raptures, and prophecy suspicious on two grounds: first, because it was impossible to distinguish illusion from truth in these manifestations; and second, because they thought that what can be known, possessed, and felt here on earth is not God. This mystical doctrine claimed that the divine could only be apprehended through pure faith and in darkness.

37. Bossuet, *Instruction*, 18:366–67.

38. Quoted by Beckwith, "A Very Material Mysticism," 49.

39. See "Béguines," in *DSAM* (1937) 1:1355. For details on female mystics' influence on negative mysticism see "Mystique," *DSAM* (1980), 10: 1907.

40. See "Béguines," in *DSAM* (1937), 1:1350.

41. Jeanne-Lydie Goré, "La Fortune de Sainte Catherine de Gênes au XVIIe siècle," in *L'Italianisme en France au XVIIe siècle* (Paris: Didier, 1969) 63–77.

42. See Brémond, *Histoire littéraire du sentiment religieux*, 11:3–56.

43. Bossuet, *Instruction*, 18:371.

44. Gallicanism designates a doctrine that advocated a certain independence of the French Catholic Church from papal authority. In theological terms, this doctrine negates the absolute supremacy of the pope, and was proclaimed by the Council of Constance in 1417. However, the supremacy of the pope was already reaffirmed in the course of the fifteenth century and then definitively established with the proclamation of papal infallibility in 1870. Historically, Gallicanism is linked with the religious politics of the French sovereigns. Jansenists supported the movement toward the end of the seventeenth century, and by the eighteenth century political Gallicanism and Jansenism were overtly linked.

45. Guyon, *La Vie de Mme*, 3:191.

46. Ibid., 3:97.

47. Cited by Françoise Mallet-Joris, *Jeanne Guyon* (Paris: Flammarion, 1978), 436.

48. Around 1726, Madame de Lambert wrote: "Molière in France has created the same disorder [ridicule for learning] with his comedy *Les Femmes savantes*. Since this time, learning in women has become as shameful as the worst vices," *Oeuvres morales* (1890), 215.

49. On the question of the "précieuses" as a literary and a political creation see Domna Stanton, "The Fiction of *Préciosité* and the Fear of Women," *Yale French Studies*, 62 (1981), 107–34.

50. Bossuet's literary and rhetorical devices are analyzed by Fénelon in his *Réponse à la relation*, in *Oeuvres*, ed. J. Le Brun.

51. Bossuet, *La Relation sur le quiétisme*, in *Oeuvres*, ed. Abbé Velat

and Yvonne Champailler (Paris: Gallimard, 1970), 19, 1106–1107. Translations from this work are mine.

52. Ibid., 1127.

53. Ibid., 1116.

54. Ibid., 1126.

55. Ibid., 1107.

56. Ibid., 1152.

57. Ibid., 1107.

58. Ibid., 1124.

59. Ibid., 1113.

60. Ibid., 1106.

61. Ibid., 1145.

62. Ibid., 1127, 1132, 1136, 1137.

63. Ibid., 1175. Montanus was a priest from Phrygia. He had been a pagan priest serving the mother earth Cybel before he became a Christian. He founded a sect, preaching in the Orient and in Rome that certain souls were in direct relation with God. He was accompanied by two women, Priscilla and Maximilia, his prophetesses whom he had detached from their husbands and with whom, according to Eusebus, he had a sexual relationship.

64. Bossuet harped on the image Guyon gave of herself as the woman of the Apocalypse: ibid., 1109, 1110, 1111, 1113.

65. Ibid., 1172.

66. Ibid., 1157.

67. Ibid., 1107.

68. Ibid., 1113.

69. Ibid., 1150.

70. Ibid., 1135.

71. Ibid., 1101. *Instruction*, 18:632, already showed that Bossuet wanted the public to think that she had recanted, for such an act on her part justified his behavior toward her.

72. Bossuet, *Relation*, 1125.

73. Ibid., 1135.

74. Cited by Mallet-Joris, *Jeanne Guyon*, 436.

75. Bossuet, *Relation*, 1105.

76. Ibid., 1105.

77. Ibid., 1105.

78. The Princesse Palatine wrote in her *Mémoires*: "This woman must be mad and I don't understand why she was incarcerated in the Bastille rather than shut up in an [insane asylum]." Cited by Mallet-Joris, *Jeanne Guyon*, 435. My translation.

79. Guyon, *La Vie de Mme*, 319.

80. Guyon, *Récits de captivité: inédit*, ed. Marie-Louise Gondal (Grenoble: Jérôme Millon, 1992), 54.

81. Fénelon, *De l'éducation des filles* in *Oeuvres*. In this book published in 1687, Fénelon shows no awareness that the problem of women's education was connected with their social condition. He did not see that it was not an intellectual, philosophical, or religious problem but rather a political one, an argument held by his contemporaries, Marie de Gournay, the women of the salons, and Poullain de la Barre. The education for women that Fénelon proposes does not aim at modifying women's traditional place in family and society but at consolidating it; his theories merely tend to prepare women to better help men in their endeavors. This reactionary position is very much the same as Rousseau's description of what female education ought to be in his *L'Emile*. For an assessment of Fénelon's view on women see Carolyn Lougee, *Le Paradis des Femmes: Women, Salons and Social Stratification in Seventeenth-Century France* (Princeton, N.J.: Princeton University Press, 1976).

82. See *Madame Guyon and Fénelon. La Correspondance secrète*, especially letter XLII, 126.

83. The pope condemned Isabella to silence in 1601, as Bossuet did in the case of Guyon in 1693. A certain number of Jesuit missionaries in foreign lands continued, nevertheless, to write to Isabella. When she died, the clergy forbade the mob to take relics from her body. The General of the Company of Jesus forbade that any Jesuit would write her *vita*. Nobody, however, found any fault with the book she wrote with Gagliardi, the *Breve Compendio*, in which there are no mentions of extraordinary graces, miracles, or bodily manifestations. The condemnation of Clement VIII only targeted certain papers of hers, in which there is mention of revelations and visions, papers which Gagliardi had gathered and imprudently disseminated. See Brémond, *Histoire littéraire du sentiment religieux*, 11:11, 19.

84. Ibid., 11:5–13.

85. Ibid., 11:11.

86. Bossuet, *Instruction*, 18:535.

87. Bossuet, *Relation*, 1126.

88. See Albert Chérel, *Fénelon au XVIIIe siècle.* (Paris: Hachette, 1917).

89. Bossuet, *Relation*, 1176.

90. Jean Rousset, *Anthologie de la poésie baroque française* (Paris: Armand Colin, 1961).

91. Voltaire, *Siècle de Louis XIV* (Paris: 1847). Translations from this work are mine.

92. Bossuet, *Relation*, 1105.

93. Voltaire, *Siècle de Louis XIV*, 453.

94. Ibid., 452.
95. Ibid., 452.
96. Ibid., 511.
97. Cited by Brémond, *Apologie*, 198.
98. Sigmund Freud, "Female Sex," 21:221–46; idem., "Some Psychical Consequences of the Anatomical Distinction between the Sexes," 19:241–60; idem., "Three Essays on the Theory of Sexuality," 7:1–243; idem., "Femininity," 22:112–35, in *The Standard Edition of the Complete Psychological Works of Sigmund Freud*, ed. James Strachey, 24 vols. (London: Hogarth, 1953–74).
99. Sarah Kofman, *The Enigma of Woman: Woman in Freud's Writing*, trans. Catherine Porter (Ithaca, N.Y.: Cornell University Press, 1985).
100. Ibid., 66.
101. Bossuet, *Relation*, 1133.
102. Ibid., 1145.

Chapter 8. Guyon's Autobiography at the Crossroads of History

1. See, for example, Philippe Lejeune, *L'Autobiographie en France* (Paris: Colin, 1971), and idem., *On Autobiography*, trans. Katherine Leary (Minneapolis: University of Minnesota Press, 1989); Yves Coirault, "Autobiographie et Mémoires (XVIIe–XVIIIe siècles), ou existence et naissance de l'autobiographie," *Revue d'Histoire Littéraire de la France*, 6, (1975), 937–56. For the Anglo-American tradition see, for example, Wayne Shumaker, *English Autobiography: Its Emergence, Material and Form* (Berkeley: University of California Press, 1954). For a history of the criticism on autobiography, see the essay appended to William C. Spengemann's *Forms of Autobiography: Episodes in the History of a Literary Genre* (New Haven, Conn.: Yale University Press, 1980), and the introductory essay in James Olney's anthology, "Autobiography and the Cultural Moment," in *Autobiography: Essays Theoretical and Critical*, ed. James Olney (Princeton, N.J.: Princeton University Press, 1980).
2. This is also Coirault's position in "Autobiographie et mémoires," 949.
3. Paul Delany, *British Autobiography in the Seventeenth Century* (London: Routledge, 1969).
4. William C. Spengemann, *The Forms of Autobiography: A Collection of Critical Essays* (Englewood Cliffs, N.J.: Prentice, 1981), xiii.
5. Georges Gusdorf, "De l'autobiographie initiatique à l'autobiographie genre littéraire," *Revue d'Histoire Littéraire de la France*, 6 (1975), 979;

idem., "Conditions and Limits of Autobiography," in *Autobiography: Essays Theoretical and Critical.*

6. Bynum, *Jesus as Mother*, 83. For an account of the critics who argue for the discovery of the individual in the twelfth century, see her entire chapter: "Did the Twelfth Century Discover the Individual?" 82–109.

7. Karl Joachim Weintraub, *The Value of the Individual: Self and Circumstances in Autobiography* (Chicago: University of Chicago Press, 1978).

8. See, for example, Nancy K. Miller, "Women's Autobiography in France: For a Dialectics of Identification," in *Women and Language in Literature and Society* (New York: Praeger, 1980); Domna Stanton, *The Female Autograph* (New York: New York Literary Forum, 1984); Sidonie Smith, *A Poetics of Women's Autobiography* (Bloomington: Indiana University Press, 1987); Faith E. Beasley, *Revising Memory.*

9. Georges Gusdorf acknowledges the importance of this text in pietist literature as well as in the history of autobiography. Karl Joachim Weintraub studies Guyon's *La Vie de Mme* in *The Value of the Individual* but seems to equate the value of an autobiography with its "truthfulness," or orthodoxy. Consequently he views Madame Guyon's autobiography as inferior to that of Suso or of Teresa of Avila.

10. See the letter from James Keith to Lord Desford of July 5, 1718, as cited in Henderson, *Mystics of the North-East*, 159. See also Albert Chérel, *Un Aventurier religieux au XVIIIe siècle. André-Michel Ramsey* (Paris, 1926), 106ff.

11. Letter of James Keith to Val Nalson of November 5, 1718, as cited in Henderson, *Mystics of the North-East*, 164.

12. Georges Gusdorf, "De l'autobiographie initiatique à l'autobiographie genre littéraire," 981.

13. Marie-Louise Gondal, "L'Autobiographie de Mme Guyon. La découverte et l'apport de deux nouveaux manuscrits," *XVIIe Siècle*, 164 (1989), 307–23.

14. The manuscript that served for the published text of vols. 1–3 has not been found, but there exists a copy similar to the published text, corrected in the hand of the author, at the Bodleian Library in Oxford. Madame Guyon had entrusted this copy to her Scottish disciple, Michael Ramsey. The manuscript of vol. 4 was found by Marie-Louise Gondal at the Jesuit Library in Chantilly: Madame Guyon, *Récits de captivité: inédits*, ed. Marie-Louise Gondal (Grenoble: Jérôme Millon, 1992).

15. See Dewald, *Aristocratic Experience.*

16. Guyon, *La Vie de Mme*, 3:56.

17. See for example Guyon, *La Vie de Mme*, 3:94.

18. Michel Beaujour, *Poetics of Literary Self-portrait*, trans. Yara Milos (New York: New York University Press, 1991).

19. Dewald, *Aristocratic Experience*, xi.

20. De Certeau, *Fable*, 13, 77.

21. The appearance of a new childhood narrative supports Philippe Ariès's thesis, according to which a new interest for children appears in the seventeenth century. See Philippe Ariès, *Centuries of Childhood: A Social History of Family Life*, trans. Robert Baldick (New York: Vintage, 1972).

22. Guyon, *La Vie de Mme*, 1:10.

23. Ibid., 1:8.

24. Ibid., 1:9.

25. Ibid., 1:10.

26. Ibid., 1:11.

27. Ibid., 1:7.

28. Ibid., 1:10.

29. Ibid., 1:13.

30. Ibid., 1:30.

31. Ibid., 1:17.

32. Ibid., 1:13.

33. Ibid., 1:14.

34. Ibid., 1:15.

35. Ibid., 1:16.

36. Ibid., 1:16.

37. Ibid., 1:16.

38. Ibid., 1:50.

39. Ibid., 1:51.

40. Ibid., 1:51.

41. Ibid., 1:130.

42. Here are a few examples of maternal metaphors used by Guyon: metaphors of motherhood and childbirth for writing (*La Vie de Mme*, 2:118–19); that of the pain of childbirth for those she counsels (ibid., 2:182); that of spiritual hierarchy and motherhood (ibid., 2:143–44); that of spiritual motherhood as manifested in her mission, writing and spiritual communication; that of the woman of the apocalypse (herself), pregnant with God's designs (ibid., 2:149–50); that of God as mother, with herself associated to divine maternity in her suffering and her illnesses (ibid., 2:192); that of herself as the mother of a people (ibid., 2:97, 210–11); that of Jesus as mother (ibid., 2:198–99); that of her followers as siblings (ibid., 2:209); that of spiritual mother of several priests (ibid., 2:218–20), etc.

43. Ibid., 2:19.

44. Ibid., 1:273.

45. Gusdorf, "De l'autobiographie initiatique à l'autobiographie genre littéraire," 986.

46. Ibid., 979.

47. Guyon, *La Vie de Mme*, 3:238–39; idem., *Récits de captivité*, 176. The last chapter of the third volume of *La Vie de Mme* is truncated, and a few sentences of the epilogue of the fourth volume, *Récits de captivité* have been added to it. This is the autobiography published by Poiret in 1720.

48. Ibid., 3:242.

49. Ibid., 3:242.

50. Ibid., 3:241.

51. Ibid., 3:241.

Conclusion

1. De Certeau, *Fable*, 48–70.

2. Ibid., 31–39.

Bibliography

Primary Sources

Bossuet, Jacques Bénigne. *Instruction sur les états d'oraison. Oeuvres complètes de Bossuet.* Ed. Lachat. Vol. 18. Paris: Louis Vivès, 1862–66.

———. *La Relation sur le quiétisme. Oeuvres.* Ed. Abbé Velat and Yvonne Champailler. Vol. 19. Paris: Gallimard, 1970. 1099–1177.

Cowper, W. *Correspondence of W. Cowper.* 4 vols. T. Wright, London, 1904.

———. *Guyon, Jeanne Marie (Bouvier de la Motte). Poems Translated from the French of M. de la Mothe Guyon.* London: J. Johnson, 1811.

Du Creux, François. *Historiae Canadensis.* Paris: 1664.

———. *History of Canada.* Trans. Percy J. Robinson. Ed. James B. Conacher. Toronto: Champlain Society, 1951.

Fénelon, François de Salignac de la Mothe. *Correspondance de Fénelon.* Ed. Jean Orcibal. 13 vols. Paris: Klincksieck, 1972.

———. *De l'éducation des filles. Oeuvres.* Ed. Jacques Le Brun. Paris: Gallimard, 1983

———. *Réfutation du système de Malebranche.* Paris: 1684.

———. *Réponse à la Relation. Oeuvres.* Ed. Jacques Le Brun. Paris: Gallimard, 1983.

Gournay, Marie de. *Egalité des hommes et des femmes. Fragments d'un discours féminin.* Ed. Elyane Dezon-Jones. Paris: Corti, 1988. 111–27.

———. *Le Grief des Dames. Fragments d'un discours féminin.* Ed. Elyane Dezon-Jones. Paris: Corti, 1988. 129–33.

Guyon, Madame. *Courte apologie du Moien Court. Les Opuscules spirituels de Madame J. M. B. de la Mothe Guion.* Ed. Pierre Poiret. Cologne: Jean de la Pierre, 1720.

———. *Instruction chrétienne d'une mère à sa fille. Les Opuscules spirituels de Madame J. M. B. de la Mothe Guion.* Ed. Pierre Poiret. Cologne: Jean de la Pierre, 1720.

———. *Les Justifications de Madame J. M. B. de la Mothe Guion, écrites par elle-même, suivant l'ordre de Messieurs les Evêques ses examinateurs, où l'on éclaircit plusieurs difficultés qui regardent la vie intérieure* [. . .]. 3 vols. Cologne: 1720.

———. *Moyen Court et très facile de faire oraison. Les Opuscules spirituels de Madame J. M. B. de la Mothe Guion.* Ed. Pierre Poiret. Cologne: Jean de la Pierre, 1720.

———. *La Passion de croire.* Ed. Marie-Louise Gondal. Paris: Nouvelle Cité, 1990.

———. *Poésies et cantiques spirituels sur divers sujets qui regardent la vie intérieure, ou l'esprit du vrai Christianisme.* 4 vols. Cologne: Jean de la Pierre, 1722.

———. *Récits de captivité: inédit.* Ed. Marie-Louise Gondal. Grenoble: Jérôme Millon, 1992.

———. *Les Torrents spirituels. Les Opuscules spirituels de Madame J. M. B. de la Mothe Guion.* Ed. Pierre Poiret. Cologne: Jean de la Pierre, 1720.

———. *La Vie de Mme J. M. B. de la Mothe Guion écrite par elle-même.* Ed. Jean-Philippe Dutoit. 3 vol. Paris: Libraires associés, 1790.

Supplément à La Vie. Anonymous manuscript, which can be found in the Bodleian Library, together with a manuscript of her autobiography.

La Combe, Père. *Apologie* in *Revue Fénelon* (September 1910–11), 67–87 and 139–64.

Lafiteau, Joseph F. *Moeurs des sauvages américains comparées aux moeurs des premiers temps.* 2 vols. Paris: Saugrain, 1724.

Lambert, Madame de. *Oeuvres morales.* Paris: 1890.

Le Masson, I. *Eclaircissements sur la vie de Jean d'Arenthon.* Chambéry: Jean Gorrin, 1699.

Marie de l'Incarnation. *Correspondance.* Ed. Dom Guy Oury. Solesme, 1971.

Martin, Dom Claude, comp. *La Vie de la Vénérable Mère Marie de l'Incarnation.* 1677. Reproduction. Solesmes: 1981.

Nicole, Pierre. *Réfutation des principales erreurs des quiétistes contenues dans les livres censurés par l'ordonnance de Mgr l'arch. de Paris du 16 oct. 1694, précédée de l'ordonnance de l'arch. de Paris.* Vol. 1. Paris: 1695.

Porète, Marguerite. *Le Miroir des âmes simples et anéanties.* Paris: Albin Michel, 1984.

Poullain de La Barre, François. *De l'éducation des Dames.* Paris: DuPuis, 1674.

——. *De l'égalité des deux sexes, Discours physique et moral, ou l'on voit l'importance de se défaire des Préjugez.* Paris: DuPuis, 1673. 2nd ed. 1679. Rpt. in *Corpus des oeuvres de philosophie en langue française.* Paris: Fayard, 1984.

——. *De l'excellence des Hommes, Contre l'égalité des sexes.* Paris: Du-Puis, 1675.

Sahler, Benjamin, ed. *Madame Guyon et Fénelon. La Correspondance secrète.* Paris: Dervy-Livres, 1982.

Scudéry, Madeleine de. *Clélie, histoire romaine.* 1654–60. 10 vol. Genève: Slatkine Reprints, 1973.

——. *Mathilde d'Aguilar.* 1667. Genève: Slatkine Reprints, 1979.

Thwaites, Reuben Gold, ed. *The Jesuit Relations and Allied Documents.* Cleveland, Oh.: Burrows, 1890–1901.

Voltaire [Francois Marie Arouet]. *Le siècle de Louis XIV.* Paris: 1847.

Secondary Sources

Ariès, Philippe. *Centuries of Childhood: A Social History of Family Life.* Trans. Robert Baldick. New York: Vintage, 1972.

Ariès, Philippe, and Georges Duby, eds. *Histoire de la vie privée.* Vol. 4. Paris: Seuil, 1987.

Backer, Dorothy. *Precious Women.* New York: Basic, 1974.

Baruzi, Jean. *Saint Jean de la Croix et le problème de l'expérience mystique.* Paris: Alcan, 1924.

Beasley, Faith E. *Revising Memory: Women's Fiction and Memoirs in Seventeenth-Century France.* New Brunswick, N.J.: Rutgers University Press, 1990.

Beaujour, Michel. *Poetics of Literary Self-portrait.* Trans. Yara Milos. New York: New York University Press, 1991.

Beauvoir, Simone de. *The Second Sex.* Trans. H. M. Parshley. New York: Bantam, 1970.

Beckwith, Sarah. "A Very Material Mysticism: The Medieval Mysticism of Margey Kempe." *Medieval Literature: Criticism, Ideology and History.* Ed. David Aers. Brighton: Harvester, 1986. 34–55.

Bell, Rudolph. *Holy Anorexia.* Chicago: University of Chicago Press, 1985.

Bergamo, Mino. *La Science des saints. Le Discours mystique au XVIIe siècle en France.* Grenoble: Jérôme Millon, 1992.

Bloch, Marc. *The Royal Touch.* London: Routledge, 1973.

Bordo, Susan. R. "Anorexia Nervosa: Psychopathology as the Crystallization of Culture." *Feminism and Foucault: Reflections on Resistance.* Ed.

I. Diamond and L. Quinby. Boston: Northeastern University Press, 1988. 87–118.

―――. "The Body and the Reproduction of Femininity: A Feminist Appropriation of Foucault." *Gender/Body/Knowledge: Feminist Reconstructions of Being and Knowing.* Ed. Alison. M. Jaggar and Susan. R. Bordo. New Brunswick, N.J.: Rutgers University Press, 1989. 13–33.

Brammer, Marsanne. "Thinking Practice: Michel de Certeau and the Theorization of Mysticism." *Diacritics* 22:2 (1992): 26–37.

Brémond, Henri. *Apologie pour Fénelon.* Paris: Perrin et Cie., 1910.

―――. *Histoire du sentiment religieux en France depuis la fin des guerres de religion jusqu'à nos jours.* Vol. 11. Paris: Bloud, 1921–33.

Bruneau, Marie-Florine. "Mysticisme et Psychose: l'autobiographie de Jeanne Guyon." *DAI* XLII (1981): 237 A-238 A. University of California, Berkeley.

Bynum, Caroline Walker. *Fragmentation and Redemption.* New York: Zone, 1991.

―――. *Holy Feast and Holy Fast.* Berkeley: University of California Press, 1987.

―――. *Jesus as Mother.* Berkeley: University of California Press, 1982.

Caron, Elisabeth. *Les Essais de Montaigne ou les échos satiriques de l'humanisme.* Montréal: CERES, 1993.

Charcot, J. M., and P. Richer. *Les démoniaques dans l'art, suivi de la foi qui guérit.* Ed. P. Fedida and J. Didi-Huberman. Paris: Macula, 1984.

Chérel, Albert. *Un Aventurier religieux au XVIIIe siècle. André-Michel Ramsey.* Paris: Perrin, 1926.

―――. *Fénelon au XVIIIe siècle en France.* Paris: Hachette, 1917.

―――. "Mme Guyon directrice de conscience." *Revue Fénelon* (1910).

Clendinnen, Inga. "'Fierce and Unnatural Cruelty': Cortés and the Conquest of Mexico." *New World Encounters.* Ed. Stephen Greenblatt. Berkeley: University of California Press, 1993. 12–47.

Clermont, Norman. "La Place de la femme dans les sociétés iroquiennes de la période du contact." *Recherches Amérindiennes au Québec* 13:4 (1983): 286–90.

Cognet, Louis. *Crépuscule des mystiques.* Paris: Desclée, 1958.

―――. "La spiritualité de Mme Guyon." *XVIIe Siècle* (1951–52): 269–75.

Coirault, Yves. "Autobiographie et Mémoires (XVIIe–XVIIIe siècles), ou existence et naissance de l'autobiographie." *Revue d'Histoire Littéraire de la France* 6 (1975): 937–56.

Collectif Clio, *L'Histoire des femmes au Québec depuis quatre siècles.* Montréal: Quinze, 1982.

De Certeau, Michel. "The Gaze: Nicolas de Cusa." Trans. Catherine Porter. *Diacritics* 17:3 (1987): 2–38.

——. *Heterologies: Discourse on the Other.* Trans. Brian Massumi. Minneapolis: University of Minnesota Press, 1986.

——. *The Mystic Fable.* Trans. Michael Smith. Chicago: University of Chicago Press, 1992.

——. "Mysticism." Trans. Marsanne Brammer. *Diacritics* 22:2 (1992): 11–25.

——. "Mystique au XVIIe siècle." *L'Homme devant Dieu; Mélanges offerts au Père Henri de Lubac.* Vol.2. Paris: Aubier, 1964. 267–91.

——. "On the Oppositional Practices of Everyday Life." *Social Text* 1:3 (1980): 3–43.

——. *Political Writing.* Trans. Tom Conley. Minneapolis: University of Minnesota Press, 1996.

——. *La Possession de Loudun.* Paris: Gallimard, 1980. (To be published in English translation by the University of Chicago Press.)

——. *The Practice of Everyday Life.* Trans. Steven F. Rendell. Berkeley: University of California Press, 1984.

——. *The Writing of History.* Trans. Tom Conley. New York: Columbia University Press, 1988.

——. "Writing vs. Time: History and Anthropology in the Work of Lafiteau." *Yale French Studies* 59 (Summer, 1980): 37–64.

Davis, Natalie Zemon. "Gender and Genre: Women as Historical Writers, 1400–1820." *Beyond Their Sex. Learned Women of the European Past.* Ed. Patricia A. Labalme. New York: New York University Press, 1980. 153–82.

——. *Women on the Margins: Three Seventeenth-Century Lives.* Cambridge: Harvard University Press, 1995.

——. "Women on Top." *Society and Culture in Early Modern France.* Stanford: Stanford University Press, 1975. 124–51.

Delacroix, Henri. *Les Grands mystiques chrétiens.* Paris: Alcan, 1938.

Delany, Paul. *British Autobiography in the Seventeenth Century.* London: Routledge, 1969.

Deroy-Pineau, Françoise. *Marie de l'Incarnation. Marie Guyart femme d'affaires, mystique, mère de la Nouvelle France.* Paris: Laffont, 1989.

Deslandres, Dominique. "Marie de l'Incarnation et la femme amérindienne." *Recherches Amérindiennes au Québec* 13:4 (1983): 277–85.

Dewald, Jonathan. *Aristocratic Experience and the Origins of Modern Culture: France 1570–1715.* Berkeley: University of California Press, 1993.

Dictionnaire de spiritualité ascétique et mystique: Doctrine et histoire. 20 vols. Paris: Beauchesne, 1937–92.

Dronke, Peter. *Women Writers of the Middle Ages.* Cambridge: Cambridge University Press, 1984.

Finke, Laurie. *Feminist Theory, Women's Writing.* Ithaca, N.Y.: Cornell University Press, 1992.

Foucault, Michel. *The Order of Things*. New York: Vintage, 1973.

Freud, Sigmund. *The Standard Edition of the Complete Psychological Works of Sigmund Freud*. Ed. James Strachey. 24 vols. London: Hogarth, 1953–74.

Giard, Luce. "Epilogue: Michel de Certeau's Heterology and the New World." *New World Encounters*. Ed. Stephen Greenblatt. Berkeley: University of California Press, 1993. 313–22.

———. "Remapping Knowledge, Reshaping Institutions." *Science, Culture and Popular Belief in Renaissance Europe*. Ed. Stephen Pumfrey, Paolo L. Rossi, and Maurice Slawinski. Manchester: Manchester University Press, 1991. 19–47.

Gondal, Marie-Louise. "L'Autobiographie de Mme Guyon. La découverte et l'apport de deux nouveaux manuscrits." *XVIIe Siècle* 164 (1989): 307–23.

———. *Madame Guyon 1648–1717: Un Nouveau visage*. Paris: Beauchesne, 1989.

Goré, Jeanne-Lydie. "La Fortune de Sainte Catherine de Gênes au XVIIe siècle." *L'Italianisme en France au XVIIe siècle*. Paris: Didier, 1969. 63–77.

Green, Rayna. *Native American Women: A Contextual Bibliography*. Bloomington: Indiana University Press, 1983.

Greenblatt, Stephen, ed. Introduction. *New World Encounters*. Berkeley: University of California Press, 1993. vii–xviii.

Gusdorf, Georges. "Conditions and Limits of Autobiography." Trans. James Olney. *Autobiography: Essays Theoretical and Critical*. Ed. James Olney. Princeton, N.J.: Princeton University Press, 1980. 28– 48.

———. "De l'autobiographie initiatique à l'autobiographie genre littéraire." *Revue d'Histoire Littéraire de la France* 6 (1975): 957–1002.

———. *Dieu, la nature, l'homme au siècle des Lumières*. Paris: Payot, 1972.

Hanley, Sarah. "Engendering the State: Family Formation and State Building in Early Modern France." *French Historical Studies* 16 (1989): 4–27.

Heidenreich, Conrad. *Huronia: A History and Geography of the Huron Indians 1600–1650*. Ontario: McClelland, 1971.

Henderson, G. D. *Mystics of the North-East*. Aberdeen: Spalding Club, 1934.

Herlihy, David. *Opera Muliebria: Women and Work in Medieval Europe*. New York: McGraw, 1990.

Jaenen, Cornelius J. "Amerindian Views of French Culture in the Seventeenth Century." *The Canadian Historical Review*, 55:3 (1974): 261–91.

———. "L'Autre en Nouvelle France/The Other in Early Canada." *The Canadian Historical Association, Historical Papers* (1989): 1–11.

————. *Friend and Foe: Aspects of French-Amerindian Cultural Contact in the Sixteenth and Seventeenth Centuries*. Toronto: McClelland and Steward, 1976.

————. "Perceptions françaises de la Nouvelle France et de ses peuples indigènes aux XVIIe et XVIIIe siècles." *Recherches Amérindiennes au Québec* 13:2 (1983): 107–14.

Jegou, Marie-Andrée. *Les Ursulines du Faubourg Saint Jacques à Paris 1607–1662*. Paris: Presses Universitaires de France, 1981.

Jones, Ann Rosalind, and Peter Stallybrass. "Fetishizing Gender: Constructing the Hermaphrodite in Renaissance Europe." *Body Guards: The Cultural Politics of Gender Ambiguity*. Ed. Julia Epstein and Kristina Straub. New York: Routledge, 1991. 80–111.

Kelly, Joan. "Early Feminist Theory and the *Querelle des Femmes*, 1400–1789." *Signs* 8 (1982): 4–28.

————. *Women, History and Theory*. Chicago: University of Chicago Press, 1984.

Kieckhefer, Richard. *Unquiet Souls: Fourteenth-Century Saints and Their Religious Milieu*. Chicago: University of Chicago Press, 1984.

Kofman, Sarah. *The Enigma of Woman: Woman in Freud's Writing*. Trans. Catherine Porter. Ithaca, N.Y.: Cornell University Press, 1985.

Kors, Alan C. *Atheism in France: 1650–1729*. Princeton, N.J.: Princeton University Press, 1990.

Kuhn, Thomas S. *The Structure of Scientific Revolutions*. Reprint. Chicago: University of Chicago Press, 1970.

Laude, Patrick D. *Approches du quiétisme*. Paris: Biblio 17, 1991.

Le Brun, Jacques. "Biographies spirituelles françaises du XVIIe siècle. Ecriture féminine? Ecriture mystique?" *Esperienza religiosa. Escritture femminili tra medioevo ed età moderna*. Ed. Marilena Modia Vasta. Vol. 20. Università di Catania: Bonanno Editore, 1992. 135–50.

————, ed. Introduction. *Oeuvres*. By Fénelon. Paris: Gallimard, 1983. ix–xxvii.

————. *La Spritualité de Bossuet*. Paris: Gallimard, 1982.

Lejeune, Philippe. *L'Autobiographie en France*. Paris: Colin, 1971.

————. *On Autobiography*. Trans. Katherine Leary. Minneapolis: University of Minnesota Press, 1989.

Lemoine, George Louis. *Les Ursulines de Québec depuis leur établissement jusqu'à nos jours*. 4 vols. Québec: C. Darveau, 1866–78.

Lochrie, Karma. *Margery Kempe and Translations of the Flesh*. Philadelphia: University of Pennsylvania Press, 1991.

Lougee, Carolyn C. *Le Paradis des Femmes: Women, Salons and Social Stratification in Seventeenth-Century France*. Princeton, N.J.: Princeton University Press, 1976.

Maclean, Ian. *Woman Triumphant (1610–1652)*. Oxford: Oxford University Press, 1977.

Mallet-Joris, Françoise. *Jeanne Guyon*. Paris: Flammarion, 1978.

Masson, Maurice. *Fénelon et Mme Guyon*. Paris: Hachette, 1907.

Mathieu, Nicole-Claude. "When Yielding Is Not Consenting." *Feminist Issues* 9:1 (1989): 3–49 and 10:1 (1990): 51–90.

McGinn, Bernard. *Meister Eckhart and the Beguine Mystics*. New York: Continuum, 1994.

Miller, Nancy K. "Women's Autobiography in France: For a Dialectics of Identification." *Women and Language in Literature and Society*. Ed. Sally McConnell-Ginet, Ruth Borker, and Nelly Furman. New York: Praeger, 1980. 258–73.

Montrose, Louis. "The Work of Gender in the Discourse of Discovery." *New World Encounters*. Ed. Stephen Greenblatt. Berkeley: University of California Press, 1993. 177–217.

Olney, James, ed. "Autobiography and the Cultural Moment: A Thematic, Historical and Bibliographical Introduction." *Autobiography: Essays Theoretical and Critical*. Princeton, N.J.: Princeton University Press, 1980. 3–27.

Orcibal, Jean. "Le Cardinal Le Camus, témoin au procès de Mme Guyon." *Le Cardinal des Montagnes, E. Le Camus, évêque de Grenoble (1671–1701)*. Ed. Jean Godel. Grenoble: Presses Universitaires de Grenoble, 1974. 123–40.

———. "Une Controverse sur l'Eglise, d'après une correspondance inédite entre Fénelon et P. Poiret (1710–1711)." *XVIIe Siècle* 25–26 (1955): 396–422.

———, ed. Introduction. *Correspondance de Fénelon*. By Fénelon. 13 vols. Paris: Klincksieck, 1972. 7–16.

———. "Mme Guyon devant ses juges." *Mélanges de littérature française offerts à Mr. Pintard*. Ed. Noémie Hepp, Robert Mauzi, and Claude Pichois. Strasbourg: Centre de Philologie et de Littératures Romanes de l'Université de Strasbourg, 1975. 409–23.

———. "L'Originalité théologique de John Wesley et les spiritualités du continent." *Revue Historique* 222 (July–September 1959): 51–80.

Oury, Dom Guy. *Marie Guyart (1599–1672)*. Trans. Miriam Thompson. Cincinnati, Oh.: Specialty Lithographing, 1979.

Petitdemange, Guy. "L'Invention du commencement: *La Fable mystique* de Michel de Certeau." *Recherche de Science Religieuse* 71:4 (1983): 497–520.

Petroff, Elisabeth A. *Medieval Women's Visionary Literature*. New York: Oxford University Press, 1986.

Pumfrey, Steven, Paolo L. Rossi, and Maurice Slawinski, eds. *Science, Culture and Popular Belief in Renaissance Europe*. Manchester: Manchester University Press, 1991.

Rapley, Elizabeth. *The Dévotes: Women and Church in Seventeenth-Century France.* Montreal: McGill-Queen's University Press, 1990.

Richardson, Ruth. *Death, Dissection and the Destitute.* London: Routledge, 1988.

Rousset, Jean. *Anthologie de la poésie baroque française.* Paris: Armand Colin, 1961.

Schweitzer, Franz-Joseph. "Von Marguerite Porète (+ 1310) bis Mme Guyon (+ 1717): Frauenmystic im Konflikt mit der Kirche." *Frauenmystic im Mittelalter.* Ed. Peter Dinzelbacker and Dieter R. Bauer. Stuttgart: Schwabenverlag, 1985. 256–74.

Scott, Joan Wallach. *Gender and the Politics of History.* New York: Columbia University Press, 1988.

Shumaker, Wayne. *English Autobiography: Its Emergence, Material and Form.* Berkeley: University of California Press, 1954.

Smith, Sidonie. *A Poetics of Women's Autobiography.* Bloomington: Indiana University Press, 1987.

Spengemann, William C. *The Forms of Autobiography: A Collection of Critical Essays.* Englewood Cliffs, N.J.: Prentice, 1981.

———. *Forms of Autobiography: Episodes in the History of a Literary Genre.* New Haven, Conn.: Yale University Press, 1980.

Stanton, Domna, ed. *The Female Autograph.* New York: New York Literary Forum, 1984.

———. "The Fiction of *Préciosité* and the Fear of Women." *Yale French Studies* 62 (1981): 107–34.

Timmermans, Linda. *L'Accès des femmes à la culture (1598–1715).* Paris: Champion, 1993.

Tooker, Elizabeth. "Women in Iroquois Society." *Extending the Rafter.* Ed. Michael Foster and Deborah Welch. New York: New York State University Press, 1984. 109–23.

Trudel, Marcel. *Initiation à la Nouvelle-France.* Montréal: Holt, 1968.

———. "The Meeting of Cultures." *Beginnings of New-France.* Toronto: McClelland, 1973. 150–62.

Trumback, Randolph. "London's Saphists: From Three Sexes to Four Genders in the Making of Modern Cultures." *Body Guards: The Cultural Politics of Gender Ambiguity.* Ed. Julia Epstein and Kristina Straub. New York: Routledge, 1991. 112–41.

Vauchez, André. *Les Laïcs au Moyen Age: pratiques et expériences religieuses.* Paris: Editions du Cerf, 1987.

Verdeyen, Paul. "Le Procès d'inquisition contre Marguerite Porète et Guiard de Cressonessart (1309–1310)." *Revue d'Histoire Ecclésiastique* 81:1–2 (1986): 47–94.

Vuarnet, Jean-Noël. *Extases féminines.* Paris: Arthaud, 1980.

Wajeman, Gérard. *Le Maître et l'hystérique*. Paris: Navarin/Seuil, 1982.

Ward, Patricia A. "Madame Guyon in America: An Annotated Bibliography." *Bulletin of Bibliography* 52:2 (June 1995): 107–11.

Weinstein, Donald, and Rudolph Bell. *Saints and Society: The Two Worlds of Western Christendom*. Chicago: University of Chicago Press, 1982.

Weintraub, Karl Joachim. *The Value of the Individual: Self and Circumstances in Autobiography*. Chicago: University of Chicago Press, 1978.

Weisner, Merry E. "Spinning Out Capital: Women's Work in the Early Modern Era." *Becoming Visible: Women in European History*. Ed. Renate Bridenthal, Claudia Koonz, and Susan Stuard. 2d ed. Boston: Houghton, 1987. 221–49.

Welch, Deborah. "American Indian Women: Reaching beyond the Myth." *New Directions in American Indian History*. Ed. Collin Calloway. Norman: University of Oklahoma Press, 1988. 31–48.

$\mathfrak{I}$ndex

275